New Novels in African Literature Today
27

Editor: Ernest N. Emenyonu
Department of Africana Studies,
University of Michigan-Flint
303 East Kearsley Street, Flint, MI 48502, USA

Deputy Editor: Nana Wilson-Tagoe
Department of Black Studies, University of Missouri,
Kansas City, MO 64110, USA

Assistant Editor: Patricia T. Emenyonu
Department of English, University of Michigan-Flint

Associate Editors: Francis Imbuga
Literature Department, Kenyatta University,
PO Box 43844, Nairobi, Kenya

Emmanuel Ngara
Office of the Deputy Vice-Chancellor,
University of Natal,
Private Bag X10, Dalbridge 4014, South Africa

Charles E. Nnolim
Department of English, School of Humanities
University of Port Harcourt, Rivers State, Nigeria

Ato Quayson
Centre for Diaspora & Transitional Studies,
Room 202, Medical Arts Bldg, 170 St George Street,
Toronto, Ontario, Canada, M5R 2M8

Kwawisi Tekpetey
Department of Humanities,
Central State University,
PO Box 1004, Wilberforce, OH 45384, USA

Iniobong I. Uko
Department of English, University of Uyo,
Uyo, Akwa Ibom State, Nigeria

Reviews Editor: James Gibbs
8 Victoria Square, Br·
jamesgibbs@btintern

African Literature Today

1-14 were published from London by Heinemann Educational Books and from New York by Africana Publishing Company

*Backlist titles available in the US and Canada from Africa World Press
and in the rest of the world from James Currey, an imprint of Boydell and Brewer*

Note from the publisher on new and forthcoming titles

James Currey Publishers have now joined Boydell & Brewer Ltd.
African Literature Today will continue to be published as an annual volume under the James Currey imprint. North and South American distribution will be available from The University of Rochester Press, 68 Mount Hope Avenue, Rochester, NY 14620-2731, USA, while UK and International distribution will be handled by Boydell & Brewer Ltd., PO Box 9, Woodbridge IP12 3DF, UK.

Call for papers

ALT 29 Teaching African Literature Today*

The issue will focus on experiences of teaching African Literature. Submissions can be on 1) Theoretical /pedagogical issues; 2) Productive teaching innovations; 3) Research reports on the teaching of African Literature; 4) Teaching African Literature across racial/cultural/national boundaries; 5) Problems of teaching African Literature in specific cultural/geographical areas; 6) Problems of teaching specific works/genres; 7) Student responses to African Literature 8) Teaching African Literature on-line – problems and prospects; 9) Teaching African Literature in an era of technology.

Guidelines for Submission of Articles

The Editor invites submission of articles or proposals for articles on the announced themes of forthcoming issues:

Ernest N. Emenyonu, *African Literature Today*
Department of Africana Studies, University of Michigan-Flint
303 East Kearsley Street, Flint MI 48502, USA
email: eernest@umflint.edu
Fax: 001 810 766 6719

Submissions will be acknowledged promptly and decisions communicated within six months of the receipt of the paper. Your name and institutional affiliation (with full mailing address and email) should appear on a separate sheet, plus a brief biographical profile of not more than six lines. The editor cannot undertake to return material submitted and contributors are advised to keep a copy of all material sent. Please note that all articles outside the announced themes cannot be considered or acknowledged and that articles should not be submitted via email. Articles should be submitted in the English language.

Length: articles should not exceed 5,000 words

Format: two hard copies plus disk of all articles should be submitted, double-spaced, on one side only of A4 paper, with pages numbered consecutively. Disks may be formatted for PC or AppleMac but please label all files and disks clearly, and save files as Word for Windows or Word for Macintosh.

Style: UK or US spellings, but be consistent. Direct quotations should retain the spelling used in the original source. Check the accuracy of your citations and always give the source, date, and page number in the text and a full reference in the Works Cited at the end of the article. Italicise titles of books or plays. Use single inverted commas throughout except for quotes within quotes which are double. Avoid subtitles or subsection headings within the text.

References: to follow series style (Surname date: page number) in brackets in text. All references/works cited should be listed in full at the end of each article, in the following style:
Surname, name/initial. *title of work*. place, publisher, date
Surname, name/initial. 'title of article'. In surname, name/initial (ed.)
title of work. place of publication, publisher, date
or Surname, name/initial, 'title of article', *Journal*, vol. no.: page no.

Copyright: it is the responsibility of contributors to clear permissions

Reviewers should provide full bibliographic details, including the extent, ISBN and price, and submit to the reviews editor
James Gibbs, 8 Victoria Square, Bristol BS8 4ET, UK
jamesgibbs@btinternet.com

New Novels in African Literature Today
27

A Review

Editor:	Ernest N. Emenyonu
Deputy Editor:	Nana Wilson-Tagoe
Assistant Editor:	Patricia T. Emenyonu

Associate Editors:	Francis Imbuga
	Emmanuel Ngara
	Charles E. Nnolim
	Ato Quayson
	Kwawisi Tekpetey
	Iniobong I. Uko

Reviews Editor:	James Gibbs

JAMES CURREY
HEBN

James Currey
is an imprint of Boydell & Brewer Ltd
PO Box 9, Woodbridge, Suffolk, IP12 3DF, UK
www.boydell.co.uk
and of Boydell & Brewer Inc.
668 Mt Hope Avenue, Rochester, NY 14620, USA
www.boydellandbrewer.com

HEBN Publishers Plc
1 Ighodaro Rd, Jericho
P.M.B. 5205, Ibadan, Nigeria
www.hebnpublishers.com

1 2 3 4 5 13 12 11 10 09

British Library Cataloguing in Publication Data
New novels in African literature today. -- (African
  literature today ; v. 27)
  1. African literature (English)--20th century--History
  and criticism. 2. African literature (English)--21st
  century--History and criticism.
  I. Series II. Emenyonu, Ernest, 1939-
  820.9'96'09045-dc22

ISBN: 978-0-85255-572-9 (James Currey paper)
ISBN 978-978-081-370-3 (HEBN paper)

Contents

Notes on Contributors

Sophie I. Akhuemokhan is a senior lecturer in English at the department of English, University of Benin, Nigeria.

Ada Uzoamaka Azodo is associate faculty in African and African Diaspora Studies in the department of African and Diaspora Studies, Indiana University, Northwest at Gary Indiana, USA. Her most recent work, *Gender and Sexuality in African Literature and Film*, was published in 2007 by Africa World Press.

Sery Bailly is a lecturer in African Literature in the department of English, University of Abidjan-Cocody, Ivory Coast.

Brenda Cooper is a professor of English in the Faculty of Arts, University of Cape Town, South Africa and has published critical works in African literature including *A New Generation of African Writers*, published in 2008 by James Currey.

Tej N. Dhar is a professor of English in the Faculty of Arts, Asmara University, Eritrea and has published critical articles on African literature.

Joseph McLaren teaches African and African American literature in the department of English, Hofstra university, Hempstead, New York, USA.

Charles E. Nnolim, is a professor of English in the department of English, University of Port Harcourt, Nigeria. He has published extensively in the field of African literature.

Machiko Oike is an assistant professor of English at Hiroshima University, Japan. She has published critical articles on African literature.

Clement Abiaziem Okafor is a professor of English in the department of English, University of Maryland, Eastern Shore, Maryland, USA. He has published several articles in the field of African literature.

Christopher Okonkwo is an associate professor in the department of English, University of Missouri, Columbia, USA. He has published articles in the field of African literature and his book, *A Spirit of Dialogue*, was published in 2008 by the University of Tennessee Press.

Florence Orabueze teaches African literature in the department of English at the University of Nigeria, Nsukka.

Omar Sougou is an associate professor and teaches francophone African literature at the Université Gaston, Berger, Senegal.

Editorial Article
The African Novel in the 21st Century:
Sustaining the Gains of the 20th Century

Ernest N. Emenyonu

In 1986 Wole Soyinka made history by becoming the first African and the first black person to win the coveted Nobel Prize for Literature. By the turn of the new millennium, three other African writers, all novelists, had won the Nobel Prize for Literature. This conferred on the African novel, and African writing in general, a legitimacy, relevance and authenticity which centuries of denigration and distortion had sought to deny.

With the publication of Chinua Achebe's *Things Fall Apart* in 1958, the literary world woke up to a new invention – African dynamics in the art of the novel. The modern African novel which emerged in the middle of the twentieth century brought with it new motifs, new symbolisms and new techniques in the fictional representation of human reality which were to force redefinitions and expansions of E.M. Forster's 'aspects of the novel'. The African novel emerged to 'fight' the battles of and for African communities in various locations on the continent. The African novelist emerged as a true voice of Africa and Africans, and, as the conscience and sensitivity of the society, boldly challenged untenable myths and stereotypes of Africa and Africans in the wider world. The African novelist debunked the age-old concept of 'art for art's sake', taking on the issues of the human condition in Africa and aligning him or herself with the cause of the people. 'Art for art's sake' was repudiated in the new definition of the function of art as an inevitable, socially relevant and vital force. In this capacity, the African novel entertained, instructed and moralized through direct and indirect didactic messages. The African novelist in particular, and the African writer in general boldly and bluntly attacked the ravages of colonialism on the continent of Africa and proceeded to tell the story of the colonial encounter from the African point of view.

In one of the most forcefully encapsulated prose passages in African fiction of the twentieth century, Chinua Achebe, the pioneer of this new orientation, fiercely attacked the European colonization of Africa:

> Does the white man understand our custom about land? How can he when he does not even speak our tongue? But he says that our customs are bad, and our own brothers who have taken up his religion also say that our customs are bad. How do you think we can fight when our own brothers have turned against us? The white man is very clever. He came quietly and peaceably with his religion.

We were amused at his foolishness and allowed him to stay. Now he has won our brothers, and our clan can no longer act like one. He has put a knife on the things that held us together and we have fallen apart. (TFA 176)

Achebe, along with his contemporaries, who saw their roles as those of 'teachers, educators, and pace-setters', defended their sense of mission in a number of literary essays. In his article, 'The Novelist as Teacher' (1965), he succinctly declared:

> I would be quite satisfied if my novels (especially the ones I set in the past) did no more than teach my readers that their past – with all its imperfections – was not one long night of savagery from which the first Europeans acting on God's behalf delivered them. Perhaps what I write is applied art as distinct from pure. But who cares? Art is important but so is education of the kind I have in mind. And I don't see that the two need be mutually exclusive. (4)

Clearly, therefore, Achebe and his contemporaries, saw their artistic roles as those of 're-education and regeneration' and believed the novel was an arena in which to wage 'wars' against imperialism, colonialism, corruption, dehumanization and ignorance first abroad and later at home. Without a proper understanding of the African writer's theory of the function of the novel in Africa, the reader may be tempted to see the African writer at the time as engaging in matters outside the realm of the novel as a work of art.

To accomplish the task which the African novelist set for him or herself, it was obvious that he/she had to step outside the box of literary traditions or conventions. One particular case was the language of expression, its re-configuration and manipulation. The contemporary African novel for the most part had to be written in the language of the former colonial masters. This did not come without a price. In the case of the English language, it had to be altered in several artistic and linguistic ways to 'force' it to bend to African surroundings and sensitivities. Achebe, the innovator of this mechanism, explained the process clearly:

> The African writer should aim to use English in a way that brings out his message best without altering the language to the extent that its value as a medium of international exchange will be lost. He should aim at fashioning out an English which is at once universal and able to carry his peculiar experience. (61)

It is through this process that African traditional narrative devices (the use of proverbs, sayings, songs, anecdotes, folk tales, etc.) have found their way into the pages of the modern African novel. The world celebrated with unprecedented fanfare in 2008, the golden jubilee of the publication of *Things Fall Apart*, a vindication of Chinua Achebe's vision for the African novel.

The African novel flourished in quality and quantity in the second half of the twentieth century. Multinational publishers helped in no small way to nurture and nourish its emergence and development. Heinemann Publishers in the United Kingdom deserves the greatest credit. The recent withdrawal of patronage by most of the multinational publishing companies has dealt a very severe blow to current efforts to sustain the gains of the twentieth century. This withdrawal was essentially a response to market forces and economic realities and not because new novels from Africa have nothing new or of value to offer to Africa and the world. This issue of ALT provides more than ample evidence of this fact. New voices are emerging from all parts of the African continent not only to reinforce the voices of the generations before them, but also to reveal the new realities, visions and concerns of Africa and its people.

The African novel of the twenty-first century has come a long way. It now has an African literary foundation and tradition as its heritage. The nurturing must continue, this time from within, using African resources and initiatives. From this angle the establishment of several literary prizes to encourage creative productivity in all parts of the continent is a step in the right direction. One must commend such exceptional initiatives as the Nigerian Liquefied Natural Gas (NLNG) Company's Nigerian Prize for Literature whose annual award of $50,000 makes it currently the highest indigenous literary prize on the African continent. Other initiatives, in particular, that of the Association of Nigerian Authors (ANA) which has resulted in the establishment of over a dozen annual literary prizes for poetry, women's writing, drama, prose on environmental issues, prose fiction, children's literature (prose), children's fiction, Igbo literature, playwriting, teen author prize (prose), and teen author prize (poetry), deserve praise and are worthy of emulation by individual, associations, corporate bodies and agencies throughout the continent of Africa. The same is true of literary prizes such as: The Wole Soyinka Prize For Literature in Africa (cash prize $20,000) awarded every other year by The Lumina Foundation, Lagos, Nigeria, and The PAT UTOMI Book Prize (cash prize one million Naira). Another positive initiative announced at the Cape Town Book Fair in 2008 was the re-launch of Heinemann's African Writers Series (AWS) starting with the republication of eight titles in the new Classics series. In 2009 Dambudzo Marechera's *The House of Hunger* was the first of other lapsed titles in the series to be put back into print; and new manuscripts are now being read with the aim of building a new body of work.

WORKS CITED

Achebe, Chinua. *Things Fall Apart*. New York: Anchor Books Edition, 1959.

——. 'The African Writer and the English Language', *Transition*, IV, 18, 1965.

——. 'The Novelist as Teacher' in G.D. Killam, *African Writers on African Writing*, Evanston, Northwestern University Press, 1973.

Resurgent Spirits, Catholic Echoes of Igbo & Petals of Purple: The Syncretised World of Chimamanda Ngozi Adichie's *Purple Hibiscus*

Brenda Cooper

> Vibrant bushes of hibiscus reached out and touched one another as if they were exchanging their petals. The purple plants had started to push out sleepy buds, but most of the flowers were still on the red ones. (*Purple Hibiscus*, 9)[1]

Chimamanda Ngozi Adichie strives for a holistic vision in her novel, *Purple Hibiscus*, one that integrates Igbo customs and language with Catholic ritual and which incorporates men into her gender politics and embraces the literary traditions of her elders – Chinua Achebe, Ngũgĩ wa Thiong'o and Alice Walker. If this sounds high flown, we need to understand that Adichie attempts to represent this syncretised world through the material culture and everyday realities of life in modern Nigeria. Solid objects – tables and chairs, grains of rice and ceramic ornaments – are syncretised with bodies and infused with spiritual life. They create a world where the boundaries between the living and the dead, the animate and the inanimate, the big and the small, the literal and the symbolic, words and things, are breached.

Where does this implicit belief in the power of the old gods sit in a novel by a Catholic African author? She says in an interview that she is 'interested in colonized religion, how people like me can profess and preach a respect of their indigenous culture and yet cling so tenaciously to a religion that considers most of indigenous culture evil' (Adichie in interview with Anya 2003: 15). In this paper, I will be tracing precisely how she juggles the pieces that make up the kaleidoscope of her vision. I will also demonstrate that the pieces sometimes slip away from her reach, and I will be suggesting possible reasons for this.

Purple Hibiscus is the story of Kambili, who is the fifteen-year-old first person protagonist. She lives in the violent and repressive atmosphere of her father, who physically abuses her meek mother, herself and brother, Jaja, by beating them into submission. Yet he is a pillar of the community. He is an avid Catholic churchman, a very successful businessman and, most puzzlingly, he is also a brave and incorruptible defender of democracy in Nigeria.

1

In other words, Papa's political integrity, grit and courage appear to be at odds with his domestic crimes of violence and his cruelty towards his family. His obsession to root out any surviving remnants of his indigenous culture means that he also behaves abominably towards his own father, who he calls a heathen and who he disowns. He thereby infringes some of the most sacred traditions of respect for the elders. He is a sycophantic anglophile, slavishly mimicking white ways and narrow Church doctrine. Yet he loves the children he nearly murders with his violent abuse of them. We will attempt to account for the contradictions in his portrayal later. This is, however, not his story. It is the story of Kambili. Before we can tell it, we need to make sense of the narrative structure on which it rests.

Purple Hibiscus works around a complex time-space axis. The novel's time line is divided into four parts. The first part begins on Palm Sunday with a family row when Papa smashes Mama's precious ceramic dancing figurines displayed on a shelf or what is described as an *étagère*. Papa's rage is provoked by Jaja, who refuses to go to communion. The bulk of the novel takes place in the second part, which is a flashback to before Palm Sunday, and the events leading up to Jaja's previously unheard of rebelliousness and the smashing of the ballerina ornaments. The third part takes us beyond Palm Sunday reaching its climax with Papa's violent death. The final part is situated in 'the present' and describes life after Papa. Repeated physical abuse and domestic violence provide the thread joining up all of the parts. Alongside this domestic realm, still in the temporal zone, is the growing crisis in the public political arena of the repressive Nigerian state.

Alongside this temporal to-ing and fro-ing, are spatial journeys to and from Enugu where the family lives. Events begin in Enugu but quite soon we are flashed back from there as the family travel to their village house in Abba for Christmas. Here the children interact with their father's sister, Aunty Ifeoma, and her children, from Nsukka. During this visit to Abba, the children are allowed to go to their grandfather's compound. Although the visit is very short, Papa-Nnukwu's compound and his shrine become powerful spaces within the novel.

In Abba, Aunty Ifeoma persuades Papa to let Jaja and Kambili come to visit her in Nsukka where they participate in an entirely different kind of family life. They stay in Aunty Ifeoma's flat in Nsukka and especially Jaja becomes entranced by her tiny, fabulous garden and her purple hibiscuses, in particular. During their visit, Papa-Nnukwu becomes gravely ill and their aunt brings him to the flat where he dies.

The children return to Enugu, Jaja armed with stalks of purple hibiscus from Aunty Ifeoma's garden. All of this takes the narrative back to Palm Sunday and to the point where the novel began. Jaja's revolt against his authoritarian, disturbed father continues after the smashing of the figurines and he decides that he and Kambili are going to spend Easter with their aunt and cousins in Nsukka, not least of all to say goodbye to them as they emigrate to America. They return to Nsukka, go on a Catholic pilgrimage to Aokpe and learn about Papa's sudden death from poison, seated at his desk in his office. The suspicion is that the state has murdered him, as it assassinated his editor. They return at once to Enugu, where, in a quite shocking climax to the novel's violent tensions, Mama confesses to having poisoned Papa. Jaja insists on taking the rap and is imprisoned, since everyone believes Mama to be attempting to confess in order to protect her son, rather than the other way around. *Purple Hibiscus* ends with Kambili and Mama visiting Jaja in prison, the final space of the novel, with the good news of his impending release, given that the Head of State had died a few months earlier and suspicion had, not improbably but incorrectly, fallen on 'the old regime' as responsible for Papa's murder.

Throughout the novel, we see Kambili's inability to cope emotionally with the mixed feelings of love and terror for her father, and adoration and disdain for her passive, abused mother, all of which she is unable either to acknowledge or understand. Kambili stutters, chokes on her words, stammers and whispers. How does she find her voice and how does this link to the syncreticities with which Adichie is grappling?

> [Papa] said that the stories about mmuo, that they were spirits who had climbed out of ant holes, that they could *make chairs run and baskets hold water*, were all devilish folklore. (*PH*, 85, my emphasis)

During the family's visit to their home village, Abba, Aunty Ifeoma secretly, given Papa's disapproval of 'heathen customs', takes Kambili and Jaja to Abagana for the Aro festival to look at the procession of *mmuo* spirits (73). She also sneaks in contact between them and their forbidden grandfather, who she brings along.

On the way, Papa-Nnukwu and Aunty Ifeoma have an apparently bantering conversation in the car, but one which, nonetheless, seriously introduces the nature of indigenous belief in the 'High God, the *Chukwu*' and the *chi*, which is a person's own spirit. Papa-Nnukwu promises that his spirit will intercede 'so that *Chukwu*, will send a good man to take care of you and the children' (83). Aunty Ifeoma quips that his spirit should rather 'ask Chukwu to hasten my promotion to senior lecturer' (83). For all its lightheartedness, this exchange establishes the signifi-cance of the spirits and their role in a changed world, where women pray for promotion, rather than for a man to earn the money to care for them.

This new world is exemplified by the traditional procession of *mmuo*, which is integrated into modern Nigeria, with cars 'bumper to bumper' and people dressed in every which style – 'wrappers blended into T-shirts, trousers into skirts, dresses into shirts' (85). Papa branded the *mmuo* as 'devilish folklore' (85) but the novel repeatedly distances itself from the rigidity of his beliefs and it does so here through Papa-Nnukwu, who passionately believes in their power and points to 'our *agwona-tumbe*', which is 'the most powerful *mmuo* in our parts, and all the neighboring villages fear Abba because of it' (86). As Kambili watches a huge *mmuo* float past she thinks that 'it was eerie, watching it, and I thought then of chairs running, their four legs knocking together, of water being held in a basket, of human forms climbing out of ant holes' (87).

These *mmuo* silently and unspokenly pervade the novel, acting on solid objects, inhabiting these baskets and chairs and animating them. It becomes clear that looming, living everyday objects both haunt and comfort Kambili and appear in visceral shape and form in all the moments of stress or emotion in her life. This the novel never directly states, given that it does not abandon its Christian base, albeit that it attempts to re-vitalise it with African traditional beliefs and practices.

For example, right at the start, at the moment of the smashing of Mama's beloved figurines, Kambili's emotions are expressed in terms of living objects, of the walls narrowing and bearing down on her and 'even the glass dining table was moving toward me' (7). A few pages later, when she is filled with the terror induced by her father, she becomes convinced that 'the compound walls would crumble' and 'squash the frangipani trees' and that 'the Persian rugs on the stretches of gleaming marble floor would shrink' (14). In Papa-Nnukwu's yard, Kambili's conflict and the discomfort resulting from Papa's prohibitions regarding contact with her grandfather, results in her being stuck to a bench and unable to get up – 'the bench held me back, sucked me in' (66).

Flesh and objects meld as spirits inhabit the material world and exert power over visceral, vulnerable human bodies. Kambili's body dissolves into the furniture in terror, when Papa arrives, unexpectedly, at the flat in Nsukka, just after Papa-Nnukwu has died – 'I froze on my seat, felt the skin of my arms melding and becoming one with the cane arms of the chair' (187).

There had been solid objects, which were also alive at home in Enugu and that is the étagère with their precious ceramic dancing ballerina figurines, before they were smashed. We must look at them more closely to see how objects are animated through the resurgent spirits that occupy them and what happens when they are abused and also how this relates to the Catholicism that the author unambiguously professes.

> He picked up the missal and flung it across the room, toward Jaja. It missed Jaja completely, but it hit the glass étagère, which Mama polished often. It cracked the top shelf, swept the beige, finger-size ceramic figurines of ballet dancers in various contorted postures to the hard floor and then landed after them. Or rather it landed on their many pieces. It lay there, a huge leatherbound missal that contained the readings for all three cycles of the church year (7).

Purple Hibiscus begins with a mystery. The opening part is entitled 'BREAKING GODS' (1). How can the breakage of these ornaments constitute the destruction of gods? These figurines are Mama's coping ritual against the physical violence to which Papa subjects her. After he beats her up, instead of crying, she washes the little ballerinas in soapy water. Mama says the figurines do not matter, but Kambili knows they do:

> I would go down to see her standing by the étagère with a kitchen towel soaked in soapy water. She spent at least a quarter of an hour on each ballet-dancing figurine. There were never tears on her face. The last time, only two weeks ago, when her swollen eye was still the black-purple color of an overripe avocado, she had rearranged them after she polished them. (10–11)

It is significant that the weighty object that is the weapon in the destruction of the figurines is a book of church readings. At first this appears to be an example of the Christian church's attack on indigenous belief. However, this cannot be the case, given that these European made ballerinas, dancing on their French styled display case, are hardly simply indigenous, nor is Papa's brand of imitative Christianity the only one available.

What we witness in the novel is the attempt to re-fetishise objects linked to pre-colonial rituals, but syncretised with the Church and with European culture and integrated into a global modernity. The figurines, in other words, are Mama's protecting spirits, albeit hybridised in the African Catholic home. The étagère was her shrine; the spirits of old have resurged. Papa has desecrated the sacred space and he will be punished.

Is this far fetched? I do not think so. These figurines relate to the character of Papa-Nnukwu, who is a role model and a spiritual guide to the children, albeit that he is a 'traditionalist' and has not converted to Christianity. He carries the moral high ground in his sole, quiet and uncompromising refusal to be bullied by Papa, who tries to make him throw away 'the chi in the thatch shrine in his yard' (61). However, 'he would not throw away his chi' (61). His shrine is sacred and during their short visit to him in his compound, Kambili watches a gray rooster 'walk into the shrine at the corner of the yard, where Papa-Nnukwu's god was, where Papa said Jaja and I were never to go near' (66). The implication is that going near the shrine would be a violation of a sacred space, which echoes with the shrine of Mama's precious objects.

How, precisely, do these Igbo beliefs and customs integrate with the Catholicism to which the novel subscribes? There are echoes of Igbo throughout and particularly of the inclusion of Igbo songs and styles within church ritual.

We have already seen the respect afforded Papa-Nnukwu and his beliefs, in the multiple spirits, for example, which inhabit the novel. Papa-Nnukwu's age and frailty and his death, however, are indicators that his way of life is not the direction of the future. The moral high ground rests with Catholics like the young and progressive Father Amadi, who is the family's priest in Nsukka, and with Aunty Ifeoma and her family, who attempt to integrate the spirituality of Papa-Nnukwu into their Catholicism.

What the novel uncompromisingly rejects is bigoted, Eurocentric white priests, like Father Benedict, and the brand of Catholicism into which he has brainwashed Papa, who is a caricature in his over-zealousness. For Father Benedict, 'Igbo was not acceptable' and only Latin permissible for saying Mass. However, Igbo could be used in offertory songs – 'he called them native songs, and when he said 'native' his straight-line lips turned down at the corners to form an inverted U' (4). Papa becomes an undignified mimic when he changes his accent so as to sound British when speaking to Father Benedict – 'he was gracious, in the eager-to-please way that he always assumed with the religious, especially with the white religious' (46). The novel's goal, however, is not to polarise Papa and Papa-Nnukwu, but to infuse Igbo customs into Catholic spirituality.

The pathway to a more syncretic religion is via Igbo language, songs and rituals and these echo throughout the novel. English integrates with Igbo as in ''*ne, ngwa.* Go and change,' Mama said to me, startling me although her Igbo words were low and calming'' (8). The words may be explained, but the timbre of the language is what is metonymically and concretely communicated. Later, and likewise, Kambili says of Father Amadi that she 'did not fully comprehend his English-laced Igbo sentences at dinner because my ears followed the sound and not the sense of his speech' (135).

All of this is transcribed into the Catholic ritual that Adichie so enjoys, but again which her protagonist, Kambili, at first found hard to stomach. Integrated into family prayer at Aunty Ifeoma's home, 'after we said the last Hail Mary' Amaka broke into Igbo song, to Kambili's enormous shock, causing her to snap back her head at the sound of Igbo in this prayer context – '*Ka m bunie afa gi enu...*' (125). Kambili, at this early stage, thinks censoriously, 'It was not right. You did not break into song in the middle of the rosary' (125). This does not stop the family ritual, 'Amaka broke into song at the end of each decade, uplifting Igbo songs that made Aunty Ifeoma sing in echoes, like an opera singer drawing the words from the pit of her stomach' (125). The opera simile is interesting and buttresses the cultural fusion being enacted so approvingly by the novel. In fact, 'morning and night prayers were always peppered with songs, Igbo praise songs that usually called for hand clapping' (140). Then comes Kambili's bewildering realisation that 'Jaja had been tapping his feet to the beat of an Igbo song that Aunty Ifeoma and my cousins sang at evening rosary' (154). The writing is on the wall and Jaja's rebellion against attending Papa's brand of Catholic communion is firmly set in motion.

Nonetheless, we are left in no doubt regarding the novel's endorsement of a different kind of Catholicism and this is demonstrated by the pilgrimage Aunty Ifeoma takes them on to Aokpe, a little village in Benue, where the Blessed Virgin is supposedly appearing (99). In Aokpe Kambili has this vision: 'And then I saw her, the Blessed Virgin: an image in the pale sun, a red glow on the back of my hand, a smile on the face of the rosary-bedecked man whose arm rubbed against mine. She was everywhere' (274–5). Kambili experiences here a powerful confirmation of her Catholic spirituality, of the holy presence of the Blessed Virgin in every dimension of life, experienced through the reflected beauty of the sun. Once again, however, this Catholic 'miracle' is depicted as a hybrid one, which is Africanised in two ways. First it is in a remote village in Nigeria in which the Blessed Virgin has purportedly decided to appear, something that racists in more powerful places in the world are loath to accept. Amaka, Kambili's cousin, notes in a letter from America, after the family have emigrated, that a writer in a magazine there 'had sounded pessimistic that the Blessed Virgin Mary could be appearing at all, especially in Nigeria: all that corruption and all that heat' (300).

Second, and taking us into the next section of this paper, the Catholic experience is described through an intertext from the novel of another African writer, Ngũgĩ wa Thiongo's *Petals of Blood*. The ground underneath a big flame tree in Aokpe is 'covered with petals the color of fire' (274). This contributes to the red glow in which Kambili has her religious vision that the Blessed Virgin is everywhere.

> I think it pisses God off if you walk by the color purple in a field somewhere and don't notice it. (*The Color Purple*, 167)

Postcolonial writers attempt to escape from Western culture's metaphors, which are steeped in racism and white, male colonial imaginaries, such as those of writers like Kipling, Conrad and Carey. The English language, into which these metaphors and symbols are deeply melded, refers to Africa as a dark and savage heart and other such distorting images. Young African writers, like Adichie, now have a wealth of alternative traditions from which to draw. Three powerful intertexts frame *Purple Hibiscus* – Chinua Achebe's *Things Fall Apart*, Ngũgĩ wa Thiong'o's *Petals of Blood* and Alice Walker's *The Color Purple*. These both consolidate and enrich Adichie's integrated vision, but also set up tensions as her juggled agendas, on occasion, themselves slip and smash.

If *Things Fall Apart* charted the transformations wrought by colonialism, then *Purple Hibiscus* is a sequel, plotting postcolonial devastation, the demise of national liberation and the migration to North America of some of the best, most talented Nigerians, like Aunt Ifeoma. The opening words of the novel signal this indebtedness to Achebe –'*things started to fall apart* at home when my brother, Jaja, did not go to communion and Papa flung his heavy missal across the room and broke the figurines on the étagère' (*TFH* 3, my emphasis). Like the Europeans, who violated the sacred shrines during Achebe's novel of colonialism, the new dictators are destroying the postcolonial, hybrid, but still holy spaces. At the same time, the availability of alternative sources of figurative inspiration give rise to new symbolisms, of which the purple hibiscus is exemplary.

Kambili, at the outset of the novel, remembers how their lives changed with the visit to Nsukka and 'Aunty Ifeoma's experimental purple hibiscus', that 'began to lift the silence' (16), a silence behind which the terrible secret of family abuse lay hidden. This entwines the image of the purple hibiscus with language, with finding a voice out of the silence. This voice is both the liberation of Kambili, who is silent, or stutters and whispers, but also the voice of the young writer, Adichie, who finds her medium through the availability of literary traditions other than those of the Western canon.

How does the symbol function? The yard of the house, in which the children grow up in Enugu, is full of red hibiscus bushes. They visit their aunt and cousins in Nsukka where Jaja is captivated by Aunty Ifeoma's garden, and in particular by her purple hibiscuses. Jaja brings back some cuttings from these purple bushes and plants them in the garden in Enugu. They take root and flower and signify the changes in the relationships within the family as the children begin to seize the initiative, rebel against their father and transform their lives.

At this point it appears as if a simple binary is being established between the blood red violence of home and the purple liberation of Nsukka. This polarisation is simultaneously interrogated, in that the red versus purple is undercut by the novel's consideration of the liberating potential contained in the red and by the ultimate insistence on the necessity of red as well as purple, on Ngũgĩ wa Thiongo's petals of red, along with Alice Walker's purple fields.

The red flowers make a connection between the Marxist Socialist politics of *Petals of Blood* and the ruby glow of the Blessed Virgin. The reference to Ngũgĩ's novel during the Pilgrimage to Aokpe is unambiguous, given that the ground there was 'covered with petals the color of fire' (274). This is crucial to Adichie's religious vision, where radical liberation theologians, like Father Amadi, create the possibilities for a politicised religion, what Adichie referred to earlier in an interview as 'the commitments that some [Catholic] orders have to social justice' (Adichie in an interview with Wale Adebanwi, 2004). Ngũgĩ's insistence that ordinary people 'would continue struggling until a human kingdom came ... so that flowers in all their different colours would ripen and bear fruits and seeds' (303) would resonate with Adichie's search for a holistic vision of ordinary lives and people being incorporated in a just society.

The problem with the multiple flowers, of purple and red, only arises in relation to the character of Papa. Papa, like Ngũgĩ's heroic characters, struggles for national liberation, a struggle that has not terminated with independence, and accounts for the great lengths to which the novel goes to emphasise Papa's courageous resistance to corruption, his generosity to the poor and the fact that he is a champion of democracy, to the extent of endangering his own life.

The point here is that the purple of the hibiscus reflects its hue on him as well, when he struggles for freedom. This makes his red hibiscuses, not only the red of blood that he spills in his family, but the violence that is wrought against him by the State. So, when government agents come to terrorise the family, and Papa in particular, he throws them out and note that the sinister 'the men in black ... yanked hibiscuses off' (200). These would be red hibiscuses.

Adichie seems to be contradicting herself by insisting that Papa be judged according to his actions at home, where the terrible revenge of Mama and the figurine spirits is justified, but then also demonstrating Papa's true grit, which seems to break out of the small yet large stage of the étagère. All of this stretches our credibility to breaking point. I think that the contradiction in her portrayal of Papa, relates to Adichie's 'womanism' as opposed to 'feminism' and the influence of Alice Walker.

'Womanist', coined by Alice Walker, is defined as 'a black feminist' (1983b, xi). Walker says that 'womanist is to feminist as purple to lavender' (1983b, xii). The definition is bound up with the colour purple, which is also the title of Alice Walker's Pulitzer Prize winning novel. A crucial tenet of womanism is that it recognises the mutual suffering that black men and women together have endured, be it at the hands of the slavers or the colonisers. This it has to balance against the ways in which black men oppress black women, as patriarchs. Again, according to Alice Walker – womanism is 'committed to survival and wholeness of entire people, male *and* female' (1983b, xi, her emphasis).

This balancing is wonderfully achieved in the character of Jaja, a young man, who is battling with issues not dissimilar to those of his sister and who is appropriately included in Adichie's vision of transformation in gender terms. He is sensitive, loves beautiful flowers and is a role model for the future. This accounts for the novel's emphasis that the purple hibiscuses are Jaja's rather than Kambili's passion, in a novel which clearly charts the growth of Kambili's ability to speak, to have an identity, with a focus on women, patriarchy and voicelessness. This is why Adichie describes Kambili as disinterested in the flowers – 'I wondered if [Aunty Ifeoma] was thinking that my voice lacked the enthusiasm of Jaja's when she talked about her garden' (143). The dilemma with 'womanism' comes when women have to confront men who have indeed suffered the indignities of racism and colonialism with them and are struggling for a better world, but who simultaneously oppress them in the domestic sphere.

Adichie attempts to prevent this dilemma by depicting Papa as depraved in the domestic violence that he horribly and compulsively engages in. She falters, however, when she, nonetheless, attempts to salvage him. The violent abuse of his whole family is so heinous, that he cannot be recovered as a decent character on any level. His beating of his wife ensures that she nearly dies and loses more than one baby in the womb; he batters Kambili to an inch of her life, having scalded her and

Jaja's feet in boiling water. He is a demon, toxic to the family and we, as readers, feel only support for Mama and relief when she murders him. Adichie, however, attempts to redeem him as part of the recognition of the role of men in the struggle for freedom. As she says in an interview:

> Kambili's father, for all of his fundamentalism, at least has a sense of social consciousness that is expansive and proactive and *useful*, so while his character may be seen as a critique of fundamentalism, the God-fearing public in Nigeria can learn a bit from him as well. (Adichie in an interview with Wale Adebanwi 2004, her emphasis)

How can anyone learn from such a man, given his crimes in the home? What Adichie is battling with here is a simultaneous commitment to domestic struggle and also to a more macro party politics. These dimensions, often referred to as the public and the private, are not, by definition, in contradiction with each other. Quite the opposite is true and Adichie herself, elsewhere in the novel, attempts to find a way of profoundly implicating them, precisely through the nature of the étagère and the little figurines dancing on its glass shelves.

Let us then return to these compelling and powerful miniature figurines. Susan Stewart in her *On Longing*, which is a study of *Narratives of the Miniature, the Gigantic, the Souvenir, the Collection* suggests that miniatures occupy a 'privatized and domesticated world' (Stewart 1993: 172). It is a woman's world, where knickknack shelves satisfy the longings of women, who seek limited mastery over space. I am suggesting that Adichie's project of taking this space and magnifying it to occupy central stage is a radical feminist move. Stewart elaborates that 'the miniature becomes a stage on which we project ... a deliberately framed series of *actions*' (1993: 54, her emphasis). This explains this rather quaint word, 'étagère', that Adichie uses and repeats, underlining its significance. 'Étagère' is a French word for display shelves, and it is tellingly linked to an old French word for staging, as in a play. This small display unit becomes the stage upon which all the big events of the novel are played out. The smallness of the miniature is enlarged by the sacredness of their being occupied by the spirits of tradition and the étagère looms large as the shrine, at the heart, at the centre, of all existence, for all its deceptive, apparent smallness

The daily life rituals and possessions, the special places in the home, in this view, are the basis and framework for political action. This is why the novel details solid objects of everyday life in so much concrete detail. The medium is the message where small is big, the personal is political and ordinary daily life, embodied in the things that surround us, is where the sacred spirits live, and from which Nigerian culture should arise and grow.

The contradiction in the representation of Papa, however, is the site where *Purple Hibiscus* is caught in the crossfire of its own multiple agendas. At one level, and unambiguously, the novel is locating the stage centrally within the home where men are judged politically in terms of their domestic relationships; at another level, it is examining the politics of Nigerian corruption and brutality, militarism and violence and suggesting, in somewhat weaker tones, that even patriarchal, wife-bashing men may somewhat redeem themselves in an African context, where struggle against colonialism and then post-independence fall-out, involved both genders.

Having said this, the attempt at mingling of religions and cultures, as also embodied in the purples flowers, which do not stand alone, is wise and lovely when applied to men and women, like Jaja as well as Kambili. Remember how 'vibrant bushes of hibiscus reached out and touched one another as if they were exchanging their petals' (9). And Aunty Ifeoma's garden includes 'roses and hibiscuses and lilies and ixora' and these 'grew side by side like a hand-painted wreath' (112). The image of the wreath is important. These blue flowers are artifacts, a feat of science, the result of intensive experimentation on the part of Phillipa, Aunty Ifeoma's botanist colleague at the university. They are the result of scholarship and human endeavour and not the involuntary gifts of nature. Jaja has to take cuttings and plant and tend them, hiding them and their meaning from Papa to enable them to grow. But grow they will, and only very uneasily beside the red hibiscuses of Papa's own struggles, both against the dictators and his own, terrible, blood-letting demons.

The novel ends with Jaja's and Kambili's plans to plant new orange trees in Abba and for Jaja to plant purple hibiscus and for Kambili to plant ixora. This reverberates with Alice Walker's *In Search of Our Mothers' Gardens*, where the child questions:

'Mama, why are we brown, pink and yellow, and our cousins are white, beige, and black?' Ans.: 'Well, you know the colored race is just like a flower garden, with every color flower represented.' (Walker, 1983b: xi)

Walker's description of her mother echoes Aunty Ifeoma, given that she was a magnificent grower of flowers and Walker's 'memories of poverty are seen through a screen of blooms – sunflowers, petunias, roses, dahlias, forsythia, spirea, delphiniums, verbena' (241).

And yet, Adichie is also aware that this bouquet may not be so harmoniously possible. Elsewhere in the novel, she understands that the 'big' politics at a public, national level is not important when children are abused at home:

Jaja's defiance seemed to me now like Aunty Ifeoma's experimental purple hibiscus: rare, fragrant with the undertones of freedom, *a different* kind *of freedom from the one the crowds waving green leaves chanted* at Government Square after the coup. A freedom to be, to do. (16, my emphasis)

If you are fighting for freedom from domestic abuse, if you are searching for an individual identity and a voice without a stutter, liberated from terror at home, then a coup, or a rally in Government Square becomes less important, miniaturised by these bigger albeit purportedly smaller concerns. This perception is muted when Adichie, simultaneously, partially forgives Papa his crimes and portrays him as a brave fighter for democracy, standing, shoulder to shoulder with women, against the Nigerian state, red and purple entwined in an embrace. This sets up a polarisation between the 'public' and the 'private' in a novel that specifically and simultaneously contests this particular false binary through the other central image, that of the miniature figurines on the étagère, which Papa smashes. His domestic violence, in fact, interrogates the big picture and re-defines the political from within its standpoint.

Right near the end of the novel, Kambili hopes that the silence that has grown up between herself and Jaja after all the family tragedies and his incarceration, will be broken; she hopes that they will be able eventually 'to clothe things in words, things that have long been naked' (306). *Purple Hibiscus* has given us many naked things, broken things, living things, things with the spirits of old gods still living in them. Adichie has clothed them with the words appropriate to their concrete material realities and transformed them into new metaphors, metaphors for a global world, metaphors constructed in America, in the Catholic Church and in the Shrine of the Igbo village.

NOTES

*   A longer version of this article appeared in Brenda Cooper, *A New Generation of African Writers*, Woodbridge: James Currey, 2008.
1   Chimamanda Ngozi Adichie, *Purple Hibiscus*, London: Fourth Estate, 2004. All quotations are taken from this edition.

WORKS CITED

Achebe, Chinua. *Things Fall Apart*, London: Heinemann Educational Books, 1958.
Adebanwi, Wale. 'The Chimamanda Ngozi Adichie Interview'. *Nigeria Village Square*, www.nigeriavillagesquare1.com/books/adichie_interview.html, 2004.
Adichie, Chimamanda Ngozi. *Purple Hibiscus*, London: Fourth Estate, 2004.
Anya, Ike. 'In the Footsteps of Chinua Achebe: Enter Chimamanda Ngozi Adichie'. *Sentinel Poetry* Issue 12, November (2003): 11–16.
Ngũgĩ wa Thiong'o. *Petals of Blood*, London: Heinemann Educational Books, 1977.
Stewart, Susan. *On Longing: Narratives of the Miniature, the Gigantic, the Souvenir, the Collection*, Durham & London: Duke University Press, 1993.
Walker, Alice. *The Color Purple*, London: The Women's Press, 1983a.
—— *In Search of our Mother's Gardens*, San Diego, New York, London: Harcourt Brace Jovanovich, 1983b.

Ambivalent Inscriptions:
Women, Youth & Diasporic Identity in Buchi Emecheta's Later Fiction

Omar Sougou

African diaspora subjects articulate identities constructed far away from their homelands or motherlands both in fiction and critical theory. Besides the African Americans and the Afro-Caribbeans, the African diaspora includes long-term voluntary or forced exiles and new immigrants of African descent in other parts of the world. A black diaspora emerged in Britain gathering members of the already constituted African Caribbean diaspora and emigrants from Africa. Their presence has generated a rich literature – creative as well as expository – that explores the implications of settlement in the mother country, and translates the formation of an imagined identity away from the land of origin or the motherland.

Buchi Emecheta's fiction is one useful locus to consider such an experience, especially her later novels, *Kehinde* and *The New Tribe*. Therein home and belonging are problematized in the life stories of the main protagonists. Of course, as customary in Emecheta's work, gender relations are inscribed in the process, and more so in *Kehinde.* This paper intends to explore the relationships of the migrant subjects to home, namely the motherland. Such an inquiry is based on the development of the concept 'home' from *Gwendolen* or *The Family* to these two later works. It seeks to pursue an earlier reflection on the subject that focused on *Gwendolen* and the *Rape of Shavi*. Thus, it proposes to follow and examine the attitudes that are filtered through the characters' experiences and postures in relation to the notion of belonging that has been so far predicated on Africa. The African Caribbean diaspora and African immigrants imagine or strive to preserve an identity with Africa, endeavouring likewise to keep alive the ties with the motherland and to come to terms with ambivalence. Their turning to their homelands even symbolically proves cathartic sometimes in the face of ostracism and other trials suffered in the mother country. However, in Emecheta's *Kehinde* and *The New Tribe* there is a twist in the rapport of the émigrés and their offspring to Africa. Africa/Nigeria is gradually removed as home and superseded by the mother country in a plot that is at odds with the familiar one, and in which the empire is appropriated as the seat of conquered identity.

13

Reflecting on the issue of displacement, Susan R. Suleiman suggests a taxonomy of the different categories of subjects: émigrés, exiles, expatriates, refugees, nomads and cosmopolitans. For her, all of 'these words designate a state of being "not home" (or being '"everywhere at home", the flip of the other side of the same coin), which means, in most cases, at distance with one's native tongue.' She raises questions as to whether this distance is 'falling away from some original wholeness and source of creativity, or is it on the contrary a spur to creativity? Is exile a cause for optimism (celebration, even) or its opposite?'[1] These interrogations overlap with the frame of reference of many a critic approaching literature by the diaspora, and they apply to Emecheta's writing. Hers is one of celebration of the self, as can be seen in *Second-Class Citizen, In the Ditch,* and *Head Above Water,* her autobiography. Clearly, exile spurred her creativity as manifested by her own statements and the number and location of her publications. She broaches the issue of migration in her two debut novels, and shows through her characters what it means to be an African and a woman in Britain. Immigrants' expectations are not always as conjectured. Their relationship to the motherland is not easy either.

Emecheta's *Kehinde* and *New Tribe* are set in and between the African and the Western worlds. The subjects she creates and locates in the African and Western spaces migrate to the West, or travel from the West to Africa. The novels refract a manner of seeing and a will to construct an identity in 'the "inter" – the cutting edge of translation and negotiation, the in-between space – that carries the meaning of culture' (Bhabha 1994: 38). Like the previous novel, *Gwendolen*, they are partly set in the West, and are literary expressions of the imagined identity of the new diasporic subjects trying to make sense of their relationships to the motherland.

Correlatively, discussing nationalism and the cultural forms of diasporas, Robin Cohen makes a point relevant to the novels we are concerned with: 'diasporas are positioned somewhere between the nation-states and 'travelling cultures' in that they involve dwelling in a nation-state in a physical sense, but travelling in an astral or spiritual sense that falls outside the nation-state's space/time zone' (1997: 135-6). The diaspora members found in fiction are usually torn between choices that involve argument and/or negotiation with themselves and their homelands.

Gwendolen insistently suggests the need for Africans and African Caribbeans to identify with a place to call home outside the boundaries of Britain. That location is clearly defined in the dedicatory note of the novel as Africa, the motherland, in opposition to Britain, the mother country. Africa is presented as the root, the mother of all, Caribbeans and Africans alike. The name Iyamide, 'My mother is here' denotes in *Gwendolen* the desire to keep the bond with and to acknowledge Africa as the land of identification, the signifier of belonging. Numerous tropes in this novel refer to the centrality of Africa for the doubly displaced African Caribbean and the African immigrants.

Kehinde and *The New Tribe* revisit this theme and remain in the pattern of Emecheta's novels such as *Second-Class Citizen*, *Naira Power*, and *Double Yoke* marked by the movement of the characters between Nigeria and England. Both novels present British Nigerians hankering after their homeland. Nigeria is seen as an antidote to life in Britain that is mostly synonymous with loneliness, insignificance, and anonymity despite the material gains. The home country appeals to the protagonists who contemplate to return there to enjoy fulfillment and recognition. *Kehinde* focuses partly on the eponymous heroine's husband's return to Nigeria. Albert, a long term expatriate, resigns from his work to go and enjoy the oil boom effect in Nigeria. His children and his wife join him later. *The New Tribe* introduces a British-born boy, son of a young Nigerian woman, who engages in an identity quest that leads him to Nigeria. Through these paradigms the novels interrogate the concerns of long-standing residents abroad and young people born and bred outside their parents' homeland, the new diasporic subjects. The choices they make and the dilemma resolution each individual manages in his/her own posture and interests constitute the driving force of both narratives.

The novels of Emecheta have hitherto displayed an ambivalent attitude towards the mother country that would be recognized by most of her readers. The later part of her fiction deploys a responsive strategy that seems intent on resolving the contradictions inherent in biculturalism. The overall result seems to work against Nigeria which turns into a hostile land, a place of chaos for the returnees. Both novels' main protagonists turn their backs on Nigeria, the site of a traumatic experience, antithetic to the commonly held view of home as a place of healing and comfort. The motherland is oppressive for the woman Kehinde as well as for the fostered child, Chester, now a grown-up looking for his roots. Each narrative displays an ambivalent consciousness that gradually leads the protagonist to despondency that only running back to the mother country soothes. Such a reversal of ideal conversely echoes the turning of tables that takes place in *The Rape of Shavi* and partly in *Gwendolen* as a means to write back to the empire's pretensions. The motherland becomes a soul-killing space and the mother country graduates into home offering steady peace and security. This process is dramatized in a three tier narrative across the two novels through Kehinde, Chester, and Esther.

Kehinde rests on a motif achieved by way of a dialogic relationship the heroine entertains with her stillborn twin Taiwo 'the one who has tasted the world first'. Kehinde adds to her own voice the intermittent utterances of Taiwo, the subconscious manifestation of her superego. The device allows the expression of a dual consciousness that helps both narrator and character to ease out of dilemma. Kehinde's responses to Taiwo occur at critical moments when choices are to be made. One major instance is the episode dealing with her decision to terminate her pregnancy in which she is chided by the supernatural Taiwo: 'Into

Kehinde's mind, interrupting her thoughts, came a voice, the same as she often heard when she was lonely or confused. 'Our mother died having you. I died so you could live. Are you going to kill your child before he has a chance of life?' (*K* 17).

The event triggers a reminiscence meditated through Kehinde's own voice that runs on for four pages. Thanks to this analepsis the reader discovers that Kehinde's origins and childhood that are deeply entrenched in traditional life and beliefs. The young Kehinde moors her identity to Igbo culture in disagreement with her Christian aunt. The latter took her away from her birthplace, where it was believed that she killed her twin sister and survived their mother, and gave her a Christian name: Jacobina. The young Kehinde resentfully accounts for the happening:

> When she had snatched me away from the negative situation in which I was born, she had thought she was saving me from the clutches of superstition. She did not know that I would grow into a child who would not let her identity die... I was haunted by my past, so that Aunt Nnebogo put me on the hem of the skirt of her love ... However for me to get well, she had asked a special *ibeji* carver to make me my Taiwo. (21)

This identity clearly defined in childhood gradually separates itself from home, Nigeria, in the grown-up Kehinde. While Albert is eager to return home, and asks her to stay in London until their house is sold, she doubts whether she will go. Although she is uncertain, it is clear that she holds on to her identity as a woman, and predicates it on her body. She intends to have full control over it in deciding to have no more children even if she goes back to Nigeria after the abortion her husband persuades her to undergo. On the other hand, she admits: 'My dreams about home are confused. I haven't a clear vision of what I'm supposed to be looking for there' (22).

The writer weaves into Albert's decision the agency of his sisters, who prompt him to return home, in order to challenge and deride the traditional prerogatives sisters have in their brothers' houses. It is also another way to suggest that tradition dies hard. It dogs people even abroad and seeks to keep them under its sway. Tradition thus counters individual identity with its demands, especially on the woman.

On the other hand, even if man is shown as an insensitive being in the depiction of Albert, a shift takes place in the treatment of the heroine's father. He is respectable, and is part of the supernatural and symbolic language of the novel. Beside the archetypal female *chi* present in Taiwo's figure, in Kehinde's dream, it is her father's spirit that means to come back and take care of her in the form of a would-be male child whose embryo was removed from her womb. This aesthetic feature and Taiwo's voice combine with Kehinde's and the narrator's to give the novel the look of a scripted oral life story that 'clearly exists in that liminal space between the public and the private, between oral and written discourses ... another of those sublimated women's articulations' (Davies 1992: 15).

Kehinde's inconsistent posture regarding the abortion parallels her confusion about home. Yet, her son and daughter readily accept Nigeria as their home although they were born and raised in England. They are eager to go and discover the land where their parents hail from. A similar eagerness seizes Chester in *The New Tribe.* He relates to Africa through a dream. He is a representation of the black children who are adopted by white couples. His story ties in with Julia's, a white baby-girl abandoned in a telephone booth and adopted by the local curate, Arthur Arlington, and his wife, Ginny. The press reports about the foundling govern Chester's mother's choice of the Arlington couple as his foster parents. He and Julia grow up in the same home like siblings under the care of a thoughtful foster-mother. Neither of them shows awareness of difference with respect to the other. Yet, as the narrator points out, Chester is conscious of his separate identity:

> [He] could not remember the exact moment when he knew he was adopted.... It began as a glimmer and gradually becomes a solid awareness, established, but somehow imprisoned inside him. However, even at the age of four or five, he felt a sense of unbelonging. He instinctively knew that broaching the subject with his parents would cause pain, and he kept silent, but he was sure it would come to light one day. (*NT* 9–10)

It is at school that Chester is made aware of being different; he feels demonized when the headmaster calls him 'little devil'. The narrative pursues the exposition of preconceived attitudes towards black children in the school's giving him the part of the leader of the three kings in a Christmas nativity play.

The title 'Chester, king of the Orient' elicits from him questions about the Orient to which Ginny answers, and unwittingly points out to the young boy his not really being part of the colour determined foster family.

> 'What is the Orient Mummy?'
> 'It means the East, where the wise men came from,' she responded.
> 'What is the East?' he pursued. Ginny was silent for a moment, then she said, 'Africa's in the East. Where your people came from.'

In bed that night, he thought about her words. 'Your people'. He thought the Arlington were his people. The sense of unbelonging strengthened. (*NT* 12)

Ginny's attempt to explain re-inscribes Edward Said's comments on Orientalism, a discursive practice that reflects the relationship of power, domination, and hegemony of the Occident over the Orient. The Orient, like Africa, is the colonized and dominated other through the policy of imperialism that Said's archival investigation traces back to Balfour and Cromer. As Said posits in *Orientalism*,

> the argument, when reduced to its simplest form, was clear, it was precise, it was easy to grasp. There are Westerners, and there are Orientals. The former dominate; the latter must be dominated, which usually means having their lands occupied, their internal affairs rigidly controlled, their blood and treasure

put at the disposal of one or another Western power. That Balfour and Cromer could strip humanity down to such ruthless cultural and racial essences was not an indication of their particular viciousness. Rather it was an indication of how streamlined a general doctrine has become by the time they put it to use – how streamlined and effective. (1978: 36)

School implements this discourse in *The New Tribe*, Chester's classmates call him the 'King of the devils', hence he forsakes his role in the play. He is made even more conscious of his awkward position as a black person in a white family and is haunted by a desire to uncover his real identity. Likewise, his question about his real mother compels Arthur Arlington to reveal to both Julia and him their different adoption stories. Henceforth, a growing feeling of estrangement nags the developing boy. His exclusion is suggestively conveyed in the scene of the moment of truth through the joining of hands that binds the white couple and the adopted white girl, leaving him out (*NT* 14).

Subsequent to the disclosure that his mother, a young Nigerian woman, parted with him because she was expecting twins by another man who was not prepared to take care of him, 'Chester started to have a recurring dream. Though it usually came at night, it sometimes came during the day as well, and nothing he could do would dispel it. It came to him in fragments at first, but after a while, it acquired concrete images and a definite theme' (16). Thus denied a city of his own to belong in, his mind constructs one that offers solace. His sense of being 'shut out' worsens because of trivial incidents that cause his father's display of anger and isolate him more, then plunge him deeper into his dream. The vision that materializes in the dream consists in a pristine village scene in which is wrought an even more dream-like and exotic self-image: that of a lost prince.

Chester is in a mood Julia Kristeva would diagnose as melancholia, an infant's state of mind caused by separation from one parent. From this depressive position, Kristeva explains, the infant 'tries to signify the sorrow that submerges him by producing in his own ego elements that, while alien to the exterior world, are to correspond to that lost or displaced exteriority: we are, then, no longer in the presence of equivalences but of symbols in the proper sense of the word' (*NT* 15). Moreover, her remark based on Gérard de Nerval's poetry tones with Chester's predicament:

> The triumph over melancholy consists as much in the constitution of a symbolic family (ancestor, mythical personage, esoteric community) as the constitution of a symbolic object: the sonnet. This construction, due to the author, replaces the lost ideal in the same movement as it turns melancholy's lugubrious shades into lyrical song. (*NT* 17)

If the low-spirited poet curbs his mood thanks to a lyrical song, Chester resorts to a fictive world of his own, his dream of Africa, the land of his ancestors and people. It comes as a blurred memory of a time and place he has never known which he conceptualizes as a kingdom, and yearns to visit. He escapes into this dream world to make up for his lack: his missed parents, and the isolation he feels in his foster family.

Oddly enough, Chester remains in a world he meant to shun by giving up the part of the leader of the three kings. His dream bestows on him a princely status, the pursuit of which spurs the story forward. The narrative engages him in a quest for a kingdom. The device refers to a known stereotypical figment, one might call the 'prince syndrome' in the African diaspora imagination. 'In his vision, he [Chester] was at home in his kingdom, the prince everybody wanted. He had grown up somewhere else, but his city was there waiting for him to take possession. The vision that had been haunting him since he was child of seven took shape before his eyes' (*NT* 40).

The vision derives from an African folktale that Ginny adapted and impressed on his mind in his childhood in order to 'keep alive for Chester some memory of where he came from' (*NT* 8). By way of consequence, the contrived bed-time story plays a key role in the identity quest Chester embarks on, and which leads him to Nigeria. So just like Kehinde, he goes home, but unlike her, he leaves Britain for the first time in pursuit of this dreamt home. Kehinde travels back home, prodded by Taiwo: 'Why don't you go to Nigeria and find out what is happening, before it is too late? Have you forgotten that in Nigeria it's considered manly for men to be unfaithful? Even if he didn't want women they would come to him' (*K* 46). The two journeys tally with each other; and Chester's discovery of home resembles Kehinde's reunion with it.

In *Kehinde* just as in *The New Tribe,* there is no notable change in the way Nigeria has been presented so far in Emecheta's novels. Home turns into an oppressive place for Kehinde, whereas Albert blooms and exudes more confidence. He has a good professional position, while Kehinde's applications for work are turned down on a regular basis. Her homecoming signifies isolation and disempowerment: loss of the power she had in London as an economically independent woman and of her matrimonial privilege and status. She finds a highly educated co-wife, Rike, holder of a doctorate and university teacher. Rike embodies one version of educated women referred to as the *acada*. They epitomize successful independent women who use men to their advantage. In the language of the novel, they may operate as checks to women's empowerment by entrenching the very traditions that enlightened women like them are supposed to resist. Her attitude seems to reify the traditional idea that security lies in marriage, be it in polygamous *ménage*. In opposition, Kehinde stands by more individuation and dissents from the local culture and social demands.

What complicates the situation is not Albert's change of status and his confidence but his new wife. She foils Kehinde's defensive arguments that no Nigerian woman would stand competition with an educated been-to like her. Indeed, some deep sensitivity and a closeness of vision transpire in the manner the narrator renders Kehinde's state of mind by fusing their two voices:

> Here women were supposed to stick together and a wife to give her husband room enough to be a man. This was not new to her so why was he finding it difficult to accept? She felt she was being cheated, undervalued. She looked at Albert's young wife, a much more educated woman, bowing down to tradition. But through it, she had acquired a home and a big extended family for her children to belong to. In spite of her doctorate, she had got herself hooked to a man eighteen years her senior, with a wife and two children in England. Kehinde knew she did not stand a chance against Rike, with all her sophistication. They were not playing by the same rules. (*K* 89)

This representation of the stakes in polygamy discloses a new positioning of the local female elite in the social formation in which the novel is set; there appears readiness to accommodate and to play by the rules of the dominant social discourse. *Kehinde* thus prolongs in some way the debate in *Naira Power* by further reducing the dialogic treatment of the question there to a monologic one. Kehinde refuses to compromise and returns to London thanks to the helping hand of a friend, Mariommo, which also reiterates a familiar pattern in Emecheta's writings that the West is more congenial to women's development. Home is no place for the been-to woman to blossom. As much can be read in Kehinde's resolve to return to her home in London, a haven of selfhood. Nigeria is stressful and leaves her distraught. The narrative also curtails Albert's success as if to enhance the negativity of Nigeria. His successful career plummets. Yet, Kehinde's daughter elects to stay and study in Nigeria, even though her decision is bound with her wanting to be with her boyfriend.

However destructive her original home is, once in London, her co-wife's intellectual achievement urges her to study for a degree, although such a degree might mean taking substandard jobs as many qualified Africans do in the metropolis. She also voices her recognition of Mary Elikwu, a graduate Nigerian woman in London who left her violent husband, as a role model. Following an initial rejection of Mary because of her independence, Kehinde ruefully admits:

> She had been on my conscience since the night of Albert's party. She has foresight, going to college and having herself educated, after so many children.... The saving grace for us is the big 'E' of education. This girl, Rike, doesn't even have to live with us, because her education made her independent, yet she is content to be an African wife in an Igbo culture. How come we in England did not see all this? I think perhaps Mary Elikwu did. (*K* 95)

The dispute with the empire that erupts from now and again in the novel becomes subdued by a discourse of accommodation to the space it grants Kehinde who now makes it her permanent home, once her motherland is deserted. Significantly, the chapter entitled 'The Rebel' closes the novel like a final statement. Its contents corroborate the new posture that home

has induced in Kehinde who has become a transformed person determined to affirm her freedom by taking in a lover, to the discontent of her
son.

Thus ends a story of a strained homecoming. Rather than being what
Belinda Edmonson calls, with reference to the journey of Paule Marshall's
protagonist, 'a meditation on the irrevocable *loss* of the African. . .
identity' *Kehinde* is a narrative of identity relocation outside its original
space. And Edmonson further notes: 'if the movement is First to Third
World, it is also, as Avey's status signifies, from one coordinate of the
black diaspora to the other: the two become contrasting possibilities to
each other' (163). In this regard, Kehinde travels from the First to the
Third World and back to the First which amounts to reducing the possibilities to one.

While Kehinde lives and acts as a knowledgeable person, Chester has
only a remote idea of Nigeria reinforced by his meeting with one Nigerian,
Mr Enoch Ugwu, the agent of his induction to Nigerian culture. He even
gives him a meaningful Igbo name, Illoefuna: 'your community will not
be extinct' (*NT* 86). Just as Kehinde and Chester's motives differ, so does
the outcome of each person's adventure to the motherland. The endings of
the two novels raise questions. The characters dis-identify with the
Nigeria that still enjoys a half-hearted treatment in each. This attitude
present in Emecheta's earlier fiction is rehearsed in them, but with a
marked distancing from the motherland in favour of the land of adoption:
the mother country. The discourse on the relationship to the motherland
seems to be moving to a close and the internal conflict is resolved.
Kehinde's divided loyalties seem to have come to an end. The balance
finally tilts towards England, the land that provides more.

The novels privilege the manichean categories: the West the land of
order versus Africa the place of disorder that refer back to orientalism, as
exemplified by Ginny's idea of Nigeria as 'one of those dreadful African
countries where .... chaos, poverty and violence reigned' (*NT* 8). Although
this reductive representation is challenged by her subsequent surprising
discovery, following research, that 'Nigeria was a country of many
languages and peoples, with a rich history and its own traditional way of
doing things' (*NT* 8), it is this same chaotic view that Kehinde has of
Nigeria. She registers the smell, the noise, the traffic, the overwhelming
disorder, and the lack of discipline in the manner of an alien visitor. This
is a fair dart of social criticism but it overstates the vilification of home;
there is nothing attractive there.

From Kehinde's repugnance for an inhospitable home to Chester's dis-
illusionment in *The New Tribe* there is one constant that lies in their way
of coping with the environment that confronts them. Albeit Chester has
never been to Africa, his reactions are milder. Kehinde is a subject who
has come to terms with an identity she has accepted as a shifting one. She
lets run its full course and orients it towards England. Chester, on the

other hand, is a subject in constitution, as it were, with Africa as a reference. It is worth noting that not even the cautioning of Esther Willoughby, his black British girlfriend, could deter him from his projected journey to his dreamland. Her word of caution, purposefully placed at the initial stage of his plan, states the foregone conclusion:

> 'Oh, I see, you're looking for your roots.' Chester's face clouded, and Esther felt she should explain.
> 'You don't seem ready to accept reality, Chester. We don't belong in Africa, we're British. Black British maybe, but this is our home now.'
> 'You are patronizing me.'
> 'I'm sorry Chester, I didn't mean to. It's just that all that roots stuff is so dated. Look how black people have changed the face of British culture. Don't you want to be part of that.' (*NT* 113)

Esther's point abides by the 'we're here to stay' philosophy, which, valid as it stands, does not necessarily preclude identifying with, or claiming, Africa. Esther's statement closes, by transference, the mock dialogue in *Kehinde*. Thus, while Kehinde negotiates with and claims both cultures with strong leanings towards the West, Esther's point carries further Kehinde's acts at the close of the novel. Their combined views differ from the one propounded in *Gwendolen*. The unbelonging subjects have adopted the mother country as their motherland, and they are resolving the anxiety of ambivalence that inhabits them. After rejoining to Taiwo, 'this is not my home. Nigeria is my home,' Kehinde concedes to be one with her, and accepts her opinion: 'We make our choices as we go along.... This is yours. There is nothing to be ashamed of in that' (*K* 108).

In Esther's assertion may lie an answer for a critic who concludes a study of *Kehinde* with this comment: 'it is intriguing to imagine the effect this obvious resolution will have on Buchi Emecheta's future fiction' (Hawley 1996: 347). Esther's standpoint and, indeed, *The New Tribe* as a whole moves a step beyond another reading, by Brenda Berrian, of the direction *Kehinde* takes with regard to the vexed issue of cultural allegiance:

> By combining and synthesizing aspects of Igbo, Yoruba and British culture in *Kehinde* Emecheta creates a protagonist who supports her preference for dual citizenship, requiring a coming to terms with herself and reaching a level of comfort with multiple assimilations and exposures. The natural ambivalence is the allegiance to one's emotional language and birth country in connection with Kehinde's original sense of loss within the core of her childhood years for a part of herself – her Taiwo. (1996: 181–2)

The New Tribe follows the route Esther delineates before the action starts. As the title of the novel suggests, she and Chester represent a new diasporic breed: the second or third generation descending from immigrants. The novel shows Chester chasing a futile dream as Esther puts it, and adds: 'maybe the reality of Africa would wake him up and make him accept his life as it was' (*NT* 115). The warm feeling of homecoming when landing on Nigerian soil subsides into suffocating unease that matches the effects of the heat on him. In binding the heat to 'the undisguised chaos' (*NT* 116) Chester notices around him and which makes him wonder how he could 'find his kingdom in such a vast and chaotic country' (*NT* 119), the text subtly or unconsciously reiterates the chaos/order construct that places Africa on the negative end of the binary opposition earlier mentioned. No doubt, as in *Kehinde*, there is a valid intended critical effect in presenting the country in this way so as to draw attention to its negative sides further manifested in the hidden culture in terms of bribery and cunning extortion.

The quest reveals the dark aspects of human relationships, pointing to the deceptive dealings that foreigners are subjected to. Chester's experience mirrors numerous ones based on considering the foreigner as a rich person to fleece. The text foregrounds such occurrences to present the search for identity as a voyage into a covetous country where everything turns around gifts and money. The traveller quite often runs into unexpected hurdles. The compact space allotted to the quest is replete with incidents that expose the vanity not just of the dream but of the place. Crude as their representation may be, the dream and its pursuit appear as a strategy that not only serves to deride such idealistic ventures on the one hand, but also those who cash in on the gullible African diasporans searching for their roots. The novel caricatures the type through Jimoh, a swindler, who uses Chester, the naïve pursuant of his African origins. Stories about such incidents and individuals abound. That Emecheta uses them to relate Chester's home discovery is purposeful in at least two respects: to satirize the type on the one hand, and to emphasize the extent of the victim's helplessness on the other. Chester's bewilderment and his blunders lay bare the incongruity of his adventure.

The failure in the search for roots is ultimately over-determined and the narrative inalterably follows the pre-ordained path to this end. Then the story becomes a cautionary tale and another instance of dissociation from the motherland. At this point the early demonization of Chester as a child by the headmaster and his classmates backfires on the ancestors' land through the incidents that litter the searching protagonist's way. Everything from the uncertainty of his escort to the haphazard directions to the Obas' abodes seems programmed to show how debilitating the homeland is.

The New Tribe attempts to balance the horrible and the admirable, just as *Kehinde* does. Such love-hate reactions cumulate and result in a dubious attitude. Chester is shown quite often in the grip of awkward feelings that increase his confusion, enhance his doubts about home, and undermine his imagined identity especially when he learns that the Nigerian local king has gone to England for medical treatment, a telling incident not only for what it stands for in its face value, but for what is unsaid. It is a witty statement on the dependence apparent in the ironical questioning put in Chester's mouth (*NT* 132).

An eight-week-long trek with Karimu and Mowunmi leads them to the charismatic churches that are also the target of Emecheta's satire in *Kehinde*. One of them is actually the cause of Kehinde's plight in Nigeria. Albert's second wife belongs to a congregation that is shown enticing her husband into the ways of polygamy. *The New Tribe* derides such churches with specific reference to Mowunmi's flock: 'In spite of copious prayers, singing and speaking in tongues, and many offerings on Chester's part, Chester's kingdom was not revealed. Karimu saw that he had to think again, and suggested that, as a last resort, they visit the palace of the Oba of Chamala' (*NT* 133).

The new style Oba is portrayed as a graduate of an American university, ridden with the 'cargo mentality' to use Armah's phrase from *Fragments*. The satirical and allusion-laden treatment of the Oba culminates in his unmasking as the armed robber chasing Chester and Karimu, and in the ironic concealment of the cause of his death as an attack by road armed robbers:

> Some days later, Karimu showed Chester a report in the *Daily Echo*. The Oba of Chamala had been attacked on the road by armed robbers, and had died later. His people were in deep mourning. For a few days, obituaries and tributes filled the papers. These extolled the enlightened leadership of one of the new generation of educated Obas, who was both a devout Christian and a worshipper of his ancestors. He would be missed. (*NT* 141)

The eventful six-month visit to Nigeria ends in a Lagos hospital to which a malaria-stricken Chester is brought by a picturesque white-robed congregation that claims to have carried him walking from Benin to Lagos, a miracle that adds to the dreamlike language the novel taps into.

The illusion in which Chester has been engrossed dissipates as he regains consciousness responding: 'I'm home,' when Esther tells him she has come to take him home, to England. Almost like a well-rehearsed cue Esther's retort reiterates a point she made at the beginning of Chester's project: 'No Chester. Africa is no longer our home. We have stayed away in the market too long, as Nigerians say. Our home is Liverpool!' (*NT* 145). It is important to note that this final decision is made by a strong educated woman, who comes to rescue her male sweetheart. This utterance echoes and upholds, not only Taiwo's 'home sweet home' in London, but also the symbolic meaning in Kehinde's ripping down the House for Sale sign when she returns from Nigeria, a gesture that both claims her ownership right to the house and affirms her will to remain in Britain. Chester reaches the same conclusion at the end of the story. Although his depiction as a sympathetic and non-assuming character may preclude interpretation of his departure a 'repudiation of the duty of the exile to return to the land of his ancestors' (Okafor 2004: 128), one would contend that the resolution of *New Tribe* is problematic.

All in all, the reader is far from the unbelonging subjects of *Gwendolen*, Mrs Odowis and Sonia, who wished 'they could feel their beating hearts each time the British national anthem was sung' (*G* 164). Emecheta's later characters have accepted the mother country as home. After initial reluctance due to the racism time and again decried in *Second-Class Citizen*, *In the Ditch,* and *Gwendolen*, they are now ready to merge into British society, to be part of the changing culture, as Esther suggests in *The New Tribe* enhancing Kehinde's resolve in *Kehinde*. They are socialized as hybrid subjects claiming agency in this change. Likewise they mean to play their part in what Edouard Glissant calls the 'drama of relation', which is tantamount to imagining an identity that lays claim to both African and British cultures. Discussing hybridity, Glissant asserts: 'all societies are accultured. Any acculturation is likely to be transformed into the motif of a new culture. It is essential here to stress not so much the acculturation and deculturation mechanisms as the dynamics capable to freeze or to get over them' (1997: 429, my translation).

The divided loyalties and the wariness of 'turning hybrid' (Kane 1972: 113) identified in Emecheta's earlier works have been gradually neutralized. The subjects consent to naturalization and become one with the adopted motherland that Ginny symbolizes in *The New Tribe*. Her relationship to Chester is metonymic of the diasporic subjects' to Britain. She becomes a trope for the surrogate and foster mother/land that is finally adopted and accepted by immigrants in the same way as Chester accepts curate Arthur Arlington as a father whose estate he largely inherits. Quite suggestively, Chester muses: 'He had noticed since his illness and recovery that something had changed inside him. He no longer felt isolated and adrift, his head had cleared. Perhaps Karimu was right, and the water from the River Niger had washed away all his confusion and headaches. Yes, he would go to Liverpool, and get on with his life' (*NT* 148).

His mother has made contact to see him and has also revealed that his biological father is an African American. Thus ends a 'once upon a time story', and indeed *The New Tribe* ends with those very words that could also mean as well that qualms about identity and belonging are in the past for Emecheta and her immigrant or British-born black characters. The choice has been made. The two novels suggest, then state, in the stories of their main protagonists that they and their creator have opted either for dual citizenship or a diasporic identity that locates itself in the mother country. This choice privileges the centre in the postcolonial discourse, and reinforces the affiliation to the metropolis. As a result, the previous anger with the mother country subsides and the motherland develops into the desired yet unwanted other. The burgeoning homecoming in the *Rape of Shavi* and in *Gwendolen* withers in the final returns of Kehinde and Chester, the prodigal daughter and son of the mother country. The wavering and half-hearted feelings are brought to an end. The dialogic treatment of the theme narrows down to a single-voiced one that promotes an identity at one with the adopted land where one's heart lies. Kehinde, the African-born and Esther and Chester, the British-born, all lay claim to a British and a diasporic identity.

NOTES

1   'Homeland' and 'Motherland' are used alternately to denote the land of origin: Africa. 'Mother Country' refers to Britain. *Mother/lands: Black Women's Writing from Africa, the Caribbean and South East Asia,* ed. Susheila Nasta. London: The Women's Press, 1991, holds useful essays on the subject.
2   Further references to these works, whenever convenient, will be *K* for *Kehinde* and *NT* for *The New Tribe* followed by page numbers
3   Omar Sougou, *Writing Across Culture,* Chapter 6.
4   Ayi Kwei Armah debunks this myth in *Osiris Rising,* Popenguine: Per Ankh, 1994, Chapter VI.

WORKS CITED

Armah, Ayi Kwei. *Fragments*. London: Heinemann, 1974
—— *Osiris Rising*. Popenguine: Per Ankh, 1994.
Berrian, Brenda F. 'Her Ancestor's Voice: The Ijebi Transcendance of Duality in Buchi Emecheta's *Kehinde*'. *Emerging Perspectives on Buchi Emecheta*. Ed. Marie Umeh. Trenton, New Jersey: Africa World Press, 1996. 169–84.
Bhabha, Homi. *The Location of Culture*. London: Routledge, 1994.
Cohen, Robin. *Global Diasporas: An introduction*. Seattle: University of Washington Press, 1997.
Davies, Carole Boyce. 'Collaboration and Ordering Imperative in Life Story Production.' *De/colonizing the Subject: The Politics of Gender in Women's Writing*. Sidonie Smith and Julia Watson, eds, Minneapolis: University of Minnesota Press, 1992. 3–19.
Edmonson, Belinda. *Making Men*. Durham and London: Duke University Press, 1999.
Emecheta, Buchi. *The New Tribe*. Oxford: Heinemann, 2000.
—— *Kehinde*. Oxford: Heinemann, 1994.
—— *Gwendolen*. London: Collins, 1989.
—— *Rape of Shavi*. London: Flamingo, 1985
—— *Naira Power*. London: Macmillan, 1982.
—— *Second-Class Citizen*. London: Allison and Busby, 1974.
—— *In The Ditch*. London: Barrie and Jenkins, 1972.
Glissant, Edouard. *Le Discours antillais*. Paris: Gallimard, 1997.
Hawley, John C. 'Coming to Terms: Buchi Emecheta's *Kehinde* and the Birth of a 'Nation'' *Emerging Perspectives on Buchi Emecheta*. Marie Umeh, ed. Trenton, New Jersey: Africa World Press, 1996. 333–48.
Kane, Cheikh Hamidou. *Ambiguous Adventure*. Trans. Katherine Woods. London: Heinemann, 1972.
Kristeva, Julia. 'On Melancholic Imagination.' *Postmodernism and Continental Philosophy*. Hugh J. Silverman and Donn Welton, eds, Albany, New York: New York University Press, 1988, 12–25.
Nasta, Susheila, ed. *Mother/lands: Black Women's Writing from Africa, the Caribbean and South East Asia*, London: The Women's Press, 1991.

Okafor, Clement Abiazem, 'Exile and Identity in Buchi Emecheta's *The New Tribe.*' *New Women's Writing in African Literature.* ALT 24 (2004):114–28.

Said, Edward. *Orientalism.* New York: Pantheon Books, 1978.

Sougou, Omar. *Writing Across Cultures: Gender Politics and Difference in the Fiction of Buchi Emecheta.* Amsterdam and New York: Rodopi, 2002.

Suleiman, Susan R., ed. *Exile and Creativity: Signposts, Travelers, Outsiders, Backward Glances.* Durham and London: Duke University Press, 1998.

Clement Abiaziem Okafor

The practice that began in Jamestown, Virginia in 1619[1] of forcibly bringing Africans to perform the exhausting task of working in the American plantations from 'sun up' to 'sun down', which later blossomed into the transatlantic slave trade that lasted about three centuries, denuded African societies of their most virile members and created the first African diaspora in the Americas. The Africans in this first diaspora were sought after for their physical strength.

The catastrophic collapse of the economies of most independent African nations has in recent times triggered another exodus from the continent. This time, however, the emigration is voluntary and involves the most educated members of the various African states. This brain drain has over the years created a second African diaspora in America and the Western world.

Call Me By My Rightful Name[2] belongs to the growing body of African literature that explores the ramifications of the African presence in the Western world. This novel makes a valuable contribution to the diasporic discourse by examining the important issues of racial memory and the search for one's roots among the Africans in diaspora from two different perspectives: Western (Clinical Psychiatry) and African (Yoruba Ifa). The novel's protagonist, Otis, is an individual with a split personality and dual identities (American and African). He is a normal bubbly American youth until he is destabilized by mysterious drumming only audible to himself. The music triggers compulsive behaviour during which his speech becomes incomprehensible to other human ears. When in his fits the gibberish he utters is recorded for study by American clinical psychiatrists for clues to the treatment suitable for the condition. Until the 'language' of the drum is decoded, Otis cannot return to a state of mental, physical or psychological normality. The whole process takes Otis back centuries to his ancestral life in Africa.

The Western (Clinical Psychiatry) Perspective

After listening to Norma's playback of her recording of the gibberish that Otis utters during his seizures, Mr Hampton suddenly realizes the enormity of his family's predicament. He comes to the painful conclusion that his son is in dire need of psychiatric counseling – a procedure that is likely to expose the innermost thoughts of his family members to a total stranger, especially since there is no black psychiatrist practising in Boston at the time. His agony is heightened further by his awareness of the racial tension prevalent in the area.

Mr Hampton is not unduly worried about his own side of the family, but he is not too confident about his wife's lineage. He knows that although his father, Daley Hampton, was very taciturn and did not communicate very much with members of his family or outsiders, he was essentially a very decent man who loved and provided for his family. Furthermore, the little he knows about his grandfather convinces him that the old man had very high self esteem. Hence, he has nothing to fear on his account. However, Hampton is worried about his wife's ancestry, since her father was lynched allegedly for lusting after the daughter of his white employer and her mother was murdered by an enraged lover. Thus, it is with great trepidation that Mr Hampton finally settles for the services of Dr Fishbein, a Jewish doctor, who is noted for his concern for the black community.

In consonance with modern Western medical practice, Dr Fishbein's approach to Otis Hampton's problems is in three stages – a clinical examination, a diagnosis, and a prescription.

The Clinical Examination
The clinical examination comprises several counseling sessions during which Dr Fishbein deftly burrows into Otis's mind to unearth not only the origin of his condition, but to record the full text of the poem that Otis chants during his seizures. Besides, the sessions also enable the psychiatrist to identify the event that triggers the seizures. In the end the evidence leads him to conclude that his patient's phobia for drum music precipitates the seizures:

> What about drum: do you like drums ? ... Not really, I don't like drums that much ... Otis shakes his head, rather forcefully. Fishbein scribbles, eyeing him. Silence. ... Otis, I can see you don't like drums. Is there anything about drums that turns you off? ... Well, I don't know. Maybe just the noise? ... Right, and as I recall, it was the sound of drums that upset you on two occasions, sent you into spasm. What is it about drums that does this to you? Try to think ... I ... I don't know. I've been trying to figure it out. (54–5)

The Diagnosis
The final outcome of the clinical sessions is that they enable the psychia-

trist to diagnose the nature of Otis's illness. Dr Fishbein's diagnosis is that the seizures that Otis suffers and the accompanying chant he recites whenever he hears African-derived drum music are manifestations of recitative xenoglossy. In his opinion, they are symptomatic of family trauma that manifests itself in a generation after the one that has experienced it. Dr Fishbein is aware that the most current medical literature on the subject, based on studies of Jewish survivors of the Holocaust, points to the possibility of racial memory of events that happened one generation before the victim was born. However, the literature does not suggest the possibility of racial memory of traumatic events occurring more than one generation before the victim's birth. Consequently, the doctor finds Otis's trauma – which traverses several generations – intellectually challenging; it could advance the state of knowledge in Clinical Psychiatry. In any case, Dr Fishbein's interest is engendered not only by intellectual curiosity but is also sustained by his earlier altruistic support of black people:

> The psychiatrist's interest in the strange case had steadily grown – partly because he had taken a personal liking to Otis, partly also because Otis's condition brought him an unprecedented challenge. Not merely a professional challenge; that came with the job. More than that, he was slowly beginning to realize, after so many years of wading through good relations with black people that cost him nothing, that it took not much more to commit himself to people as people without counting what he stood to gain. (70)

The Prescription
Having diagnosed the nature of the illness, Dr Fishbein's next step in trying to cure his patient is to establish the source of the xenoglossy. Since he is unable to identify the language involved, he seeks the assistance of a professor of linguistics at Harvard University, who is also a fellow Brown alumnus. Thereafter, the search for the implicated language resembles a serial mystery with one event leading to yet another until the puzzle is solved.

All the Harvard professor does is use his equipment to isolate the patient's chant from the African drum music that triggered it and then refer Dr Fishbein to a Boston University professor, who is an expert in Southern African languages. This expert rightly identifies the language of the xenoglossy as Yoruba, but not being a specialist in that language refers Dr Fishbein to Dr Baldwin, an anthropologist at Berkeley, who studied Yoruba. Unfortunately, although Baldwin's dictograph transcribes Otis's chant into a legible script, he is unable to decipher much of its meaning. Hence, he in turn refers the matter to Professor Bolaji Alabi, a Yoruba visiting postdoctoral fellow at Northwestern University. In the end, Alabi establishes beyond all reasonable doubt that the chant belongs to a specific family among the Ekiti of Northeastern Yorubaland in Nigeria.

Once the origin of the xenoglossia has been identified, Dr Fishbein prescribes a trip to Nigeria for his patient.

Mr Hampton's reluctant acceptance of the prescription is further strengthened when even his sister Ella – invited by his wife to try the Christian approach of praying for the son – approves of the prescribed journey too. Indeed, in her view, Otis is not ill at all. Rather, it is their ancestors who are beckoning them through him. As Ella says to her brother: 'Your son is not sick; Otie Jay. Our ancestors are talking to us through him. It took a long time coming. But God's time comes never too soon nor too late.' (90) If anything Ella's only regret is that she is not the one chosen for the mission: 'Somehow, I wish they had chosen me and made me well enough to make the journey.' (91)

Thus Otis's journey to Nigeria as well as all the events that take place during his sojourn in the country are not only aspects of the Hampton's quest for their ancestral roots, but are steps in the implementation of the prescription, with the psychiatrist coming along to monitor his patient's progress.

The Ifa Perspective

Briefly, Ifa is the compendium of traditional knowledge that pertains to every aspect of life within the Yoruba cosmos.[3] Viewed from the Ifa (Yoruba) perspective, *Call Me By My Rightful Name* portrays the actualization of the Ifa statement: *Ola silo n'ile, ola dehin s'ile* (Honor leaves the home, and honor returns to the home). Honor left the home when Akimbowale was kidnapped in his homeland while he was performing the funerary dance for his late father Akindiji and enslaved in America. Hence, honor returns to the home when Otis, who is believed to be the reincarnation of Akimbowale, returns to the very site at Ijoko-Oke to complete the funerary performance that was tragically interrupted more than a century earlier.

Seen through this perspective, the novel becomes the narrative of how Otis, a third generation descendant of Akimbowale, is chosen to be the one to bring honor back to his ancestors. It is also the account of the medium through which the intimations of the mission are conveyed to Otis. Above all, it is the chronicle of the response of the chosen one to his special vocation.

The vocation is conveyed to Otis through the medium of a dream vision. In the hypnotic trance induced by Dr Fishbein, Otis relives the experience once again:

> There's a man or maybe a woman. Saying things. A man, yes, a man. But I haven't a clue who he is. Yes, he's dancing, and there's music. Many people . It's very confusing, I can't make out their faces. Men and women. But I can't figure out any of them. God, they look so weird. And they're all in a strange place … You've never been there before?... No, never. Never been here before … Think, Otis, you could have been there sometime but forgotten? No – yes – no – no – no – No (55)

Initially, Otis does not understand the nature of the calling; hence, he is unable to respond to it meaningfully. His predicament is thus akin to that of the legendary son of the descendants of Obi Ezechi in Igbuzo oral tradition. This scion of Ezechi did not realize that he had a special duty to perform in his ancestral homeland, Igbuzo, until a remarkable event drew his attention to it. A buffalo singled out his farm in Ejime for destruction again and again. Frustrated eventually by this repeated destruction of his farm, he ran back to his home, a distance of twenty-five miles and was crowned after performing the requisite rituals.[4]

Otis's predicament in the beginning is also comparable to that of another legendary figure, this time in Yoruba oral tradition. Here, Oyepolu was punished and frustrated continuously in all his endeavours until he reappraised his life and elected to perform the duties he owed his ancestors:

> Ifa divination was done for Oyepolu, scion of those who performed cult rites at Ife. He was told that it was because he had ignored the ancestral rites that his life was in disarray. He was told to visit the ancestral shrine and pay his respects. Once he did that, life would be good for him again. He did as he was told. Things became well for him. (3)

Like the two legendary figures above, Otis continues to be humiliated and frustrated to draw the attention of his family to the duties that he has been singled out to discharge. In which case, *Call Me By My Rightful Name* may be viewed as a chronicle of the process through which Otis discovers his calling, fulfills his obligations to his ancestors and by so doing brings honour to his lineage. However, he discovers his special calling only after being subjected to a series of humiliating experiences.

Otis's first major humiliation occurs on the very day that his team mates celebrate not only his coming of age but also his great accomplishments as Tiger, the most valued player of their winning basketball team. Everyone expects him to join one of the major professional National Basketball Association teams and prosper. Nevertheless, this is the day that fate brings him down from his pedestal and humiliates him. On his way from the team party, the drum music emitting from his car radio causes Otis to have a seizure in the middle of the road. The resulting traffic disruption attracts the attention of the police, who appear to be only too eager to humiliate the young black man before his girlfriend.

Otis is humiliated again when he accompanies Norma to the Caribbean restaurant, Pleasure Island to interview a Jamaican businessman, Mr Barrett 'Guinea Man', in furtherance of her college project on the family in Maroon culture. This time, the playing of Kramanti (African) music in the restaurant makes Otis have another seizure in full public view. Fortunately, the tape recorder with which Norma has been recording her interview with Mr Barrett the 'Guinea Man' also records the unfamiliar words that Otis chants. Fortunately, too, out of this humiliating experience emanates the beginnings of the solution to Otis's problem, since the recorded 'gibberish' makes Mr Hampton realize that his son is in dire need of the psychiatric counseling that eventually resolves his crisis.

It is credible from the Ifa perspective that once the Hamptons decide to travel to Nigeria, their decision is communicated to their kinswoman, Taiwo, through an ominous event. Although Taiwo is more than one hundred years old, she suddenly has an intense and extraordinary urge to dance. The ominous feeling is so out of character for this ancient and venerable lady that it sounds incredible even to her own twin sister, Kehinde:

> But she cannot ignore her sister.
> So she asks, Are you alright, Taiwo?
>   I am, says the other. I am. Just … feel like … dancing.
> Do you think you might … want to join me in … dancing?
>   Are you serious? says Kehinde, turning again to the fire. Even the goat might laugh. (2)

Laughable or not, Taiwo's compulsive sensations indeed turn out to be the intimations of the glorious dance of destiny that eventually crowns their long and spectacular life on earth.

The omen is later reinforced by the details of Taiwo's and Kehinde's simultaneous dreams:

> It was a dream, Kehinde;
> There, I knew it. But why wonder a dream? How different is that, for us, than what passes for reality? Have we not long blurred the lines between them? (77)

In Taiwo's dream, an eagle and its strange companion are on their way to redeem the honour and reputation of their hosts. In Kehinde's own dream, there is also a sense of dreadful foreboding, for the birds are flying to a spot where some playing children are suddenly scattered as their playground goes up in smoke. In Kehinde's version of the dream, the birds are on their way to reconstruct the destroyed playground in the hope that they will be allowed to build their nests there. These events turn out to be foreshadowings of the details of Otis's sojourn, since there are uncanny correspondences between the details of the dreams and the various stages of Otis's experience in Nigeria. For instance, in Taiwo's dream, the eagle's companion is 'not of its kind' and while the eagle is very enthusiastic about the mission, the companion is there merely out of curiosity. Here, the eagle is an obvious reference to Otis, while the alien companion refers to Dr Fishbein. Thus, the eagle's flight to its destination corresponds to Otis's journey, first by air from Boston to Lagos via London and then by land to Ekitiland, which is his ancestral home. Similarly, the spot that erupted in white heat in the bush where the children had been playing corresponds to the spot where Akimbowale was captured and sold into slavery. This is the spot that Otis rushes to as soon as they get to Ijoko-Oke. Finally, the twins realize that the eagle's mission has the potential for both good and evil; it portends both life and death.

From the Ifa perspective, all the events that take place thereafter, namely, the search for the sacred spot; the identification of the family that owns the praise poem (*oriki orile*); the performance of the chant; the construction of the family tree; the completion of the interrupted dance of destiny and the death of the twin sisters are merely the concretizations of the dreams of the venerable twin sisters.

The first event, the search for the sacred spot generates much misunderstanding among the party of visiting Americans for not only does Otis make them set out famished and without eating their lunch but he also bullies the driver Lamidi into obeying his instructions rather than those of Bigelow, his boss from the embassy. In addition, he makes Lamidi drive faster than the village road conditions permit and eventually takes over, steering the vehicle into the bush:

> 'Look here! What the – Dr Fishbein, you better talk to your friends. I'm through with this shit. I have no part in their primitive mumbo jumbo stuff. They can go ahead and kill themselves over some old slave history. That's not of my business. Hey, listen to me!'
> Bigelow jumps from his seat, lands in the middle row where Hampton is seated, and thrusts his arm towards Otis to try to stop him. Hampton grabs Bigelow's arms fiercely and looks furiously into the officer's eyes.
> 'Let go of me, damn it!' (118–19)

However, like a bloodhound in pursuit of its quarry, Otis instinctively feels his way to the right location. '"Here, dad," Otis says, raising his head. "It's here."' (120). Surprisingly, the place turns out to be the very spot where Akimbowale was kidnapped more than a century earlier.

The second event, the identification of the family that owns the praise poem reveals the internal contradictions within the Ijoko-Oke community as well as the general wiliness of villagers. The Baale's initial pretence of not knowing the family that owns the chant (*oriki orile*) may be partly due to the wiliness of villagers and their general distrust of strangers. However, the Baale's action is also motivated by his insecurity about his throne occasioned by his family's subversion of the traditional political institution of Baale. The family members have turned the rotational office of Baale into a hereditary one. Consequently, he fears that the return to the village of men from the Akindiji family may pose a threat to the continued retention of the rulership position in his family. It is only when Pa Fadipe threatens to expose him that the Baale directs two of his councilors to accompany the visitors to the home of the centenarian twin sisters:

> 'Tell the truth, Osunkunle', the old man in the porch declares, with obvious effort. 'Others may not understand what that thing said, but you and I do. Do you think the truth will lie hidden for ever? Osunkunle, tell these strangers the truth'. (125)

When the visitors finally arrive at the home of the aged twin sisters, it appears that they are expected, with Taiwo recognizing Otis the very moment he enters the house. Then the twin sisters subject Otis to further physical examination which reveals the birth scars on Otis's head and left shoulder. Amazingly, these are identical to the scars that Akimbowale has on his head and left shoulder too. Eventually, the reunion of the Nigerian and the diasporic wings of the family is ritually consummated by the sharing of a kola nut during a subsequent visit.

The third event, the emendation of the text of the family praise poem (*oriki orile*) is very problematic, since even the twins find it a little difficult to reconstruct certain sections of the chant. This is not surprising, as they have not performed it for more than one hundred years. Indeed, the final emendation of the text requires the combined effort of not only the twins but that of the *babalawo* (the traditional philosopher and healer) and the expert drummer:

> The emendation comes to a spirited close, as together the old twins, the baba-lawo, and the drummer perform a song that is part of the people's cherished tradition of oral poetry. (144)

For the text of this praise poem (*oriki orile*) that belongs exclusively to a particular family to be meaningful, it has to be located within the family history. In this case, the family roots go back to Ifaturoti, the putative founder of their lineage. This ancestor lost his job at the court of the *Ooni* (King) of Ife and was exiled to Ondo as punishment for the amorous advances he made toward the wife of a senior palace official. He eventually brought his family to join him in Ondo. Hence, Otis is a member of this lineage, whose family tree is represented as follows:

IFATUROTI
|
IKOTUN married BAYONLE
|
ADEROJA married OLOHIGBE
|
ITAYEMI married EBUNOLA
|
AKINDIJI married ASHAKE
|
AKIMBOWALE
|
DALEY HAMPTON
|
OTIS JEREMIAH HAMPTON married MELBA
|
OTIS HAMPTON (AKIMBOWALE)

More importantly, the configuration of the family tree helps Otis to understand why and how the different members of their lineage have adopted different strategies to survive whichever problem and environment confronted them. For instance, Ifaturoti adapted to exile and his son, Ikotun, grew up in Ondo, his father's new abode, and became a great farmer and hunter. But his own son, Aderoja, learnt to work on ivory and went to Benin to work for its monarch and adapted so well there that he married a Bini wife. Again, since Aderoja's first son died fighting in the Bini army, his younger brother, Itayemi, was persuaded to leave Benin and return to Ondo, where his father had grown up. Itayemi again adapted so well to the life of the people in his new abode that he married two Ondo wives. He later became a valiant warrior, but eventually had to flee Ondo for the same reason his great grandfather was banished from the Ife palace. In his case, however, the offence was even greater and would have cost him his life, since his dalliance was with the wife of the King of Ondo himself. It was only his high social standing that saved him.

Itayemi begot Akindiji, who in time became a great farmer and warrior, who was famed for his valiant defence of his homeland against their northern neighbours, the Nupe. This same Itayemi begot Akmbowale and the centenarian twin sisters. Sadly, Akimbowale was captured and enslaved while he was performing the funerary rituals of his late father. In America, Akimbowale begot Daley, the father of Otis Jeremiah Hampton. Finally, Otis Jeremiah Hampton begot Otis Hampton, who has been chosen to restore the honor of the family. The lineage has survived through the ages because each generation adopted the survival strategy that was best suited to its problems and environment. Itayemi was short but utilized his powerful voice to scare away the enemy in battle, but his great grandson, Daley, adopted taciturnity as his preferred way of dealing with the unspeakable brutality of slavery on the American plantation. On the other hand, dogged stubbornness was Akimbowale's strategy for survival; hence, he was regarded as 'Stubborn Af'can. Didn't let no man give him no horse shit.' (18)

Teleologically, by far the most important event during Otis's sojourn is the performance of the funerary dance, which accompanies the recitation of the reconstructed and emended family praise poem. Preparatory to this most significant event, Otis is initiated into the cult of strong men, as recommended by the centenarian twins. In their view it is important for Otis, who is the reincarnation of Akimbowale to join this cult to which Akimbowale belonged in his former life. This ritual which requires him to severe the head of a dog with one stroke of the machete is obviously a form of training in the art of warfare. On this occasion, Otis is aided by the intoxicating drinks and the dominant loud music

After Otis spends one year learning the language and culture of the village, he is both emotionally and physically ready for the big event. Again, in anticipation, Madam Remilekun selects the costume uniform (*asho oke*) of alternating wine and silver stripes and a head piece of the same material – the same design the twins wore when the dance was interrupted more than a century before – and a horsetail fly whisk. Next, the *babalawo* consults the Ifa oracle to ensure that the occasion would be auspicious and then makes the prescribed offerings to appease the deities. Thereafter, the location in the village of Ijoko-Oke – which is not only the site where Itayemi had settled as an exile from Ondo but was also the site where Akimbowale was kidnapped and sold into slavery – is cleansed.

As prologue, Madam Remilekun and her Christian group who are decked in beautiful and colourful uniform costumes chant Christian songs, while a colourful ape masquerade entertains the gathering. These are followed by preliminary drums.

When Otis raises his hand, the drummers stop and he begins his chant and the twins and Otis dance to Otis's recitation of the family's special praise poem (*oriki orile*), while Olu the master drummer plays a reprise to each line. Furthermore, as Olu plays his reprise to each line, the venerated centenarian twin sisters recite phrases of their own that are not in the original script, but are the elaborations that they have formulated over the years. Meanwhile, the assembly marvels at the vigor of the twins who dance like women less than half their age. So joyous is their performance that the entire assembly joins in the last stanza; thereby climaxing the ritual dance of destiny and raising dust over the entire arena. Finally, when Otis notices that the twins are beginning to slow down he motions to the drummers to stop. This is the climax of the ritual and the fulfillment of the Ifa saying: 'Honor leaves the home and honor returns to the home.' This also concludes the funerary rites that were interrupted more than a hundred years ago.

The Epilogue

The venerated centenarian twins foresaw in their dream vision preceding the arrival of Otis that his sojourn is the harbinger of both life and death. It has certainly brought life by linking the lineage in the diaspora to that in Africa and has brought honor to the family by completing the funerary rituals that were tragically interrupted. Sadly, the completion of the dance of destiny signals the impending death of the centenarian twin sisters. Hence, Otis's sojourn has brought both life and death to the village. Taiwo dies soon after the dance of destiny and is followed closely by her twin sister Kehinde. In their honour, the Baale and his council declare a four-week period of mourning, with a special prohibition, which is a specific act of self denial proclaimed for each week. During the first week no market is permitted on the chosen day, and during the second, farming and hunting are prohibited. No one is allowed in or out of the village on the designated day of the third week, while music and merrymaking are prohibited during the selected day of the fourth week of mourning. In addition to the general prohibitions, Otis does not eat any food item cooked with palm oil. Besides, he ties a piece of black cloth around his head all day as a special sign of mourning.

The four weeks of mourning end in a great funerary ceremony that is accompanied by various kinds of music and dancing. This is the village's way of ushering the venerable twin sisters into the land of the ancestors, and is more elaborate than even the earlier spectacular dance of destiny. Appropriately, Otis Jeremiah Hampton in his capacity as the eldest living member of their lineage leads this farewell dance. On this solemn occasion, he is accompanied by his wife, who has now overcome her prejudices about Africa, as well as by Otis's girlfriend, Norma. This funeral dance is, therefore, a celebration of the reconnecting of the Hamptons to their ancestral roots.

In addition to the major narrative strands discussed above, the novel also explores various issues that are seminal to the diasporic discourse, namely, why were a handful of Europeans able to despoil the entire continent of Africa; to what extent did Africans collude with the Europeans in the trans-Atlantic trade itself; and finally, if African epistemology, more specifically if Ifa is indeed a compendium of all the knowledge that one needs in order to survive in the Yoruba cosmos, why did it not teach the people how to ward off the Europeans?

The answer to the question of Ifa's failure to teach its adherents how to ward off the Europeans is contained in the *babalawo*'s dialogue with Otis. The *babalawo* suggests that the fault does not lie with Ifa, but with adherents who failed to follow Ifa's clear teaching on the matter:

> If we had followed the teachings of Ifa properly, we should not have found ourselves in a situation where we surrendered ourselves and even our culture to other people. Perhaps we didn't listen to what Ifa said about togetherness being the only source of strength. Our people must have become so involved in protecting their private interests that they fell apart before the white people. (190)

It is also apparent that the Europeans were able to overpower various African communities on account of the internal contradictions inherent in those societies. In the specific case portrayed in the novel, the people who help the white people in capturing Akimbowale come from the nearby villages of Oguro and Imefun that have been looted earlier by Akindiji, Akimbowale's warrior father. Consequently, they have been nursing a grudge against his lineage; hence, they readily collude with the foreign slave traders intent on pillaging Ijoko-Oke and enslaving its citizens. Worse still, some villagers from Ijoko-Oke itself treacherously participate in the destruction of their own community. In Taiwo's and Kehinde's view, some villagers recognize those renegades, who deny their crime when they are confronted with it. Thus, as may be deduced from this case, the Europeans did not have enough manpower to conquer

Africa. They did, however, exploit the internal differences among the Africans to divide and conquer them.

Another issue highlighted in the novel is the perversion of traditional authority. The office of Baale of the village was rotational. However after the relocation of the village Oshunkunle's family subverted the traditional pattern and made the title exclusive to their family. As a result, they feel insecure when any possible contender for the throne emerges. This explains the existing feud between the incumbent Baale and Pa Fadipe's family, which culminates in the assassination of Pa Fadipe himself. It also informs the Baale's initial decision to conceal the identity of Otis's lineage. This is the Baale's way of trying to prevent Otis from becoming a threat to his family's hegemony. It is for that same reason that the permanent structure which Otis is building on his ancestral home is demolished. These incidents in the novel show that even traditional African societies have some unhealthy undercurrents that erode the solidarity of the village, since such leaders as Oshunkunle constantly scheme to protect their personal interests rather than those of the community. In the end, Oshunkunle's inability to exculpate himself from the suspicion that he has a hand in the brutal murder of Pa Fadipe and the destruction of Otis's house finally provokes the villagers into overthrowing him, burning down his home, and installing some one from another family to succeed him and by so doing restoring the former political equilibrium to the village.

A further important issue is the power dynamic between Africa and the modern Western world, herein represented by America. Here, the relationship between Bigelow and Lamidi is the metaphor for the power dynamics between the white world represented by America and the black world symbolized by Nigeria. Lamidi is very dark, with scarification on both sides of his face and very obsequious, while Bigelow exudes authority at all times. For instance, he uses his influence to ensure that the visiting party of Americans is not subjected to the normal custom and immigration procedures. His relationship with Lamidi is undoubtedly the classic master and servant one, as is exemplified in the following dialogue between them:

> 'Lamidi', says Bigelow, after the trunks have been loaded into the van, 'let's go. Embassy.'
> 'Yes, sir,' the driver bows, putting the car in motion.' (106)

This unequal relationship, which is obvious to Otis and his father, creates a dilemma for them. Their briefing by Mr Virgil Carillo, the Cultural Attache on the one hand reassures them of the protection of the powerful American government that has the means to extricate them in case the need arises. On the other hand, however, they wish to identify with the teeming population of their racial kinsmen, who constitute the overwhelming majority of the population of the country. Thus, although

Nigeria is ruled by black people, it is actually controlled by the white power of the American state. Bigelow flexes the muscle of the American state again when he orders his driver on the way to Akure to sound the car horn and make the masqueraders scamper away from the road. In the ensuing panic, the palmwine seller falls to the ground breaking the gourds of palmwine and spilling their content on the road, while the American party travels on without stopping.   Besides, when the Hamptons get to Akure, they find that there are American Peace Corps volunteers teaching even in a nearby village school, which shows how widespread American power is even in the most populous black nation on earth. Furthermore, Bigelow exhibits that power again by threatening the Baale even in his home village:

> He reminds the Baale that his guests are Americans, not ordinary foreigners. As such he must treat them with special care. His government does not like leaders who look on while Americans among them are treated badly or perhaps even harmed. If any harm is done to the visitors, he cannot say what his government will do but it will be something very serious. (138)

This unequal power relationship is demonstrated yet again when Bigelow later visits the nearby Baptist High School. Here, the school Principal assumes the posture of a mendicant begging for favours from the imposing and domineering foreign establishment. Furthermore, the embassy later dispatches two fully uniformed marines to the village school for the sole purpose of intimidating the villagers and showing them who is really in charge in their country which is supposed to be an independent and sovereign state.

While all the issues discussed above are in the foreground, the novel portrays in the background another important concern, namely, the Western Nigerian political crisis of the 1960s. Here, the ancient warfare between the Nupes and their Yoruba neighbours to the south is viewed as the paradigm for the crisis that is presently ravaging the Western Region of Nigeria. In this modern rendition of the historic conflict, the ruling class in Northern Nigeria has allied itself with a splinter group in the West in a move designed to help it to extend its sphere of influence south-wards. Thus, this political crisis, which forms the background to the various issues already discussed above, is portrayed as the Yoruba resistance to the hegemonic expansion of Northern Nigeria – the subject of the praise song (*oriki orile*) that celebrates the heroic exploits of the lineage of the protagonist of the novel, Otis Hampton.

The discussion above shows quite clearly that *Call Me By My Rightful Name* is a major contribution to the discourse on racial memory and the search for one's roots among the Africans in the Diaspora; it portrays these key issues from two perspectives: modern Western Medicine (Clinical Psychiatry) and the African (Yoruba Ifa). These perspectives, however, merge into one, since both entail a journey to the ancestral homeland of

Otis's great grandfather, who was enslaved and taken forcibly to America. In this way, the novel shows that each perspective is not only valid but also that these two worldviews offer complementary solutions to the issue of racial memory and the search for one's roots. Once the protagonist has identified his lineage then his ultimate duty is to honor his forbears by first assuming his rightful African name – Akimbowale – and then completing the funerary dance that was tragically interrupted when his ancestor was kidnapped more than a century earlier.

NOTES

1 Konia T. Kollehlon and Edward E. Eule, 'The Socioeconomic Attainment Patterns of Africans in the United States', *International Migration Review*, 37, 4 (Winter 2003), 1163–90.
2 Isidore Okpewho, *Call Me By My Rightful Name*, Trenton, New Jersey: Africa World Press, 2004. All citations are from this edition.
3 For a detailed discussion of Ifa, refer to Wande Bimbola, ed. *Ifa Divination Poetry*, New York: Nok, 1977.
4 D.C. Ohadike and R.N. Sham, Eds. *Oral Testimony from Igbuzo, Nigeria. Jos Oral Literature Texts*: *Western Igbo*, as quoted in *Call Me By My Rightful Name*.

The Ivorian Crisis
& Ahmadou Kourouma's Posthumous
Political Novel, *Quand on refuse on dit non*

Sery Bailly

Ahmadou Kourouma is best known for his first novel *Les soleils des indépendances* (1968; trans. *The Suns of Independence*). After initial difficulties with the publication in France, the novel was subsequently much acclaimed for its original use of the French language that made it sound like the author's native Malinké. It also criticized African leadership and one-party systems that prevailed all over Africa. This critical trend continued in his later works that denounced foreign forces of domination; African dictators and African regression or 'bastardisation,' to borrow the author's own expression were also not spared.

Certainly for the artistic value of his works and surely because it seemed that his criticism was primarily directed toward Africans, Kourouma was much celebrated in Europe. The first novel won three prizes namely, 'Prix de la Francité,' 'Prix de la Tour-Landry,' 'Prix de l'Académie Française,' and 'Prix de l'Académie Royale' of Belgium. His second novel, *Monné, outrages et défis* (1990; trans. *Monnew*), received three prizes including the 'Grand Prix littéraire d'Afrique Noire' for outstanding francophone African works. The author's third novel, *En attendant le vote des bêtes sauvages* (1998; trans. *Waiting for the Wild Beasts to Vote*), also captured three distinctions, while the fourth one, *Allah n'est pas obligé* (2000; trans. *Allah is not Obliged*), crowned them all with the prestigious 'Prix Renaudot.'

Such international recognition, which also went to our long-despised identity and intellectual capacity could not be ignored. I share Ayi Kwei Armah's bitingly ironic view of the condescending way in which his character Akosua Russell is lauded in his novel *Fragments* (1970). Although any inauthentic praise which continues our alienation should be condemned, it would be equally inappropriate not to acknowledge our own talented and committed artists because of colonialist criticism.

In expressing the gratitude and the pride of the government and people of Côte d'Ivoire on the day of Kourouma's national decoration (June 1, 2001), I could not refrain from mentioning the different prizes he had won. This renowned writer, who had received recognition both at home and abroad, expected his criticism in literature would lead to the demise of negative African rulers and promote socio-political progress.

In the latter part of his career, the artist grew bitter about African rebellions, which had brought about neither reforms nor respite to the suffering of African people. Thus, after his first three novels, Kourouma's criticism was directed toward the ruthlessness of rebels: events in the novel *Allah is not Obliged* refer to situations which were developing in Sierra Leone and Liberia. Hardly did the author imagine that his own country, Côte d'Ivoire, would be immersed in a similar turmoil. On September 19, 2002 a civil war broke out which led to an unprecedented crisis in the history of the country. Ahmadou Kourouma could not avoid personal involvement. The crisis had an ethno-regional dimension that compelled him to react and take a stand. In the beginning, he was at a loss because his sympathies lay with the *de jure* rulers. Later on, however, he became increasingly critical of them.

Of course, all the protagonists on the Ivorian political scene waited to see his literary representation of the crisis. Indeed, that work was well under way when he sadly passed away on December 11, 2003 in France. Some have asserted he died in exile to ensure that the interpretation of his life and his last novel would favour the cause of the rebels.

The much-awaited artistic work, entitled *Quand on refuse on dit non*, came out in 2004.[1] After Kourouma's death, Gilles Carpentier edited and published the unfinished novel with some minor changes. At the end of the book he added three documents that allow us to discern the possible evolution of the work which could have been totally restructured by the author if his death had not occurred. The reader, however, has enough elements to understand the direction in which the author was moving. Group opinions and attitudes are substantiated well enough for us to produce meaning. This is all the more easy as the novel is a sequel to *Allah is not Obliged*, and a similar logic runs as an undercurrent in both. This is why, in analyzing the novel, one can integrate characters that actually appear only in two separate fragments. The character of Birahima is consistent in the two novels, and it constitutes the essential element of continuity in terms of aesthetic and ethical references.

In his presentation of the novel, Gilles Carpentier, the editor, writes that 'More than his other books, this one falls in a political and civic perspective.' He is referring to the Ivorian crisis and for him, to be political and civic implies taking a stand for one camp or the other, in this case more likely for the rebels. Thus, when he asserts, with the faith of a neophyte, that the work is a 'true Ivorian novel,' the suggestion is that such a work of art faithfully reflects reality. The crucial point here is whether Kourouma broke with his critical tradition and adopted a non-dialectical voice. Did he end his whole career on a contradiction with himself and with what is fundamental to his artistic approach? Those who are eager to see him disparage Laurent Gbagbo and his followers, some of whom are thugs parading as patriots, do not notice the signs pointing in the opposite direction. It is true that the politics of this last novel is not easy to grasp, for its irony is sometimes illusive, and the ambivalence of the characters and actions could be baffling.

This novel confirms the image of Kourouma as a master dialectician. He is careful not to fall victim to the attractive but phony promises of the rebels, promises which are nothing but a continuation of the same old authoritarian agenda. When the editor expresses the candid hope: 'Provided there still are buses for Bouaké' (147), he is not aware that he is taking the side of the rebels. He reasons only in terms of speed (bus versus walking), not in terms of destination and meaning. But here, space is a metaphor for a continuing quest that is political in nature. Birahima and Fanta are heading for Bouaké, a town which is both the capital of the rebels and a haven for persecuted northerners. Moving in that direction is like crossing a frontier and joining the rebels. The wish expressed in the quotation is therefore intentional.

Fate did not allow Birahima and Fanta to reach Bouaké, because of Kourouma's death, and we must construe this as a kind of uncompleted initiation. But still this 'pilgrim's progress' toward the sanctuary of the rebels is full of meaning. Birahima, who undertakes this journey, is an ambivalent character who serves both as a witness of human rights violations and a critic of a political imposture.

In my celebration of Kourouma at his decoration, I praised young Birahima for turning his back on the Liberian rebellion and recommended that he should not be an object of fear. I stated:

> Birahima the child warrior is both a witness and heir whose eyes have been opened by the war. Turning his back on Worosso, he is heading for Abidjan. He is not an insurgent but the new *re-founding* conqueror. Maybe tomorrow he will be a democratic president to consolidate the extinction of the race of dictators.

Was I mistaken? Was he among the insurgents who attacked Abidjan? I doubt that. He was moving away from meaningless mass killings, from a Malinké solidarity based on deep misunderstandings (he was looking for an aunt not ethnicity) as well as questionable values. He was rejecting an unbridled violence that perverted positive ancient institutions like the society of hunters known as *Dozo* or *Donsow*.

I certainly over-estimated Birahima's Liberian initiation. I was wrong in believing that his disapproval of this negative enterprise would engage him in a positive quest. Hegelian belief in the necessity of a synthesis made me expect a new and different conqueror and not an opponent to the idea of conquest. Birahima had turned his back on his own words.

Birahima demonstrates the same critical distance and the same sense of irony that rendered him trustworthy and sympathetic. As a true anti-hero, he draws attention to his flaws and preserves his secret dreams that have nothing to do with the Messianic ambitions of the rebels.

Birahima is not a typical Northerner. Right from the beginning of the novel, we find him drinking alcohol and taking drugs (11). He expresses his admiration for Laurent Gbagbo who is supposed to be president of the Southerners (12).

One cannot legitimately describe him as a good Muslim Northerner. His food tastes and his aesthetic references set him apart from his community. He prefers palm-nut soup to peanut soup. Much as this may appear trivial, in Ivorian humour, specific soups are associated with different major political parties. Political and culinary differences merge, and Ivorians play with these differences, especially in the urban musical genre, '*Zouglou*', as a way of downplaying and deriding them. Furthermore, talking about the beauty of Fanta, the girl with whom he is in love, our hero does not choose a reference from the North: he compares her to a '*Gouro*' sculpture from the forest zone. This discloses his culture and open-mindedness. But this could be perceived as a betrayal by those for whom, physical beauty increases in refinement as one moves northward. Thus, right from the beginning, Birahima belongs without really belonging. He violates some essential codes that unite the members of his group. And this at a moment when there is a call for his people to face other groups in a Manichean confrontation opposing Northerners and Southerners.

Unfortunately for the Northerners, Birahima is not an authentic hero. When war breaks out in his country, he expresses a childish and dubious joy: 'I don't care, I don't care. Tribal war has reached Côte d'Ivoire. Hurrah!' (12) However, he does not have any particular sympathy for the Ivorian rebellion. He only wishes he could use his Liberian experience to impress and seduce Fanta with his dramatized gallantry.

When the time for heroism comes and Fanta asks him dramatically, 'Can you kill like Bété militants?' (35) His reaction is melodramatic. He says: 'With a Kalashnikov I will accompany you, I will protect you. With a Kalashnikov, I will massacre all the militants, all the young patriots, all the loyalist soldiers ... With a Kalashnikov, I will revolt, I will refuse!' (36)

Of course, Birahima is bragging in a theatrical manner. But on a deeper level, there is an unconscious link with Samory's famous phrase that serves as the title of the novel ['When You Disagree You Must Say No']. Like all parodies, it expresses a partial or ironic adherence to a doctrine or identification with a person. Birahima is a caricature of the great resistance warrior Samory Touré. By correcting him and setting the record straight, Fanta wants to give a heroic or an epic twist to the parody.

Actually, throughout the novel, we never see Birahima killing anyone. He uses his gun several times simply to scare people away. Sarcasm is his only weapon when he laughs at his aggressors running for their lives. Certainly, this has nothing to do with myths about the legendary cowardice of Southerners, compared to 'sorghum porridge' (23) presumably because they cannot stand up and resist as Samory did against colonial conquest. For Birahima, those who want to kill other people but are keen on protecting their own lives are ridiculous. Cowardly heroes ridicule themselves when they take to their heels.

Even worse, Birahima would be inclined to fight for money and seek alliance with highest bidders. In the synopsis of the unwritten last section of the novel, he is ready to join any of the three groups involved in the war (152). He believes he is justified, as the money will enable him to marry Fanta. He embraces no cause, and cannot reasonably be committed to any sacred cause or Jihad.

There are at least two ways in which he distances himself from the rebels. He derisively calls their speech a 'blablabla', that is nonsensical repetitive speech, or compares it to the tales his grandmother used to narrate (111). He points both to their irrational content and irrelevance. Obviously, this discourse has nothing in common with the Word! This self-derision, already perceptible in *Allah is not Obliged*, is a call for humility. It is the best way to foil any process of identification likely to lure people into worshipping any real or fictional hero.

The act of storing Fanta's teachings on a tape recorder constitutes another form of critical distance. Preserving information for future analysis can be perceived as a means of giving oneself time for reflection and maturation. Even though Birahima does not yet have an adequate intellectual level, he vows to acquire it later on. There can be no better way of protecting oneself against ideological manipulation. Even the fact of repeating and reformulating the issues as he does represents an act of independence, a way of using one's own brains to appropriate messages received. With a tape recorder, it is also difficult to modify information according to changing and conflicting interests. Finally, this learning method does not depend on excessive memorization. A recording machine allows more room for one's intelligence. While memory stands for uncritical or authoritarian ways, remembrance of past pains, and may pave the way for resentment, intelligence represents freedom, insight, and above all, time for healing processes and prospects for lasting reconciliation.

In the end, the only value in which Birahima believes is love. All he desires is Fanta's love. She can share her vision of history and her sympathy for the rebels with him, but she cannot convert him, for his mind is set against one-sided stories. Besides, he spends his time staring at her rather than listening to her: he wants romance not revolution, education not indoctrination.

Even in this respect, it is meaningful that Birahima boasts that he raped women in Liberia before recanting his words. He quickly realizes that this confession is damaging for his image and likely to scare Fanta away. How could she undertake such a long and perilous journey with him if she does not feel secure around him?

So, here is a man who flouts the codes of his community, and represents a caricature of heroism; here is someone who listens but refuses to believe, someone who is both a romantic and a rapist. With what kind of politics could he be associated? Certainly not the politics of submission, blind solidarities and violent confrontations! As he embarks on this ambiguous rescuing mission, he is quite well aware of his own inadequacies. To conceal his Kalashnikov, he had to wear a large 'boubou'. In his own words, he looks like 'a child in an over-sized garment'. (40) He finds himself involved in a confrontation beyond his understanding and desires.

In spite of his limitations, Birahima keeps his eyes open as he did in Liberia. He is able to see through people like El Hadji Koroma and other warlords who were looking for diamonds and misappropriating articles of humanitarian aid. He is a critical eyewitness and not a 'naïve and malicious character' as portrayed by the editor. (146)

The facts described in the novel depict two realities: material damages and human losses. The author also gives an explanation of the origin of the war, which is not surprising as the novel is a genre that is particularly concerned with causality.

The human consequences of this Ivorian crisis are twofold. A great number of refugees run for safety, undertaking long journeys without minimum life-sustaining means. In this case, the unprejudiced witness is able to observe that refugees flee from the two forces at war. As Birahima and Fanta leave Daloa, 'the town of criminals and barbarians' (37), others are flocking toward it.

But no matter how painful these trials and tribulations may be, they cannot be compared to the human losses. Like a griot performing for his audience, the narrator sets out to tell his story: 'Now let us recount what took place in this criminal country called Côte d'Ivoire. Let us recount what took place in this damned messy Bété town of Daloa' (19). This town is a synecdoche for the whole country. The extent of manslaughter which occurred is such that new expressions have become familiar, especially '*escadrons de la mort*' (death squadrons) and '*charniers*' (mass graves). There is no better proof of our savagery for according to the narrator, children, women and the elderly are not spared because this war is not a civilized one (42). In the village of Monoko Zohi, mass killings reached such a dimension that they were called '*Kabako*', meaning that things have gone beyond human control. (76).

Among those who are killed are several Islamic clergymen, but many are also killed for political as well as ethnic reasons. In Daloa, Birahima himself narrowly escaped from a collective execution because the soldiers were distracted by fighting over the belongings of those they had not yet killed. The soldiers are portrayed as greedy and stupid assassins.

To understand the reasons of the war and the ensuing bloodshed, we first need to assess the *ante bellum* situation. On several occasions, the narrator observes that history was progressing smoothly until September 19, 2002. Ivorians remained reasonable until they started getting at each other's throats (45–6).

It is surprising to note that a writer who has always been critical of Houphouët-Boigny's regime says the country was a kind of paradise. The late Ivorian President was represented as Tiékoroni, the wise old man.

Among other African dictators, he sided with the bloodthirsty Koyaga in *Waiting for the Wild Beasts to Vote.* But he is now miraculously rehabilitated. Perhaps the traumatic experience of the war may account for this pervading nostalgia even for past times of hardship and dictatorship. As a matter of fact, it is Birahima who reminds us of that contradiction; he speaks of 'The blessed period of the cunning, sententious and billionaire dictator Houphouët-Boigny.' (16)

The narrator goes on then to provide the reasons accounting for the war. Indeed, it is not the result of a curse placed on a country, which was once praised as blessed by God. Socio-political and socio-economic problems are identified as the causes of this war.

The immediate causes include the doctrine of '*ivoirité,*' the question of national identification papers, and the conflict which resulted from the October 2000 elections. As presented in the novel, the concept of '*ivoirité*' was created to legitimize certain sectional claims over the country. According to its critics at the time, the Northerners are considered non-Ivorians because they are immigrants: the true nationals are the Southerners. The narrator ironically says the latter have their 'ivoirité' in their blood which they never shed for their country. (59)

Because of discrimination, the national identity documents of the Northerners are contested if they are not torn to pieces. The issue of identification by *Carte Nationale d'Identité, (CNI)* becomes a problem of segregation, hence the coining of the expression '*Carte d'identité de l'ivoirité, (CII)*' (ID proving *ivoirité*),[2] an expression which makes discrimination more visible. (24) According to the author, many Ivorians from the North become '*sans papier*' (paperless) in their own country, (109) just like many African immigrants in France and other Western countries.

Referring to the preceding form of victimization, Birahima, who cannot be suspected of any hostility toward his community, confesses: 'And we, Dioula people are always buying false identity cards in order to obtain their ivoirité.' (16) He already made that observation at the end of *Allah is not Obliged* where he was even more critical of the Malinké ethnic group.

The nationality problem, in turn, raises the issue of the eligibility of a presidential candidate considered as the leader of the Northerners.[3] Because he was excluded from the election, some northern soldiers thought they were justified to stage a coup. They succeeded on 24 December 1999. The novel gives details of that coup, its motivations as well as the vicissitudes of the military transition (110-17). Then the October 2000 elections unleashed the first violent confrontations causing several hundred deaths in the country.

However, because these common law and political issues caused such bloodshed, the underlying reasons of the resentment have to be sought deeper. And there is no doubt that certain socio-economic problems made it more difficult to find acceptable compromises. The novel is rather explicit about the explanation and breaks it into two essential issues.

First, we have the fundamental question of land, compounded by a protracted economic crisis, which limited the growth of urban employ-ment. The competition for land became a source of great concern as more and more foreign and domestic immigrants flooded to the southern forest regions. Ahmadou Kourouma makes no secret about this land issue although, paradoxically, he shows ecological concerns (45–6). He points out that as we create plantations for cocoa and coffee, the desert moves southward. Thus, today's illusion of wealth may actually bring about long-term impoverishment.

  Birahima is an eyewitness to this confrontation between those threat-ened with 'landlessness' and those who have been made 'paperless'. As such, he cannot contest the reality of these contradictions and human suf-ferings. He is out there on the ground and his presence serves to disclose questionable interpretations of a hidden intolerance.

  Birahima protects Fanta but allows the reader to see the universe of resentment and intolerance of which she is part. The criticism of the politics of rebellion, which started in *Allah is not Obliged*, is further explored here. The prejudices against the Bété people have no particular meaning. They just happen to be handy. The flaws of the Bété are associ-ated with the ongoing war. They dislike the Dioula who do not like them either. These sweeping generalizations rarely prevent individuals from living together in the same communities. But Bété intellectuals are said to have invented the notion of '*ivoirité*' that allowed discrimination against the Northerners. The portrait of the Bété is summed up in this manner:

> The Dioulas or Malinkés don't like the Bétés, they make fun of them. They find them very violent and very gregarious (they obediently follow impulses from the group to which they belong). The Bétés are always ready to protest and to loot everything (houses and offices). They are always ready to fight. (17–18)

No wonder the war breaks out under a bellicose Bété President (Laurent Gbagbo). By sheer political tactics, it is clever to incriminate the Bété and exculpate the prestigious Baoulé who ruled for almost forty years, and would become allies of the Northerners in an effort to wrench power from the Bété.

  However, what holds for the Bété applies for all the Southerners. Fanta conveniently starts her teachings with physical and human geography, which she calls '*milieu naturel*' (natural milieu). European slave traders were not able to buy slaves on the coast of the territory for two reasons. They were scared of the indigenous people who were rumoured to find white flesh very tasty. They were also kept away from a coast that was neither accessible nor hospitable (43). Consequently, hostility is to be found in nature as well as inherently in the Bété and that of all Southerners, binding geography and history, psycho-sociology and politics, anthro-pophagy and war. One of the ways in which ideology operates is that it transforms history into nature.

  Another important instance of ideological disqualification is related to the question of work ethics. The Southerners are considered to be lazy and the Northerners as hard working people: 'Workers were needed, a lot of workers, courageous workers. Forest people are too few and above all, they are lymphatic. Real workers can only be found in the North of the country'(63). With the help of his numerous dictionaries, Birahima explains what is meant by 'lymphatic': 'Well! It means apathetic, sluggish, having no sense of initiative, in a word, one who does not know anything, one who cannot or is not willing to do anything' (65). Then we learn that southern Ivorians want to rob the Burkinabé immigrants of the lands they had acquired thanks to Houphouët-Boigny's doctrine according to which the land belongs to whoever tills it. The southern Ivorians are compared to snakes and the Burkinabé to rats that had successfully dug their holes in the country (74).

Once again, truth matters less than the ideological mode of operation. Specifically, it consists in a non-dialectical linking of forest and savannah, snakes and rats, laziness and work, geography and economics, cannibalism and culture or cultivation, nature and history. These two opposing paradigms explain why only or mainly Northerners resisted colonial conquest (Samory being the emblematic figure although he destroyed Kong) and why government troops, 'Gbagbo's soldiers,' (20) are cowardly. Once this logic is established, everything holds together, light is shed on the land issues and migration. Houphouët-Boigny graciously rewarded the hard working Northerners and immigrants, and now they are being deprived of lands conquered with their sweat and toil. He gave identity papers generously to foreigners willing to vote and now they are being withdrawn. As an open-minded Southerner, he is contrasted with Gbagbo, the Southerner par excellence and typical Bété, the ruler under whom violence is perpetrated and looting authorized!

This is how the history of the North becomes one of long degradation and destitution. Its conscience of victimization is submerged by an ideology of resentment that Birahima is called upon to share. The Northerners have been exploited in the time of forced labour; today their lands are being taken away from them. Although they fought hard for independence, starting from the 1945 elections, they are now oppressed and condemned to remain second-class citizens.

This 'geography of hostility' (North versus South) and this 'history of victimization' (north by south) are results of Joseph Gabel's concept of 'detotalization'.[4] The questions that remain are: were all slave dealers barred from all Ivorian coasts and for how long? If all the Southerners were lazy, from whom did they beg for food? Given their hostility, how did so many migrants come to settle in their midst? If Houphouët-Boigny is a benevolent dictator, does Gbagbo have any redeeming attributes?

The primary function of this ideology is to disqualify one's opponents so as to pave the way for their symbolic destruction. The second is to create empathy in order to unite, and achieving that unity means mobilizing in order to triumph over other groups. Régis Debray[5] has accurately observed that people do not unite just for the sake of it.

In this unification endeavour, Birahima represents an obstacle, for he refuses to be blinded by that ideology and thereby remains a kind of political 'infidel'. He does not condone questionable practices, no matter their source. He is then rejected from a community whose binding ideas he has naively exposed, a community, which he refuses to defend as a rebel hero.

The first violent intolerance Birahima meets is from his cousin's wife, Sita, who slaps him several times as he repeats 'President Gbagbo is a good guy! ... He is a Bété but a good guy' (13). One can imagine Birahima's fate if he had uttered these words in front of armed rebels. Vasoumalaye, who offers hospitality to him and Fanta on their way to Bouaké, faces the same hostility for his political opinions: he is a rare Dioula sympathizer of Gbagbo. His first wife, who wants Gbagbo to be tried by an international court, engages in a heated argument with him late at night (82–3). Unlike Sita, she cannot use physical violence against her husband.

This level of violence indicates tensions in the country because of the war. It is appropriate to recall that Fanta's father, a high religious character, an *imam* and head of a *Medersa*, had bought an old Kalashnikov from Liberia. In spite of the fact that Islam means peace, he feels compelled to protect himself in a country of madmen (39).

To better grasp the full measure of this violence, one must contrast it with the image of traditional Muslim women under stereotyped submission. Bafitini, Birahima's mother, and Mahan, his aunt, represent the traditional woman. Young Birahima did not travel to war-torn Liberia to find a submissive aunt. He undertook the journey because he was looking for a caring mother figure: all women are generally associated with life values of generosity and love.

The last woman to be considered is Fanta. Birahima's desire to marry her brings to the surface the hidden intolerance, which makes the love affair impossible. Her first reaction is instinctive and brutal:

> She screamed like a hyena caught in a trap, she screamed until she woke all the birds sleeping in the branches of the forest that night. The birds started flying above our heads that night under the moonlight. (138)

A mere request for marriage produces almost cataclysmic consequences. Arousing birds from their sleep means creating awareness (philosophers associate themselves with the bird of Minerva which represents wisdom); moonlight symbolizes the time of vision in a period of anomy; and hyenas scarcely assume a positive ethical significance. Fanta's instinctive reaction, then, shows the depth of her prejudices.

With disarming naïvety, the young suitor discards the three reasons given to refuse the marriage. To the first objection about age, his response is that Muhammad was married to a woman older than himself. To the concern about money, he retorts that he will enlist as a mercenary with the Liberian soldiers who are looting the western part of Côte d'Ivoire. The capital he will acquire will be used for a transportation business, comparable to that of Fofana the rich businessman in Daloa. Finally, Fanta objects on the grounds of an unequal educational level. Birahima evokes illiterate Fofana, whose third wife has a university degree and is a high school mathematics teacher (137–38). Confounded, Fanta ends the discussion and suggests that her uncle will decide later in Bouaké, which then appears not only as a haven for rebels but also a refuge against unresolved contradictions.

Actually, the love affair was doomed right from the beginning when Fanta said she loved Birahima as a brother. He was rejected as a suitor but accepted into a brotherhood. Boundaries exist and must not be violated. Birahima's whole discourse is based on some form of dialectics in which it is possible for things and people to evolve. Fanta, on the other hand, demonstrates Joseph Gabel's 'eleaticism', the belief that things do not change. Being consistent with herself, her public pronouncements echo in her private life.

However, her quest for a provider/protector on whom to depend contradicts her educational and militant aspirations. She is actually a traditional conformist willing to reproduce her alienation, and besides she is by far less progressive than Sita and Vasoumalaye's wife. Unsurprisingly, she leaves it to a father figure to decide whether she can marry Birahima or not.

In this case, however, she falls back on her uncle because she is intuitively sure he will refuse the marriage. They share the same principles and she can anticipate his decision on that basis. This is illustrated by the posthumous synopsis to Kourouma's novel. The unassuming Birahima and Mamourou, the rich uncle, represent two conflicting and even warring systems. The latter is a staunch Muslim, a powerful orator seriously committed to his moral choices, and a radical supporter of the rebellion (151). How could he accept somebody who drinks, smokes, takes drugs and above all is a Gbagbo-sympathizer? Under these circumstances, how does Birahima even dare to propose to his niece in Bouaké where he holds sway? The young suitor is logically ridiculed and ejected from the compound, which means rejected from the community. Power is the value that unites the uncle and the niece, and Birahima does not have any. Furthermore, he is an objective ally of those barring Fanta's people from the power to which they aspire. The logic of power is one of separation, exclusion and control. Mamourou behaves like his so-called enemies. One understands how the quest for tolerance can be intolerant, how religion and other cultural practices could inspire endogamy, ethical or ethnic cleansing.

Paradoxically then, Birahima who submits to Sita's blows and Vasoumalaye whose wife can violently contest his views are more liberal than those who resent their socio-political marginalization. Birahima claims that the blood that has been shed will increase the fertility of the Ivorian soil and make way for a greater economic prosperity. The irony here has a bitter edge to it, but who can laugh in a context of war? No one in his right mind willfully decides to irrigate his land with blood in order to have a better cocoa harvest! Only an unshakable belief in dialectics makes him hope that out of this tragic predicament, a new society will emerge. Undoubtedly, beneath any type of irony lies an indestructible faith opposed to the extinction of life and the end of communication. The sense of irony is always more generous than any form of cynicism.

Birahima's optimism seems to be shared by Fanta even though in a more serious and ideological mode:

> Any trial for a people either serves to pay for some sins or means the promise of an immense happiness. That immense happiness, for the Ivorian people, might be democracy. Democracy is the reduction of passions, tolerance for others. (38)

These are her father's words and they are placed under the auspices of Allah. They were uttered at the beginning of the novel when she thought the rebels would bring about a democratic change in the country. After her trip, her initiation into democracy did not yet yield any result. Let us hope she will stop seeing the world in terms of punishment or reward, north and south, victimized and victimizers. Let us hope that one day she will locate her own center in herself and view the world with her own eyes. In this way, she will assume self-confidence, and she will be ready for an authentic optimism, and therefore ready for love with Birahima or any other person.

In conclusion, Birahima's story is similar to that of Ahmadou Kourouma himself. He transcended regional, religious and political affiliations and was not a narrow believer. At the beginning, he had some sympathy for Laurent Gbagbo. But he was caught in the middle of a conflict that opposed his socio-political inclinations and his natural loyalty to his ethnic group. Those who resented his political stand applauded as he gradually became critical. They hoped he would join them in their battle. They probably expected a total and non-dialectical support that never came, for to them Kourouma, the writer, is reducible to the committed citizen.

Thanks to young Birahima, we see the resilient thread that runs through all Kourouma's works: irony and criticism triumph over ideological seriousness. The anti-hero has continuously neutralized the fascination for identification and submission. Uncritical adhesion is constantly rejected in favour of authentic solidarity. Whether he is associated with African oral tradition, with Rabelais or with negative aesthetics,[6] Kourouma has always promoted contradiction and change, confident that freedom will defeat dictatorships and a new life will spring from wanton deaths. He organizes the failure and the crisis of all forms of arrogance and conceit.

One of the major legacies Kourouma has left us is the '*Dokun cela*' ritual (the ritual of the crossroads), which he borrowed from the ancient society of hunters. The crossroad symbolizes freedom of choice, a need for enlightened minds. Heritage should prevail over heredity. In the same way dialectics, in its opposition to nature, stands for choice, which is precisely the essence of democracy.

Hostility and violence must not blind us to meanings that are favourable to human progress. They might lead us to fight unnecessary wars instead of perceiving linking meanings. Hopefully, sympathy for fleeting causes cannot obliterate profound commitments to freedom, unity and solidarity. The immortal Kourouma, the last and the final, is well rooted in a tradition inaccessible to prejudices and alienating myths. When you refuse injustice, you must say no to all injustices.

NOTES

1   There is no published English translation of *Quand on refuse on dit non*. The translations are mine.
2   The term *ivoirité* (ivorianness) refers to both the cultural features supposed to define Ivorian nationals and to a doctrine which sought to promote Ivorian national interests but ended up triggering hostility between Ivorians and the large population of foreigners mainly originating from the West African sub-region.
3   Allasane Dramane Ouattara.
4   Joseph Gabel, *Idéologies*, 1974.
5   Régis Debray, *Le feu du sacré: Fonction du réligieux*, Fayard, 2003.
6   Unlike the positive heroes with whom the readers would identify, the happy ends that would give them relief and take them back to their thoughtlessness, Kourouma's characters are not to be admired and the social contradictions described are not solved at the end of his works. The crisis that continues beyond the end of the narrative keeps the readers' minds alive and reinforces their critical capacities. That refusal of any positive synthesis and any affirmative stance justifies a reference to the critical discourse of The Frankfurt School.

WORKS CITED

Ahmadou Kourouma's novels

Les soleils des indépendances, (Paris: Seuil, 1970 [1968 first published by Les Presses de l'Université de Montréal]; trans. Adrian Adams, *The Suns of Independence*, Africana Publishing, 1981)

Monné, outrages et défis (Paris: Seuil, 1990; trans. Nidra Poller, *Monnew*, San Francisco, Mercury House, 1993)

En attendant le vote des bêtes sauvages (Paris: Seuil, 1998; trans. Frank Wynne, *Waiting for the Wild Beasts to Vote*, London: William Heinemann, 2003)

Allah n'est pas obligé (Paris: Seuil, 2000; trans. Frank Wynne, *Allah is not Obliged*, London: William Heinemann 2006; London: Anchor Books, 2007)

Quand on refuse on dit non (Paris: Seuil, 2004; '*When You Disagree, You must Say No*', no official translation yet)

OTHER WORKS CITED

Armah, Ayi Kwei, *Fragments*, Heinemann, 1974 (originally published by Houghton Mifflin in 1970)

Debray, Régis, *Le feu du sacré: Fonction du réligieux*, Fayard, 2003

Gabel, Joseph, *Idéologies*, Anthropos, 1974

Ngũgĩ's *Wizard of the Crow*:
Women as the "Voice of the People"
& the Western Audience

Joseph McLaren

The writings of Kenyan author Ngũgĩ wa Thiong'o have consistently presented women characters, from his early novels *Weep Not, Child* (1964) and *The River Between* (1965) to his middle period works such as *Petals of Blood* (1977) to his Gikuyu works translated into English, including *Caitanni Mutharaba-ini* (1980), translated as *Devil on the Cross* (1982); and *Matigari ma Njiruungi* (1986), translated by Wangui wa Goro as *Matigari* (1989). Ngũgĩ's most recent novel, also written in Gikuyu, *Murogi wa Kagogo* (2004) or *Wizard of the Crow* (2006), is the culmination of his orature-based, satiric novelistic writings after a twenty-year period. A magnum opus, *Wizard of the Crow* demonstrates his portrayal of women characters in a number of ways. His principal woman character, Nyawira, meaning 'work,' is central to 'the "Movement for the Voice of the People"' (*Wizard* 82), the organization that resists the retrogressive policies of the 'Ruler' of the 'Free Republic of Aburiria,' the fictitious African state used to satirize problematic governments in the South and elsewhere. Nyawira's relationship with the Wizard is framed against her progressive political awareness.

One of the central questions is whether Ngũgĩ depicts women as tropes rather than as 'real' characters confronted with gender issues in domestic and public spaces. Does Ngũgĩ employ women to further his argument relating to the nation, implicitly Kenya, and the role women can play in national reconstruction? Simon Gikandi argues that 'To understand the relation between Ngũgĩ's texts and their context, we need, among other things, to have a clear sense of the ways in which his life is wrapped up with the cultural history of Kenya since the 1920s' (2000: 2), but one can also consider the way Ngũgĩ's life has been affected by his separation from his homeland, which has not lessened his commitment to writing about his nation, particularly his disaffection with the Moi years.

Because *Wizard of the Crow* operates on satirical and magical realist levels, the novel appears at times to be a humorous mockery of state power. Nevertheless, Ngũgĩ addresses historically problematic issues for women, such as patriarchal systems, domestic abuse, and political marginalization, but at the same time the novel reinforces the West's general complaint concerning corruption in African leadership. In certain respects, Ngũgĩ's representation of women as providing the progressive social and cultural direction of the state helps rescue the work from being an extended ridicule of the African leader concerned with continuing internal political domination. Although Ngũgĩ's critique has similarities to the general view of Western observers, this kind of criticism has also been voiced by well-known African writers such as Wole Soyinka, who in *The Open Sore of a Continent: A Personal Narrative of the Nigerian Crisis* (1996) evokes Ken Saro-Wiwa's plight and questions the road to national rectification in Nigeria. If Ngũgĩ's earlier works dealing with anti-colonialism showed him in a binary relationship with the West, his neo-colonial critique in *Wizard of the Crow* aligns him with similar positions coming from Western governments, and from African intellectuals and scholars themselves. How does this play for certain Western readers, who may potentially substitute 'corrupt African leaders' for 'uncivilized' indigenous populations and notions of Conrad's 'savages,' going back to the period when Chinua Achebe sought to rectify the image of Africa in relation to the West? In other words, are Caliban and Prospero now speaking with the same accent? Conceivably, works which castigate African leadership can feed notions of Afro-pessimism, but if such works also demonstrate the complicity of the West in propping up certain leaders, they go beyond simple notions of blaming African leaders.

Ngũgĩ's Western Audience

The reception of *Wizard of the Crow* in the West suggests that Ngũgĩ is recognized as an established African author in exile, one whose use of satire and fable is generally appreciated although the ultimate achievement of this latest novel has been questioned. In Kenya, the evaluation of the novel in Nairobi's *Daily Nation* did not address any of the complications of Ngũgĩ's standing in his homeland but noted that the novel was 'voted *Time* magazine's Europe edition best third book of 2006.' The review further stated that 'the significance of yesterday's launch was, no doubt, the university's close proximity to Uhuru Park, which appears to be the locale for the 750 page tome that took six years to write.' The novel displayed a 'seductive playfulness' and was 'eerily reminiscent of Kanu's efforts to build a sky-scraper in Uhuru Park in the early 1990s' ('Ngũgĩ Book Launched' 1). In addition, the Western press viewed Ngũgĩ as a complex contemporary writer, as reflected in the *New Yorker* magazine review by author John Updike, who saw Ngũgĩ as 'caught in sometimes implacable political, social, racial, and linguistic currents' (Updike 2006). It was also evident to the *New York Times* reviewer that Ngũgĩ had written a major work emanating from oral techniques: 'It's hard to think of another recent novel so heavily steeped in oral traditions; at the level of language and cadence it recalls a long yarn told by firelight' (Turrentine 2006: 22). In addition, the *Times Literary Supplement* grouped Ngũgĩ's Ruler among 'a composite of Third World dictators, from Pinochet, Marcos and Baby Doc Duvalier, to specifically African tyrants such as Kenya's own Kenyatta and Moi, Malawi's Banda, the Central African Republic's Bokassa, Uganda's Amin and Zaire's Mobutu' (Van Der Vlies 2006: 21). Nnedi Okorafor-Mbachu, writing for *Black Issues Book Review* (2006), expressed the mythical connections to the character Matigari from Ngũgĩ's 1980s novel, for whom an arrest warrant was issued by the Moi regime, not realizing his fictional status. Ngũgĩ's Wizard 'has all the potential of becoming yet another one in that country' (38). The *San Francisco Chronicle* noted that '*Wizard of the Crow* may prove his [Ngũgĩ's] status, but only for those willing to wrestle with its incredibly demanding text. Nevertheless, the novel has many rewards for those willing to face its challenges' (Hellman 2006).

Wizard of the Crow demonstrates Ngũgĩ's ongoing interests in a number of ways. Most important, Ngũgĩ's espousal of writing in indigenous languages is clearly supported by the publication, which was first brought out in Kenya in the Gikuyu language as *Murogi wa Kagogo*. Although the language debate among African writers is more than a generation old, it is nevertheless significant and has a relationship to what can be identified as the linguistic hegemony of the English language. Ngũgĩ's non-fiction works such as *Decolonising the Mind: The Politics of Language in African Literature* (1986) and *Moving the Centre: The Struggle for Cultural Freedoms* (1993) have pursued this argument. The critical issues underlying Ngũgĩ's position on language are linked to his national concerns, his commitment to political equity in Kenya, from which he had been in exile for many years. Ngũgĩ's 2004 return to Kenya had tragic consequences for both Ngũgĩ and his wife. It was probably shocking for Western observers that a writer of Ngũgĩ's stature would have been subject to such a traumatic physical attack. Furthermore, Ngũgĩ's standing in Kenya appears complicated by personal relationships as well as literary ones since his criticism of the Kenyan state was accomplished from his location in the Western academy.

Wizard's expansive scope suggests a saga of the nation although the first third is constructed around a discreet period of time. One of the structures of the novel is the division into six books: 'Power Daemons', 'Queuing Daemons', 'Female Daemons', 'Male Daemons', 'Rebel Daemons', and 'Bearded Daemons'. This structure is indicative of its Kenyan serialization in the Gikuyu language. The 'Ruler' of Aburiria, the central figure of mockery, has an inflated sense of himself and is satirized in a project that has ironic Christian symbolism, a feature of Ngũgĩ's earlier novels. Furthermore, the 'Daemons' label is used to join the possibility of male–female unity, when at one point in the novel, there is the fear of '"male and female daemons working together"' and that '"Female daemons are unpredictable"' (745). The parody of the Ruler's seeming omnipotence is reflected in the bureaucratic-speak of the novel.

> The Ruler would be the daily recipient of God's advice, resulting in a rapid growth of Aburiria to heights never before dreamt by humans. The entire project, Heavenscape or simply Marching to Heaven, would be run by a National Building Committee, the chair of which would be announced in good time. (16)

The numerous examples of parody and bureaucratic-speak are suggested in the depiction of the Ruler's relationship to his ministers, a number of whom represent sycophantic characters. In portraying the Ruler as wielding absolute power, the novel constructs his underlings as absurd. For example, the ministers Silver Sikiokuu, Minister of State; and Markus Machokali, Minister of Foreign Affairs, are placed in a continual adversarial position, one trying to undermine the other in their attempt to gain privilege from the Ruler. This is one of the major satirical strands of the novel. Their surgery to enhance various features such as the eyes and ears, representing the organs of the state, is another of the reality shifts; Machokali's eyes are enlarged and Sikiokuu has oversized ears. The story-like quality of the novel is enhanced by deviations from the realistic mode, owing to African magic realism and the possible influences of Gabriel García Márquez in *One Hundred Years of Solitude* (1970) for instance.

Ngũgĩ's avoidance of the realistic mode in parts adds to the satirical context of the novel in that the humour aimed at state leadership is broadly conceived beyond the domains of Aburiria. However, certain contemporary African social concerns are stated as in references to HIV/AIDS, mentioned a number of times in the novel, but there are also other symbolic or satirical viruses, one caught by Tajirika, one of the central characters who follows the dictates of the Ruler and is the owner of the Eldares Modern Construction and Real Estate company. The illness known as 'white-ache' is used in an extended satirical section, and another illness, the impediment of Tajirika's speech resulting in his only being able to articulate the word *'If'*, forms a continuing strand of the novel's orature. The *'If'* word in Gikuyu language is supposedly 'If only', which suggests a more complex interpretation.

The Wizard of the Crow is the humiliated job seeker Kamiti, who is turned down by Tajirika. Kamiti reflects Ngũgĩ's ongoing concern during his Marxist phase for those who did not benefit from the fruits of Independence and suffer the depredations of the state that has little con-sideration for them. In a sense, the Wizard or Kamiti is a variation of Matigari from Ngũgĩ's earlier novel. Kamiti, a symbol of discarded humanity, is found on a rubbish heap and is later transformed into a Wizard by the assistance of other outcasts.

He [a beggar] then took a felt pen from his bag and wrote on the cardboard in big letters: WARNING! THIS PROPERTY BELONGS TO A WIZARD WHOSE POWER BRINGS DOWN HAWKS AND CROWS FROM THE SKY. TOUCH THIS HOUSE AT YOUR PERIL. SGD. WIZARD OF THE CROW. (77)

One of Ngũgĩ's narrative strategies is to reverse the role of police authority expected to be in league with the state. Through Constable Arigaigai Gathere, the Wizard's fame is spread among the people. A.G., as he is called, tells stories using the language of awe and respect for the powers of the Wizard. The voice of A.G. is somewhat different from that of the central narrator. For example, A.G. describes the voice of the Wizard in the following manner:

'His voice was round, soft, and soothing, so different from before that I could not tell whether he was making a statement or asking a question.' (114)

It is not only through multiple voices that Ngũgĩ is able to satirize state authority. Ngũgĩ also employs a range of scatological and olfactory references to identify the ruling class, where money is associated with stench; rotting bodies with one of the ministers, and excrement as part of the method used by Tajirika to end his later imprisonment.

Women Characters

Women have played crucial roles in a number of Ngũgĩ's novels. Generally, the representation of African women by male writers was 'a challenge to established male writers to recognize distortions' (Davies and Graves 1986: 14). Ngũgĩ's representation of Nyawira and other women characters foregrounds them as agents of change yet at the same time places them within the context of a satirical fable rather than a socially realistic work. The development of Kamiti is achieved through his relationship with Nyawira, a former secretary for Tajirika, who becomes an ally of Kamiti and his lover. The women characters in *Wizard of the Crow* are central to Ngũgĩ's motives found in his earlier novels because he maintains a Gikuyu-Mumbi representation, the balancing of the male and female principle through the Nyawira-Kamiti relationship. Nyawira signifies the power of women to resist state authority in her role as part of the Movement for the Voice of the People. In this regard, women stand for the nation and its potential abuse of the populace. Also, Ngũgĩ's representation of the Wizard and Nyawira in the natural landscape raises certain eco-critical issues while at the same time satirizing romanticized nature. This pastoral representation, which connects Nyawira to the land, may also suggest spiritual and political ramifications. The novel achieves both potentials by attributing to Nyawira a tough-minded political consciousness, which challenges the promulgations of the Ruler. Women in the novel are represented as the adversarial force, and at one point the

Marching to Heaven Building Committee considers how 'to remove the shame brought on the nation by female renegades'. The committee of men voice sexist views of women, which stem from a Biblical bias: 'Women had always been the thorn in the flesh of the human race; hardly surprising, most of the men concluded, given their descent from Eve' (225).

The Ruler views women as sexual objects and believes that he '"thoroughly understood women through and through."' However, the women who are part of the movement are for him 'acting out of character' because they are 'oblivious to his might' (235). In addition, the threat women pose affects the possibility of funding from the Global Bank, a satirical version of the World Bank. The power of the Movement for the Voice of the People is viewed as potentially causing the Global Bank to 'feel reluctant to release money to a country threatened by insurgency'. The competition for funds from Western institutions even affects NGOs and 'feminist groups,' who suspect 'male intrigue and formed a Just for Women movement for a share of the Global Bank' (245).

For the most part, Nyawira is indicative of the forces that challenge the status quo through action, especially through collective movements that interrupt the actions of the state, as in the moment where a Marching to Heaven event is broken up through the somewhat comic action of letting loose plastic snakes.

Most important, Ngũgĩ takes on the problematic question of abuse of women by reversing the power relationships and suggesting the possibilities of retributive justice. Here one can observe intertextual correspondences to Achebe's classic *Things Fall Apart*, which for Western audiences may have created a universalized image of African males as wife beaters through the portrayal of Okonkwo. However, in *Things Fall Apart*, Achebe counters generalizations of Igbo acceptance of domestic abuse through Odukwe, the brother of abused Mgbafo, who tells the *Egwugwu*, '"My sister lived with him [Uzowulu] for nine years. During those years no single day passed in the sky without his beating the woman."' Odukwe further suggests that if Mgbafo returns to Uzowulu but is beaten again '"we shall cut off his genitals for him"' (Achebe 91–2).

A similar reference is developed in Ngũgĩ's novel. Tajirika is threatened with the removal of his penis for the assaults he has committed against his wife, Vinjinia. In this section of the novel, the power relations are reversed with a woman head of a council judging Tajirika, who typifies sexist notions in a global context. He tries to defend his actions by saying that '"Wife beating is for the poor pagans"' and claims a '"Christian home"' and status in the middle class. The signs of domestic abuse are dismissed by him when he blames his wife's '"swollen face and a few scratches"' on an accidental fall (436). Here the classic domestic abuse scenario is reflected in Tajirika's blaming his neighbours for reporting the incident. This is a moment when Vinjinia becomes a representation of women generally because she says, '"I will not accept blows on my body anymore."' Tajirika's sentence, to be given 'as many blows' as he had given his wife, is a further reversal and a collective retribution: '"But if you ever appear before us again, you will not leave here with your penis dangling between your legs"' (439). The woman judge, described as doing 'a little war jig while brandishing her weapon,' a machete, obviously phallic, can be contrasted to Evil Forest in Achebe's work, but she goes beyond his judgement of reconciliation in the Mgbafo-Uzowulu dispute.

Like Chielo of *Things Fall Apart*, the woman judge is a figure of uncompromising strength and assertiveness. Ngũgĩ also suggests metaphysical characteristics by connecting the Wizard with the 'women of the people's court', who one of the Ruler's ministers perceives as a hologram or the effect of '"*virtual reality*"' engineered by the Wizard himself through his '"mirror"' and sent to '"beat up Tajirika"' (458). Placed within the context of a novel, wife beating is more than a family or village consideration but a matter related to state power, suggesting that women represent the people generally in relation to a nation or state that is abusive toward its citizens. Ngũgĩ's novel hints that the problem may be generational and also influenced from the top down, that the state indirectly sanctions such domestic abuse. When the novel describes a youth organization to address 'Research Regarding Youth and Women's Conformity with National Ideals', it mocks patriarchal dominance and abuse but also makes it apparent that this problem also affects 'the wives of the rich and the powerful' (557).

For Ngũgĩ, the dilemma of women in relation to the state is also connected to the possibilities of youth action and university students. Women and youth become the targets of retrogressive policies and the Ruler's absurd promulgation presented in a booklet titled '*Magnus Africanus: Prolegomenon to Future Happiness, by the Ruler*' which is supposed to address Aburiria's 'abandoning their traditions in pursuit of stressful modernity' (621). Here again the biting satire of Ngũgĩ is linked to actual social issues although expressed in the absurdity of megalomania.

> Women must get circumcised and show submission by always walking a few steps behind their men. Polygamous households should not form queues. Instead of screaming when they are beaten, women should sing songs of praise to those who beat them and even organize festivals to celebrate wife beating in honor of manhood. (621–2)

Although not extensively developed, the theme of female genital cutting is shown as a weapon of the state. By resorting to ultimate absurdities, Ngũgĩ draws greater attention to the problem of abuse of women, and by doing it through satire he has the potential to draw Western readers to this concern in ways that differ from those in Achebe's portrayal of the problem.

The question is whether Western readers will generally realize that domestic abuse in the African context is not exceptional and that abuse of women is a major global problem evidenced by statistics in such countries as the United States. In the novel, the act of 'wife beating' is used as well to determine manhood, when Tajirika, who thinks that 'Wife beating was a privilege if not a right of male power,' has to resort to 'imagining slapping his wife around and her screams for mercy and forgiveness' while he is in prison. These thoughts 'allowed him to think more soberly about other things that weighed on him' (376). Nyawira and Vinjinia, who reverse the power relationships, are faced with a head of state who orders that '"the leaders of rebellious youth and women"' should be '"crushed like ants"' (558).

Although the Wizard is depicted as exercising his own assault against the establishment, he is subject to a similar dilemma as that which affected Tajirika, the '*If*' speech impediment. In order to cure the Wizard, another healer or sorcerer is sought, which leads to the introduction of the Limping Wizard, an aged woman character who completes the gender balance in the area of sorcery. The 'Limping Wizard', who is 'A wizard to cure the wizard' (613) is presented in unflattering terms.

> The Limping Witch, as they now called the crippled witch, had a repulsive face. One of her eyes oozed, and when not talking her lips twitched; when talking to her, people felt compelled to look away. (626)

These descriptions are consistent with somewhat conventional representation of the onerous female witch. However, her ability to decipher the implications of speechlessness raises her to a more significant level of characterization. When she tells Kamiti that '"Speech is the beginning of knowledge. And lack of speech? The beginning of foolishness,"' she delivers a curative recitation, which implicates the 'Devil' lodged in his voice box (626–7). Her language is evocative, spiritual, and wise: '"*The body is the temple of the soul / Watch ye what you eat and drink*"' (628). As with the characterization of Nyawira, the Limping Witch is also part of the Wizard's salvation. Their escape from the forces of the Ruler is another example of the inability of the state to contain the efficacy of women. Like Nyawira's symbolic representation, that of the Limping Witch is even further beyond the real as she is part of the world of sorcery. Furthermore, at one point the Wizard and the Limping Witch are perceived as being 'one and the same' (634). In fact, the novel ultimately shows that the Limping Witch is in fact another incarnation of Nyawira, who is cast in a teacher-pupil relationship with Kamiti (722–3). Nyawira, 'not in disguise,' is a reaffirmation of the Gikuyu-Mumbi totality, where the union of the male and female creates an idealized notion of romantic love including a proffered wedding ring (764).

The novel suggests through Nyawira as a political activist and beyond the real sorceress that Ngũgĩ may be striving for the idyllic and the practical. Nyawira might suggest to Western readers the Kenyan Nobel Laureate Wangari Maathai, whose interest in the environment through the

Green Belt Movement has Pan-African implications. Maathai was also elected to the Kenyan parliament. By casting Nyawira as a central figure in the People's Assembly, she is given substance beyond the symbolic mother figure and romantic foil for the Wizard. The 'movement' has generated substantive political activity through 'spontaneous demonstrations' that 'call for the return of their collective voice'. Their call for a 'Day of National Rebirth or Self-Renewal' again shows the leadership role assigned to Nyawira and her co-members (666).

The underlying message of Ngũgĩ's work is that women are central in the transformation of the nation, when it has been afflicted by detrimental leaders such as the Ruler of this novel. The concept of rebirth, a metaphor which is obviously connected to the reproductive power of women, is used ironically in the novel to refer to the pregnancy of the Ruler, who gives birth to BABY D., 'Behold Baby Democracy'. The satire of this birth of 'multiparty democracy' is that the Ruler inevitably becomes the 'nominal head of all political parties' (698–9). This kind of political satire has contemporary relevance to real African situations such as that of Zimbabwe and Mugabe's attempts to manipulate the democratic process.

The message Ngũgĩ's novel might convey to the Western world is that critique of African leadership, a topic that reviewers of the novel were certainly aware of, is more complex analytically than simply blaming the leadership or looking for other Mobutus or Amins of Africa. Because Ngũgĩ treats the theme in satirical terms, it might appear that his goal is to ridicule rather than to propose strategies for reconstructing the nation. However, his use of women characters such as Nyawira, the Limping Witch, and Vinjinia suggests a different lesson. As characters, they clearly can appeal to the West's understanding of gender equity and political involvement of women in national rectification, but they also show that Ngũgĩ is grappling with the distinction between the symbolic importance of elevating women and their actual participation in the governing process.

One of the faults of the novel voiced in the Western press is that Ngũgĩ offers no discernable solution or satisfactory conclusion to the novel. Although this point has some merit, it does not necessarily mean that the novel has not offered through its own unfolding of character relationships a broader solution to the dilemmas of African states, a solution that might be found in balancing the voices of men and women and especially in viewing 'Women as the voice of the people'. For African countries this is not simply an African feminist message but a realization that the ascendancy of women is inextricably tied to the fate of nations, and although their actual abuse can be used as metaphor of national faults in need of rectification, the problem also needs to be addressed in the realm of real politics. Because Africa is reified in the Western imagination, its failings, many of which are shared by societies in the West, are often seen as typically African. If read in global terms, Ngũgĩ's novel can have important gender lessons for Western audiences, who, while viewing African situations from a distance, can also reflect on their own development in this area.

WORKS CITED

Achebe, Chinua. *Things Fall Apart*. 1958. New York: Anchor, 1994.

Davies, Carole Boyce, and Anne Adams Graves, eds. *Ngambika: Studies of Women in African Literature*. Trenton, NJ: Africa World Press, 1986.

Gikandi, Simon. *Ngũgĩ wa Thiong'o*. New York: Cambridge University Press, 2000.

Hellman, David. 'Allegory of Post-Colonial Africa Takes Flight'. Review of *Wizard of the Crow*, by Ngũgĩ wa Thiong'o. *San Francisco Chronicle* 13 August 2006: M1.

Márquez, Gabriel Garcia. *One Hundred Years of Solitude*. New York: Harper, 1970.

'Ngũgĩ Book Launched at University'. Review of *Wizard of the Crow*, by Ngũgĩ wa Thiong'o. *Daily Nation* 16 January 2007: 1.

Ngũgĩ wa Thiong'o. *Weep Not, Child*. London: Heinemann, 1964.

—— *The River Between*. London: Heinemann, 1965.

—— *Caitanni Mutharaba-ini*. Nairobi: Heinemann, 1980; trans. Ngugi wa Thiong'o, *Devil on the Cross*, London: Heinemann, 1982.

—— *Matigari ma Njiruungi*. Nairobi: Heinemann Kenya, 1986; trans. Wangui wa Goro, *Matigari*, London: Heinemann, 1989.

—— *Decolonising the Mind: The Politics of Language in African Literature*. London: James Currey, 1986.

—— *Moving the Centre: The Struggle for Cultural Freedoms*. London: James Currey, 1993.

—— *Murogi wa Kagogo*. Nairobi: East African Educational Publishers, 2004; trans. Ngũgĩ wa Thiong'o, *Wizard of the Crow*, New York: Pantheon, 2006.

Okorafor-Mbachu, Nnedi. Review of *Wizard of the Crow*, by Ngũgĩ wa Thiong'o. *Black Issues Book Review* 8.4 (July–August 2006): 38.

Soyinka, Wole. *The Open Sore of a Continent: A Personal Narrative of the Nigerian Crisis*. New York: Oxford UP, 1996.

Turrentine, Jeff. 'The Strongman's Weakness.' Review of *Wizard of the Crow*, by Ngũgĩ wa Thiong'o. *New York Times Book Review* 10 September 2006: 22.

Updike, John. 'Extended Performance: Saving the Republic of Aburiria'. Review of *Wizard of the Crow*, by Ngũgĩ wa Thiong'o. *New Yorker* 31 July 2006. Posted 24 July 2006. 8 February 2007 <http://www.newyorker.com/printables/critics/060731crbo_books>.

Van der Vlies, Andrew. 'The Ruler and His Henchmen.' Review of *Wizard of the Crow*, by Ngũgĩ wa Thiong'o. *Times Literary Supplement* 20 October 2006: 21.

Sophie I. Akhuemokhan

Introduction

In his 1972 book, *Rebellion, Revolution and Armed Force,* the social scientist, D.E.H. Russell, refers to 'unsuccessful' revolution, 'partially successful' revolution and 'successful' revolution. He argues that the first produces minimal social change, the second a middling degree of social change, and the third, which he feels is the ideal, major social change: 'Successful revolution is defined as substantial (or fundamental) social change resulting from rebellion' (58). Bearing this definition in mind, it becomes obvious that much of contemporary Africa is in dire need of successful revolution. Foreign rule, civilian rule and military rule have all failed to bring about positive social change on a continent that is to a large extent rapidly deteriorating in its morals and its economy. Africa is still searching for a means of social regeneration, and this is clearly one of the motivating factors behind the writing of Ayi Kwei Armah's sixth novel, *Osiris Rising (OR)*. Armah believes that the key to social regeneration lies in ancient Egyptian culture – in its uniqueness, its polish, and above all its testimony to African creativity.

With the reputation Armah enjoys as one of Africa's leading novelists, one would have expected this 1995 publication to have provoked a flood of critical response. On the contrary very little has been written on it, and a comment in an article captioned 'The Meaning of Life' could explain why. The comment is made by Kaye Whiteman, who read the novel and laid it aside for the better part of a year before attempting an assessment. Whiteman admits: 'Although I found it absorbing to read, there were things in its symbolism and its messages that gave me critic's block, and my un-understanding translated itself into inaction' (171).

Whiteman's confession is sincere, for the symbolism of the text is undoubtedly daunting at a first reading. It is a symbolism rooted in ancient Egyptian mythology – an area that is still unfamiliar to many – and so even the professional critic is liable to struggle with it. The struggle is worthwhile, however, when one begins to appreciate Armah's purpose.

Through his treatment of two mythical symbols, the ankh and *maat*, he presents a convincing critique of Africa's past and an intriguing proposal for the way forward. The Egyptian word 'ankh' is interpreted as 'life' and '*maat*' as 'justice'. These two symbols are part of a heritage that can purportedly put Africa back on its feet after centuries of grovelling in the dust. It is not too common to find African novelists who interweave myth with revolution in this manner; Wole Soyinka made a commendable attempt in *Season of Anomy* but his work was greeted with mixed feelings (cf. Booth 1981:143–65). And it is far less common to find a West African novelist who leans so heavily on North African mythology in making his point about development in the sub-Sahara. *Osiris Rising* is undeniably bold in the connections it makes between the affairs on one side of the continent and the other, and between Africa's past and its future.

Critics have commented on the text's symbolism before and acknowledged its revolutionary message, but have apparently avoided a close study of how the two work in consonance. A case in point is Whiteman, already quoted. His review is the most explicit available and comes closer than any other to addressing the issues in this essay. He alleges that the text 'draws on the characters and ideas of ancient Egypt to illuminate a parable of our times, making a statement about Africa's current condition ...' (1714). He goes on to explain this 'current condition' as one in which physical and mental abuse are sustained features of the African experience: 'If the book is a statement about slavery, and the psychic damage it did to African societies, it also describes its continuation in present times under present rulers' (1714). Whiteman even associates these slaveries with one of the symbols highlighted in this paper, which is the ankh: 'The powerful symbol of the ankh runs through the novel... as a sort of talisman of resistance to slaveries both ancient and modern' (1714). The association ends here, nonetheless. Whiteman moves on to other aspects of the novel without subsequent allusion to the relationship between symbolism and social regeneration.

Douglas Killam and Ruth Rowe's *The Companion to African Literature* is equally silent on the topic, even though like Whiteman it recognizes that the novel is a statement on Africa's previous and current conditions, as evident in its unabridged title: *Osiris Rising: a novel of Africa past, present and future*. In its brief analysis of Armah's contributions as a writer, *The Companion* asserts: 'His life has been centred on his literary work, especially on the retrieval of the African past for the reinvention of post-colonial Africa' (31). Adjusting the perspective to focus on *Osiris Rising* specifically, the contributor further remarks that the principal objective of the revolutionaries in the novel is 'to reinstate ancient Egypt as the matrix of African history and culture and begin long-term changes capable of breaking the contemporary neocolonial deadlock' (205). The exact importance of reinstating ancient Egypt, or how it can break the neocolonial deadlock, is left unsaid. These questions are mainly answered through the symbolism, in fact, although the entry in Killam and Rowe does not touch on it.

Indeed no commentary could be located in which the ankh and *maat* were explored as figures of social change. Armah appropriates these figures to make some interesting observations about Africa's social collapse and possible resuscitation; observations that engender lively debate because they hinge on an ancestry that a large proportion of Africans probably find alien. Such a controversial thesis merits attention. Consequently, the aim of this essay is to study the symbolism of the ankh and *maat*, examining their transformation from mythical objects in ancient Egypt to a cross-continental inheritance that contains the secret of successful revolution today.

The Ankh

The ankh is introduced to the reader in the opening paragraph with just enough information to arouse curiosity:

> From far off, it looked like an ellipse mounted on a cross. Close up, it was a female form, arms outstretched, head capacious enough to contain the womb. The day she asked its name, her grandmother Nwt turned an incredulous smile on her. 'Ankh. Life.' Ast asked where it came from. 'Home,' her grandmother said. Then her face hardened as if the answer had closed a window on it. (*OR* 1)

The setting is America in the latter part of the twentieth century and Ast is a mere child. She is puzzling over a carved wooden antiquity given to her by Nwt and destined to pilot her out of the land of her birth and towards a revelation of her true identity as an African. Ast's formative years are speedily dispensed with in chapter one – her precocity as a child, her undergraduate days, and the completion of a doctoral degree in *Kemt* (ancient Egyptian philosophy) – and at the start of chapter two she is already a Professor of Egyptology at the age of 27. At this juncture, an ankh appears again. This time it is the logo on a mysterious leaflet sent to her by an underground revolutionary group in Africa. The article is headed 'Who We Are and Why' and is seemingly the group's manifesto: '[It was] an unsigned article, mimeographed on yellowed paper, the text clean on the single page, its only identifying mark set at the top of the paper: the ankh' (9). In the article's clarity and logic, Ast detects the voice of her university sweetheart, Asar, an African who has already returned home; and she responds unhesitatingly by preparing to return too.

As soon as she lands on African soil, ankhs begin to surface in all manner of inexplicable circumstances. She encounters one as a key-holder on a chain attached to a single key; another as the broken pendant on the necklace of a phoney pastor; and yet another as a centerpiece holding together the thatched roof of a hut. No explanations are given and so, together with the reader, she is compelled to sort out for herself the contemporized meaning of the symbol. Towards the tail end of the plot Tete, a revolutionary character, finally provides some enlightenment. She informs Ast that the sign has become the hallmark of a radical society that bears its name, 'the cult of the ankh', adding: 'The society goes back not centuries but thousands of years into our past ... because it was devoted to life, its chosen symbol was the oldest of Africa's life signs, the ankh' (260, 261-262). Tete reveals much about the cult of the ankh – how its members are drawn from all walks of life and share the common goals of creativity and industry; how the society has consistently fought for justice and the preservation of the best of African values; and the numberless occasions when government hostility has forced it to go underground. As she rehearses the cult's saga, the reader notices that the ankh is synonymous with ideals such as industry, creativity and knowledge. Moreover the reader marks, with distress, that down through the ages these ideals have been swallowed up by the African's preoccupation with poor alternatives, i.e. consumption instead of production, and free money instead of hard work. In the nation's darkest moments, the ideals, the cult-members and the ankh go into extinction simultaneously. Irrespective of this, Tete's lecture is encouraging since plainly a new era is dawning in which the ankh is again being lifted up, and after manifold abortions Africa is now geared towards authentic regeneration.

In order to understand the nature of this regeneration it is essential to understand the nature of the ankh, the chosen emblem of reform in the text. Tete talks extensively about the sign as it pertains to the cult but says little about the sign itself. This is deliberate on the author's part because he wants to provoke his reader into becoming a researcher. Whiteman professes that Armah's ambitions are 'unashamedly didactic' (1714), and indeed while he strives to give accurate facts on ancient Egyptian mythology he also hopes his reader will continue with the fact-finding where the novel stops. Incontestably there is so much interweaving of fact with fiction that it is frequently difficult to distinguish one from the other, and the only way out is to resort to secondary sources for clarification. The effort unearths useful information, verifying a number of Armah's claims and supporting his view of the ankh as an African legacy.

Elementary descriptions of the symbol come from the dictionary. According to *The New Webster's Dictionary*, an ankh is 'a cross-shaped figure, with a looped handle, symbolizing life and prosperity [Egypt = 'life']' (36). John Cooper expatiates on this in *An Illustrated Dictionary of Traditional Symbols*: 'Ankh. An Egyptian symbol of life, all life both human and divine; the key of knowledge of the mysteries of hidden wisdom, power, authority, covenant. The ankh is formed of the combined male and female symbols of Osiris and Isis, the union of two generative principles of heaven and earth' (13). The primary quality of the ankh is therefore life, as Tete said. It embraces creation from heaven to earth and by implication also reaches into the grave, for while Osiris had affinities with heaven he was equally regarded as 'the supreme god of the dead' (Grimal 1979: 35).

It follows from this that the ankh was the badge of a peculiar family – Osiris, the divine father; Isis the mother, and Horus the son; and spoke of life in its three realms – the celestial, the terrestrial, and the sub-terrestrial. Consequently it was a sacred symbol; and it communicated truths to the ancient Egyptians in a fashion, for instance, analogous to the fish communicating truths to the early Christians. 'Fish' is interpreted as 'IXTHUS' in Greek (I-X-TH-U-(S)) The Christians would behold the symbol of the fish and would both read in it the message: I:IESOU ('Jesus') X:XRISTOU ('Christ') TH:THEOS ('God') U:HIOU ('Son') ('Jesus Christ Son of God'), and see in its design a reflection of their mission as fishers of men. The hieroglyphic ankh spoke in a comparable way to the Egyptian populace in the dynasties succeeding Osiris. They too decoded from its lineaments the signet of their benevolent pharaoh-god. All Egyptian pharaohs were conventionally believed to be gods, but Osiris was distinc-tive because while in his earthly frame he had an unusual compassion for humanity. The myth has it that he refined and educated his people, but his endeavour was cut short when he was murdered by his wicked brother, Set, who dissected his body into fourteen pieces. Being a pharaoh, Osiris resurrected as a deity and as an eternal paradigm for the Egyptian monarchy: 'Osiris is the prototype of the dead king who, having accomplished his task on earth, dies conferring his titles on his son, then comes to life again in a beatified form. Every pharaoh went through the same process' (Grimal ibid.: 36).

The stamp of Isis was in similar guise veiled in the ankh. Every devotee could locate it... She was Osiris' wife and sister, and emblematic of the female productive element in nature. Sir Paul Harvey, a scholar in classical literature, ranks her as 'a great Egyptian goddess, worshipped throughout the world of the Greeks' (1974: 299). Isis rescued Osiris from Set's first murder attempt; she could not thwart the second one and it was Horus, their son, who ultimately avenged his father's death. Horus was god of the sun. His presence in the ankh is presumed to be signified by its looped handle: '... the oval [loop] may have been eternity ... or it may have been the sun rising above the horizon' (Cooper 1978: 13). Through his son, Osiris was 'the source of renewed life' alongside being the god of the dead (Harvey ibid.).

The ankh was an emblem of this trio of gods. It incorporated their traits and relayed the entire Osiris myth graphically to those who could decipher its composite shapes. There are elements of the myth that should be remembered, because in Armah's fictional community the sign is meant to speak as eloquently to its new disciples, modern Africans, as it did to the old. It is not by mistake that the tale told by this Egyptian relic is akin to the tale of Africa generally. A case in point is the initial state of Osiris. He was noble and highly innovative, and capable of catering for his people. This is a metaphor for Africa prior to its corruption by materialism. When Tete chronicles the activities of the cult she mentions that the pioneer cult-members existed during an era when 'we had a civilization. It was prosperous then' (*OR* 261). It may not have been a golden era, as she concedes when she admits that 'some of the ways we live[d] [were] not worth saving' (261), but it was good enough in that the people were meaningfully occupied and self-reliant. Unfortunately, just as the innovative Osiris was prematurely hewn down, so the era of prosperity was truncated. The ankh again documents one of several reasons for this. Osiris' potential was calculatedly stifled by the greed of his brother, the reader recalls, and significantly this brother divided him into segments to ensure that his demise was permanent. Relating this to modern circumstances, the cult-members (and the reader) ought to comprehend that the treacherous brother is the European, being that the peculiar close-knit family circle symbolized by the ankh is Africa. Armah makes no bones about his antipathy towards the colonizers' segmentation of the land. Through the mouth of Asar, Ast's husband and mentor, he protests: 'We live in neocolonies called Nigeria, Botswana, Senegal, Rwanda, Tanzania and Mozambique. We will have to work against stiff odds to turn our dismembered continent into a healing society – Africa' (112). It is thought-provoking to see how parallel sentiments are expressed by writers on the opposite geographical pole; that is, by the Kenyans Ngũgĩ wa Thiong'o and Micere Mugo in their popular play *The Trial of Dedan Kimathi* (1988 [1976]). Woman, the female protagonist, soliloquizes: 'The way the enemy makes us thirst to kill one another…. We are told you are Luo, you are Kalenjin, you are Kamba, you are Maasai, you are Kikuyu' (14). Plainly there is some consensus among African writers that the carving up of the continent was devised to weaken it.

All the same there is a third fact concealed in the ankh which is encouraging. Despite all attempts to the contrary, Osiris rose in an improved form. This is a prophecy of Africa tomorrow, subsequent upon the knowledge of its own worth and the worth of its Egyptian legacy. Accordingly it can be perceived that in many ways the ankh is effectually a picture of Africa, past, present and future. It captures the country's bygone glory, its present state of relegation and disunity, and its future possibilities. Regardless of the fact that it was conceived to support a conservative tradition – and did so admirably – one can see why it is selected as a symbol for African nationalism and Africa's revolution in *Osiris Rising*.

There is one other weighty connotation of the ankh that calls for study. In *Osiris Rising*, it is carried by cult-members to the diverse African coasts, which is meant to be indicative of the wide-flung influence of Egyptian culture. It has been remarked hitherto that fact and fiction are neatly interwoven in the text, and the 'fact' which the novelist is advancing here is that there are bonafide links between the culture of

Egypt and that of the sub-Sahara. This is a burning issue among intellectuals, some of whom hold the view that such a link is inconsequential, assuming it exists at all. It is helpful to hear just one such opinion to understand why Armah rejects it so firmly in his novel. A convenient illustration is that of the French historian, Jean Suret-Canale, who in tune with the bulk of European scholars sees no tangible tie between the cultures of Egypt and black Africa:

> The Egyptian civilization had close links with the civilization of the Eastern Mediterranean and the Asian Middle East, but its influence in Africa beyond the valley of the Nile was extremely limited. Compared with it, the civilizations of black Africa show original characteristics which it is neither necessary nor convincing to attribute to exterior influence. (quoted in Wauthier 1964: 86)

Armah disputes this. As far as he is concerned the link is both tangible and vital, and Europe's refusal to acknowledge it is once more a tactic to weaken the continent. As Europe well knows, the ancient Egyptian accomplishment would give Africa stature in the international arena, and on the home front provide the youths with the requisite courage to decisively break away from European-oriented modes of administration – modes that have already been debunked in Europe, one might add. Using the cultists, Armah avers that successful social revolution in Africa is feasible, given new models of government and the incentive to improvise. This in effect is the crux of the cult's argument, and the primary reason why it is persuaded that black Africans should hook up with their pharaonic ancestors. The cultists believe that the prerogative of the West to continually maintain a leadership position in global affairs is to a considerable degree based on the premise that Africa is unable to do so. The reasoning of the Western powers – which sadly has become the reasoning of the Africans themselves – is that the black race is uncreative and is therefore better fitted to a position of followership. Ancient Egypt is evidence of a creative streak in the African race that *negates the accepted principle*, hence First-world politics demands that it be hoisted out of its locale. Asar puts it like this:

> Ancient Egypt was a high, original civilization. Africans were *a priori* incapable of developing civilizations. If it was necessary to indicate a source for Ancient Egyptian civilization, that source was located outside Egypt. If that proved awkward, Egypt was isolated as a unique phenomenon connected to no people in its African environment. [Thus] the study of Ancient Egypt was not a part of the study of Africa. (*OR* 217)

It is in Africa's interest to re-instate ancient Egypt as the continent's cultural nucleus, the cult-members admonish. And the matter does not end at that. Many of them are educationists, and they urge that *Kemt* be incorporated in African syllabuses, studied by every student at the tertiary level, and universally exploited to boost faith in African genius. It is the proof that Africans were once proud over-seers of a sophisticated system and are capable of a repeat performance.

Maat

Maat is a minor symbol that is not mentioned more than a couple of times in the narrative. The purpose of including it in this discussion is to demonstrate how it mirrors the function of the ankh, likewise directing Africa towards fundamental social change. Tete makes the most categorical reference to *maat* in her exegesis of the cult. She says the society was '... not a blood circle ... but a circle of souls, the friendship of committed souls, the companionship of minds and bodies connected to the source of humane life, our continent, through the source of civilization, the idea of justice, Maat' (263). This may sound obscure but it is as express a statement as the reader will get. Therefore, armed with the knowledge that the word 'justice' is somehow interchangeable with the word '*maat*', the reader patiently resumes research on ancient Egyptian mythology.

The background to the deity can be covered in a few sentences. *Maat*, or *Maet*, was an Egyptian goddess whose defining principle was also *maat* (justice). Fred Maroon and Paul Newby try to describe the original sense of this word in a book entitled *The Egypt Story*:

> Although the pharaoh was God on earth and theoretically possessed all the land, crops and animals in his domain, the system was humanized by a general acceptance that man lived under a law of universal justice. The Egyptian word for it is *maat*, and the goddess was a sedate figure with an ostrich feather in her hand.... The word *maat* has no precise modern equivalent. It seems to mean that the universe was good. (1979: 61)

Like the ankh, *maat* was held sacred and set the heart of the ancient Egyptian at rest. It was the symbol of an impartial and regulated cosmos in which hierarchy was not synonymous with oppression. Maroon and Newby take some pains to stress this: '[Society] was not only conservative; it was rigidly hierarchical... [but] this did not necessarily mean tyranny. There is evidence that the kingship was held in some affection' (61). Justice as practised in line with *maat* was supposed to be accessible to everyone. A peasant could appeal to this doctrine and win a case against a feudal lord. Nevertheless, the really striking factor about *maat* from the perspective of the twenty-first century is its credibility. The mighty and the mean alike trusted it to apportion each man his due without fear or favour. Thus it not only represented 'the principle of social and moral order' (Grimal 1969: 39), but went further to actualize it peacefully. *Maat* had probity, for its presiding deity was more than just the goddess of justice; she was also the goddess of truth.

Having grasped these details, the reader infers that the values of equity, truth and probity are incorporated in *maat* as those of enterprise, creativity and knowledge are incorporated in the ankh. This accounts for why such a minor symbol is of such import to the radicals, for in their own country and century equity, truth and probity have been thrown to the winds. The social situation has degenerated to the extent that neither government nor the governed bother to deceive themselves that such things exist. Government '[has] made moral issues irrelevant,' according to one disillusioned citizen (*OR* 56). Illustrative of this is the perverse Seth, the D.D. (Deputy Director of Security) and government's most senior official. Seth and Ast have several rendezvous, always at Seth's insistence and to Ast's irritation. A memorable meeting occurs early in the narrative, during which Ast labours in vain to make Seth understand the importance of justice in administration. Seth refuses to take her seriously and invariably declares the ideal impracticable. 'You know, justice is a vague concept, meaningless except to intellectuals,' Seth insists without apology, 'from whose point of view is a system just or unjust?' (37)

With rulers of this kind, the plebeians cannot pretend that justice or moral order are national priorities. It is a pity that they worsen matters by giving up. In despair, they shift the responsibility of reform to their children, as this brief discussion between Ast and Netta, a hostel-owner, unveils:

> 'I'm tired sister,' [Netta said]. 'I'd like to rest but I can't. Things are so chaotic we waste endless time treading water, going nowhere.'
> 'Some generation will begin the cleanup,' [Ast replied].
> 'That's what we say. It's our song of defeat. We're pushing such heavy loads onto children. I don't envy them, the cleaners'. (78)

Unknown to Netta, the cleaners are already in the picture. The cult of the ankh toils in the wings, raising *maat* as a symbol of the re-awakening of truth and equity. Of necessity, they modify certain of its symbolic implications, even as they did with the ankh. Hierarchy is a prime example. Pre-colonial *maat* made allowance for kings; the modified version is 'averse to life in palaces' (263). It finds expression in a desegregated society that reckons equally with all its members. This difference apart, however, the objectives of *maat* remain relatively constant. Like their predecessors in ancient Egypt, the cult wants to implant social and moral order in a set-up characterized by the reverse, and also like their predecessors, they are aware that this circumstance cannot come to pass by itself. The ancient Egyptians found guidance in *Kemt* and the cult suggests that present day Africans follow suit, concentrating on the spirit of *Kemt* (excellence and innovation) where the laws are undesirable. In all, the basic tenet of their argument under the sign of *maat* is the same as that under the sign of the ankh. They are convinced that the avenue to successful revolution is creativity and the starting-point is not Europe but Africa.

Conclusion

Armah utilizes the mythical symbols of the ankh and *maat* to demonstrate that substantial social change in Africa can only result from a change in the African mindset. The race must learn to think for itself if it wants a permanent remedy to its lingering social ills. It is pointless to hope that the remedies of outsiders will one day yield dividends; even in fiction, these remedies have failed. Armah points to ancient Egypt as a possible way out where all other ways have terminated in a dead-end. He declares that the ancient Egyptians have bequeathed upon Africa 'the key of knowledge... of hidden wisdom, power, authority,' as the ankh promises. Successful revolution is enveloped in this. It is difficult to summarise his thesis in an essay of this length. Suffice it to say that the text deserves more reflection than it has been given here, for as Whiteman posits after reading it a second time, it is 'a work for which the tag "novel" is inadequate' (1714).

WORKS CITED

Armah, Ayi Kwei. *Osiris Rising*. Popenguine: Per Ankh, 1995.

Booth, James. *Writers and Politics in Nigeria*. New York: Africana, 1981.

Cooper, John. *An Illustrated Encyclopaedia of Traditional Symbols*. London: Thames and Hudson, 1978.

Grimal, Pierre. *Larousse World Mythology*. London: Paul Hamlyn, 1969.

Harvey, Paul. *Oxford Companion to Classical Literature*. Oxford: Clarendon, 1974.

Killam, Douglas and Ruth Rowe. *The Companion to African Literatures*. Oxford: James Currey, 2000.

Maroon, Fred and Paul Newby. *The Egypt Story: Its Art, Its Monuments, Its People, Its History*, London: Andre Deutsch, 1979.

Ngũgĩ wa Thiong'o and Micere Githae Mugo. *The Trial of Dedan Kimathi:* Ibadan: Heinemann, 1988 [1976].

Russell, D.E.H. *Rebellion, Revolution and Armed Force: A Comparative Study of Fifteen Countries with Special Emphasis on Cuba and South Africa*. New York: Academic, 1974.

Soyinka, Wole. *Season of Anomy*. London: Rex Collings, 1980.

Wauthier, Claude. *The Literature and Thought of Modern Africa*. London: Heinemman, 1964.

Whiteman, Kaye. 'The Meaning of Life.' *West Africa*. 4–10 November 1996: 1714.

A New African Youth Novel
in the Era of HIV/AIDS:
An Analysis of Unity Dow's
Far & Beyon'

Machiko Oike

Few would deny that HIV/AIDS is one of the most pressing issues infecting and affecting Africa and that African literature, which has proudly been a 'literature of engagement', must address the problems 'now, and right now', to borrow Mandela's phrase (Mandela 2000). What surprises and disappoints readers of African literature is the almost total silence on the part of African literature – or, let us say, 'serious' African literature. Most novels dealing with HIV/AIDS are written by lesser known writers, published locally, intended to satisfy local reading needs, and thus can be classified to a degree or another as 'popular' literature.[1] One of the few exceptions to this trend is *Last Plague* written by an internationally renowned Kenyan author, Meja Mwangi. The novel is published in Kenya by East African Educational Publishers, for a purpose. The local publication (even though by a well-established African publisher with international distribution through African Books Collective) ensures effective circulation to the home audience.

What has been ignored at the international level has been espoused at the local level as an increasing number of young adult novels overtly tackle the issues of HIV/AIDS.[2] The lament over a 'shortage' (Mitchell and Smith 2003: 513) of youth novels dealing with HIV/AIDS, which was made only five years ago, has now become a thing of the past. The proliferation is surprising because discussing HIV/AIDS means mentioning sex and death, both being taboo topics almost everywhere in the world, and especially in Africa, where children should 'respect' adults by not interfering in adult matters (Ntsimane 2005). The growing number of youth titles reflects the urgent need keenly felt in society to break the silence and address the matter in an unprecedentedly radical way.

The present paper focuses on Unity Dow's *Far and Beyon'*, one of these new youth novels dealing with the problems of HIV/AIDS, and shows that the dire situation of HIV/AIDS is producing a new type of young adult novel. For that purpose, however, it is first necessary to map this recent phenomenon of proliferation of youth novels on HIV/AIDS, before turning to a close examination of *Far and Beyon'* itself.

The growing number of youth novels dealing with HIV/AIDS can be classified into three categories according to the pedagogical formality in their approach to the issue. The first category consists of sets of textbooks intended to be used in school classes such as life orientation, English, and health, social or cultural studies. They have questions and discussion topics listed at the end, and are accompanied by teachers' guides. One of the most comprehensive is the HIV/AIDS Readers in the Heinemann Junior African Writers Series. It is composed of 13 story books and 10 information books, one of which is on the UN Convention on the Rights of the Child, another a positive life story narrated by Botswana's Miss HIV Stigma-Free. The series is divided into four levels, and the story books for level D, that is, for readers aged 14–18, are substantial and rewarding reads.

Dancing Queen by Margie Orford (2004), for example, is a story of an aspiring dancer narrated from multiple viewpoints. The story begins dramatically as the hovering spirit of the heroine looks down at her own funeral and laments her frustrated dream of escaping from rural poverty to dancing stardom, followed by her untimely death from AIDS at the age of 18. Her boyfriend and her female friend take turns to recount with regret how they failed to rescue her from her molesting uncle and greedy aunt, who virtually killed her. The story ends with the now cleansed and serene voice of the heroine hoping that her baby niece, a prospective dancer, will learn from her story of and fulfill her dream.

Of course, not only the Heinemann publishing giant but also local publishers have made their contributions. As the most seriously afflicted area, Southern Africa responded to the grave situation in the early 1990s by producing the Macmillan Boleswa AIDS Awareness Programme which is composed of more than ten short fictional narratives. Uganda, a leading star in the fight against the epidemic, also launched the Fountain Living Youth Series in 2002, which features stories by the country's established novelists.

The second category of youth novels dealing with HIV/AIDS includes books which, though not forming a series as above, are designed to be used as textbooks and, therefore, come with teachers' guides. Worthy of note is *Stronger than the Storm* by Lutz van Dijk (2000). Dutch-German, van Dijk composed the novel through conducting numerous interviews with township youth with the collaboration of Karin Chubb, a South African lecturer and activist (van Dijk 2004). It describes how a township high-school girl comes to terms with her HIV status. Thinasonke, active in a drama club and struggling with township life, contracts HIV through being gang-raped by three boys, one of whom is making a desperate attempt to cleanse himself of HIV by way of sleeping with a virgin. In the midst of her despair, Thinasonke finds love and understanding from her teacher who organizes a sex-education play; from her eldest brother who was traumatized from detention in the 1980s; and most of all, from her boyfriend Thabang, a stigmatized AIDS orphan. The novel reaches its denouement when her eldest brother intervenes in a bloody confrontation between Thabang and the rapists and conducts a kind of healing ceremony for all concerned.

The novels in the third category are individual youth novels whose committed writers understand that their primary responsibility as professional African writers is to deal with HIV/AIDS issues. One is about a Boer middle-class boy who contracts the deadly virus through his first girlfriend, an adventurous beauty, but who comes to terms with his condition through associating with a frail but courageous elderly woman in a wheelchair (Kitching 2001). Another is about a township high-school girl, an only daughter loved by her TV director father and actress mother, who feels pressure to have sex to keep her university boyfriend, but who thinks twice after learning that her cousin has become an HIV-positive teenage single mother (Mazibuko 2003).

Some of these novels sound optimistic, and it is doubtful that they can encourage and empower readers in difficult situations. Even *Stronger than the Storm*, undoubtedly one of the best works in the genre, is not free from such disappointing optimism. After meticulously delineating the violent contradictions defining young girls and boys in society, the story comes to an almost abrupt happy ending in celebrating the African healing power. While savouring the peace and tranquility achieved at the denouement, the readers cannot help asking themselves: "Is my life so easy and rosy?" The more beautifully life is crafted in fiction, the more dismally their reality emerges; their harsh reality overwhelms them, leaving them powerless and almost numb.

It is clear that in the face of what is called AIDS fatigue, literature is expected to play an important role in motivating youth for the cause (Chetty 2005; Mitchell and Smith 2003). By entangling a protagonist just like the reader in the problem of HIV/AIDS and inviting the reader to tackle the knotty situation through putting him/herself in the shoes of the protagonist, literature can nurture warm understanding as well as cool criticism in the mind of the reader. The young reader can feel compassion for the characters living with HIV/AIDS, interpret their predicament, make a wise choice for him/herself, and help to change the society. For that purpose, the novels should not only be optimistically positive but also, and more importantly, realistically gloomy. This is a difficult task set for youth novels in the era of AIDS, and *Far and Beyon'* by Unity Dow is among the few which are able to meet the challenge.

Far and Beyon' belongs to the third category of the HIV/AIDS novels for youth, and of course, the novel is no exception in that it gives positive messages to youth. The heroine, after suffering from an illegal abortion, returns to school through her quick wit, and organizes a school cultural festival which protests against sexual abuses in school through artistic expression. She then finds out at the end of the novel that she is HIV negative and dreams about going 'far and beyon'. The tentative success of the heroine in realizing her dream amid sexual violence in times of HIV/AIDS reminds the reader of the author's brilliant profile as the first female judge in the Botswana High Court and a staunch advocate of women's rights; and hence, the positive message of the novel is doubly emphasized.[3] In the words of a reviewer, the story presents 'a victory that will move teens everywhere who feel silenced by authority' (Rochman 2002: 1518), and seems to follow the narrative of the self-fulfilling heroine common in school novels for teenagers.

On closer examination, however, it turns out that the novel does not prescribe a solution; instead, it lays bare the contradictions in sexual power games in society without showing any easy way out. A close analysis follows of how *Far and Beyon'* abstains from climaxing in hopes and achievements, as most youth novels do, yet still conveys messages to youth. First, the paper examines how this novel represents with an exceptionally realistic touch the sexual violence experienced by women in various social positions. Then, the paper analyses in terms of plot and characterization how the novel rewrites the coming-of-age narrative common in youth novels. Finally, the paper points out that the novel manages to show a glimpse of hope in the midst of despair and help the heroine and her readers live and read on.

Attention should be focused first on the novel's representation of women suffering and struggling in various positions. Among them, the novel represents most meticulously girls in the same generation as the heroine, Mosa. The most typical is Cecilia, an AIDS-afflicted friend of Mosa's childhood lying on her deathbed with her baby daughter, who is also dying. In her last words, she admonishes Mosa 'to be careful' and not to 'end up like me' (179), warning that Mosa is no exception to the risk of sexual marginalization and its fatal result. Other girls in the novel are lucky enough not to have developed AIDS symptoms yet, but they are also at risk. A junior sister of Mosa's classmate is 14 years old and has been sexually abused by her uncle. The family deliberately moves the girl to a remote village and continues to pay due respect to the culprit who is the head of the family (135). School is another field of sexual power play.[4] The principal intimidates one of the junior students to surrender her to a 'big man' in the village (128-9). A teacher notorious as a sexual harasser makes tenacious advances to Sinah, Mosa's classmate (128). Most of all, Mosa herself has had a similar experience with a police officer, a school guest for a life-orientation programme, resulting in her pregnancy, dismissal from school, and illegal abortion (94-6).

While students are thus abused, teachers are protected, and if transferred due to sexual misconduct at all, they are transferred with promotion (133). In fact, in order to escape an accusation of having sexual affairs with several students, a teacher volunteers to be transferred to Mosa's school because its principal is notorious for engaging himself in such affairs with impunity (90). Talking at a teachers' meeting about a pregnant student to be expelled, a teacher accepts the case as natural and inevitable: 'Girls will always fall pregnant. That is the way things are. That is nature' (143). Happy to conceal the responsibility of the teacher, the principal adds: 'If these girls are loose, there is nothing we can do about it' (143). It is best to expel 'the really bad ones' (143), he continues, 'before they corrupt the rest of the school' (143-4). The cause of sexual 'corruption' at school is ascribed not to the abusive teachers in power but to the essentially 'loose' girls, and thus, sexual violence persists.

It is not only girls of Mosa's generation who are sexually abused; the predicament has been handed down from mother to daughter. For instance, Mosa's mother has been raising her four children single-handedly, working as a house help. Her latest partner was an ever-drunken tyrant who nearly killed her. Uneducated, she believes in witchcraft and accuses her best friend of jealously killing her two AIDS-inflicted sons, that is, Mosa's elder brothers. Mosa is 'afraid of ending up like her mother: poor, unmarried and struggling to raise a family alone' (78), but as her only daughter, she feels that she is 'more likely to follow her mother's step' (78). Another example is found in the mother of Sinah, Mosa's classmate. Sinah does not inform her mother that she has been molested by a teacher, because her mother 'cannot do anything about it, and that would worry her and make her feel useless' (127). Sinah laments: 'What can my mother do? … What am I going to do?' (127).

Of course, educated and therefore supposedly empowered women challenge discrimination; however it is 'an uphill battle' (177). Among such women, Julia, a young militant feminist lawyer, deserves a special notice as a character closest to the author. In contrast to the masculine system of law, which uses 'any little opportunity to put a woman down' (177), Julia and her colleague help Cecilia, Mosa's childhood friend dying of AIDS, to obtain financial support from the father of her baby, though in vain. With 'their being young and female . . . working against them' (173), a mere deputy registrar, far lower in rank than lawyers, scoffs at them and refuses to proceed with the case. After the case is finally presented to court, the judge bluntly dismisses it. The total defeat of Julia shows that whether lawyer or student, as far as she is a woman, she is a loser. 'Furious' and 'close to tears,' Mosa laments: 'Was there no relief from this constant battering? At home? At school? Now even within the cradle of justice?' (177).

Female teachers at school are powerless as well. On the one hand, a few progressive teachers dare to invite community leaders to school and ask them to lecture the students, and indirectly their male colleagues also, about life and sex. Unfortunately, this opportunity only causes another case of abuse, which results in Mosa's pregnancy. On the other hand, most male teachers accept the status quo and shrug it off 'without any sign of surprise' (90) when they see their unremorseful colleagues molesting girl students. The novel is thus eloquent in showing that deeply entrenched sexual discrimination overpowers even educated women.

The bold and relentless representation of mundane sexual violence in the novel is exceptional for young adult novels – even among the radical works which consciously address the difficult issues of HIV/AIDS as a part of necessary sex education. The uncompromising and realistic voices of women ringing in the novel come from the numerous life stories the author has learned first-hand through her activities for human rights. In the *Kunapipi* interview, Dow talks about her many years of experience with abused women and their unforgettable stories whose details no legal reports were allowed to contain. Fiction was her recourse, because only fiction can 'take all this material' and 'reach a wider audience' (Dow 2004: 56).

Of course, the heroine does not sit down lamenting; on the contrary, like Julia and the author, she stands up against sexual humiliation and *almost* wins a triumph. The heroine and her friends organize a school cultural exhibition with the education minister as one of their distinguished guests in which they protest against sexual abuse by way of drawings and a play. In addition to this victory at school, the heroine finds out her HIV status to be negative at the end of the novel. A careful examination, however, would reveal that *Far and Beyon'* deliberately revises the progressive narrative of maturity of a teenage girl.

The plot and characterization of this novel attempt an alternative teenage story in times of AIDS. The first point to note is that the story remains open-ended, without offering any solution. That is to say, it is suggested that the victory of Mosa and her friends could be overturned any minute. When Mosa is thrilled after the exhibition at a promise made by the education minister to investigate the matter, her mother warns her that the minister may forget a promise made to mere girls and that any investigation, if carried out at all, may prove their allegation of abuse to be false. Mosa is still trying new tactics to ensure the attention of the minister, when the novel abruptly ends the episode of Mosa and her girlfriends, and turns to Mosa and her brother musing over their childhood in the last chapter. Thus, the victory of the girls still remains in question.

Interestingly, the girls themselves realize that their battle will be futile. On the day of the exhibition, a girl announces the opening of the show in a trembling voice, 'shaking' as if 'she might even dissolve into tears' (186). The girls presenting the drawings wear 'genuine fear on their faces . . . at the possible consequences of their daring act' (187). The girls performing on the stage desperately express 'a cry for help, an indictment and a challenge all rolled into one' (190), and Sinah shouts the harassing teacher's name in a 'suicidal' (190) improvisation. As the exhibition proceeds, all the girls concerned are 'clustered together in the back of the hall, like criminals waiting to be sentenced,' seized by 'cold fear' over 'the consequences of their actions'?(189). There are no happy girls shouting with the joy of victory, usually found in school novels for teenagers. The girls as well as their readers all know the 'consequences' in their real life to be different from those in the triumphant stories.

Most of all, Mosa is not the type of cheerful and invincible heroine of those school novels. In fact, she is more tired of the sexism than angry at it. Her matured and hardened tiredness is clear in a scene in which she and her brother Stan argue about sexual discrimination. When the boy tries to calm her down, telling her to stop fighting and 'relax and enjoy life a little bit' (148), she implores him to look at her:

> He was expecting sparks of anger from Mosa's eyes, but what he saw was something else. A tiredness. Eyes brimming with a plea for understanding. 'I am not fighting, Stan. I am thrashing to stay alive. Can you understand that?' (148)

She does not insist on justice or demand for rights but makes 'a plea for understanding' of her predicament. Although she is 'tired' of fighting, she has to battle on just to 'stay alive' under the imminent threat of AIDS. Note that with an experience of pregnancy by a seasoned womanizer, she is at risk. In another scene, revealing to her brother her decision to test her blood for HIV, Mosa with a 'faraway look' (115) murmurs over her tiredness:

> Oh, Stan, I am just tired of feeling like I am being taken over by all kinds of forces: teachers, men, foreigners, other students. ... I feel besieged. ... I don't know anymore. I'm tired. I feel I've gone through some major growing up these past two years. I feel old, Stan. I need a way to survive the pettiness around me. (115)

Here is a heroine, only 19 years old, who is already tired of fighting – not for success but for survival in times of AIDS.

This representation of Mosa's tiredness in the middle of the novel sounds more powerful than the beautiful and hopeful ending. This is because here at a moment of frustration in a coming-of-age narrative emerges a new signification in the era of HIV/AIDS. Facing the dire situation of HIV/AIDS every day, the readers cannot help asking, 'How can this life make sense to me?' They request a story which explains the meaning of violence and death surrounding them. In reply, Mosa murmurs that she is tired – tired of being the heroine of their HIV/AIDS story. She is tired of being the angry heroine of a banal romantic victory who fights injustice, much less of being the repentant heroine of a cautionary judgmental tragedy who learns lessons. Tired as she is, as long as the story goes on, Mosa cannot cease to be a heroine and must lead the story, in the same way as the readers who cannot cease to exist and who need to 'thrash to stay alive' as long as their life goes on. Here emerges a new story, a new readership and a new signification system. Sober and wise readers learn that they must live without victory or lessons, or in a word, without meaning. The story in times of HIV/AIDS does not provide a meaning for life, but, through abstinence, encourages the readers to live on.

To mitigate the gloom, the story offers occasional glimpses of a bright future encouraging Mosa and her readers to live and read on. First of all, hope lies in the family which is paradoxical since the novel is eloquent in attacking the traditional family system and its deeply entrenched sexism. However, the novel also admires the family's flexibility and lays hope there. In contrast to the European idea of a family advanced by her teacher, the family for Mosa is not a static structure, but a moving group of people which has 'expanded and shrunk and expanded and shrunk over the years' (87). The family has been supporting its members by either accepting or sending away close and distant relatives. For example, through going against established customs and accepting the surviving illegitimate daughter of her late brother killed by AIDS, Mosa, her brother and her mother rebuild their relationship and achieve 'a consolidation of the family' (59) around the little girl. Mosa's eccentric vagabond uncle also brings in new knowledge and strange ideas whenever he interrupts his wandering by paying a surprise visit to her family. In time of crisis Mosa remembers his encouragement that a girl could 'go far and beyon'' (69). In this way, the novel shows that in its flexibility the African family can support those affected by AIDS.

Ancestors also play an important role in healing the suffering of AIDS. For instance, when Mosa's childhood friend, Cecilia, is dying of AIDS, an uncle brings soil from ancestral ground where generations of umbilical cords are buried. An elderly woman then dissolves with water the soil 'enriched over the years by the souls, departing and arriving, of members' (181) of the family, and bathes Cecilia with it. Cecilia in turn puts the water onto her dying baby, and with a calm smile, she passes away. Interestingly, after thus following the traditional procedure of parting, the family are flexible in adapting the burial custom of separating graves for adults and children, and dare to bury Cecilia's baby girl next to her. Thus, the power of ancestors is mobilized in confirmation and revision of tradition to negotiate the rapidly increasing deaths due to AIDS.

The family ties on which Mosa depends for her survival are crystallized in the last chapter as a bond between her, her brother and their ancestors. The siblings sit on a rock, a favourite spot of their childhood. After happily disclosing her test result to be negative, Mosa explains that on the day of the HIV test, she came there onto the rock and obtained power from their childhood memories and their ancestors to live on whatever the result may be:

> I sat up on this rock and tried to recapture what I could of our childhood. I wanted to remember. And I did, and that gave me strength to go ahead. I felt the presence of my ancestors around here, and I asked them for strength. Not in so many words. Just being here, and feeling and thinking and remembering. That gave me strength. (197)

Stan agrees that they can 'hear the voices from the past' (197) and together they reminisce about every detail of their childhood. Enchanted in 'the magic of their newly found reunion' (199), hand in hand, they revisit plains, shrubs and hills where they once worked, played and fought, while they remember their loving mother, strict aunt, and 'precious uncle who believed even a girl could go "far and beyon"' (198–9).

But this is pale euphoria in the midst of desperation. The beauty and tranquility of the last scene lure readers to believe in the happy-ever-after. However, the dismal everyday situation of Mosa and her readers do not allow such dreams to supersede reality. The dream can be easily shattered. First, Mosa's mother may be HIV positive, and Mosa and her brother also can fall positive anytime in future. Again, the long absence of her vagabond uncle may mean his death in wandering. The sexual power relations which the novel has meticulously and relentlessly represented cannot be wiped away by this tentative happy ending.

The result is not pessimism but realism written for sober teenagers experiencing sexual violence, witnessing the death of those closest to them, and surviving the times of AIDS. The author, the characters and the readers are all 'implicated' (149) in this sexual power game, as Mosa says, and there is no escape to a happy ending. Hence, instead of celebrating a victorious heroine in romance, the author represents battered women and girls, refuses to provide an easy solution, and suggests the ever changing family as a narrow hope. The author is barely, but only barely, able to convey a positive message to disillusioned and tired girls by way of narrating a story of bitterly frustrated maturity – a new youth novel of realism in the era of AIDS.

NOTES

1   The following list is a tentative bibliography of HIV/AIDS novels, not referred to in the paper, with HIV/AIDS as the main theme and HIV/AIDS as an important factor:
    • Carolyne Adalla, *Confessions of an AIDS Victim,* Nairobi: East African Educational, 1993;
    • Doreen Baingana, *Tropical Fish,* Amherst: University of Massachusetts Press, 2005;
    • Steve Chimombo, *The Hyena Wears Darkness,* Zomba, Malawi: WASI, 2006;
    • Wamugunda Geteria, *Nice People,* Nairobi: East African Educational, 1992;
    • Rayda Jacobs, *Confessions of a Gambler,* Cape Town: Kwela, 2003;
    • Violet Kala, *Waste Not Your Tears,* Harare: Baobab-Academic, 1994;
    • Namige Kayondo, *Vanishing Shadows,* Oxford: Macmillan Education, 1995;
    • Marjorie Oludhe Macgoye, *Chira,* Nairobi: East African Educational, 1997;
    • Patrice Matchaba, *Deadly Profit,* Cape Town: David Philip, 2000;
    • Felix Mathenjwa, *Lingering Hope,* Zulu original, [Cape Town?]: Actua, 2000;
    • Phaswane Mpe, *Welcome To Our Hillbrow,* Pietermaritzburg, SA: University of Natal Press, 2001;
    • Sharai Mukonoweshuro, *Days of Silence,* Harare: Wonder, 2000;
    • Karyn Pieterse, *Mosadi,* Wandsbeck, SA: Reach, 2005;
    • Joseph Situma, *The Mysterious Killer,* Nairobi: Africawide Network, 2001;
    • Johan Steyn, *Father Michael's Lottery,* Scottsville, SA: University of KwaZulu-Natal Press, 2005.

2   Among the youth novels on HIV/AIDS not mentioned in the paper are: Henning Mankell, *Playing with Fire*, Swedish original, Crows Nest, Australia: Allen and Unwin, 2002; Sandile Memela, *Flowers of Nation*, Scottsville, SA: University of KwaZulu-Natal Press, 2005; Kekelwa Nyaywa, *The Plague at My Door*, Randburg, SA: Ravan, 1996; Lutz van Dijk, *Crossing the Line*, Pietermaritzburg, SA: Shuter and Shooter, 2006; Onne Vegter, *Whitney's Kiss*, Bellville, SA: Voices in Africa, 2004.

3   For a profile of Dow, see the introductory note to her interview with *Kunapipi* (Dow 2004: 47). Dow herself also recounts that one of her cases challenging patriarchal customary law made her 'a household name in Botswana' (Dow 2001: 327).

4   For sexual violence in schools in Southern Africa, see Burton 2005; Jewkes et al. 2002.

WORKS CITED

Burton, Patrick. *Suffering at School: Result of the Malawi Gender-Based Violence in Schools Survey*. Pretoria, SA: Institute of Security Studies, 2005.

Chetty, Adhis. 'The Use of Written Fiction based on HIV/AIDS in our Classrooms: An Effective Antidote against "HIV/AIDS Fatigue" amongst Youth?' *Stories from the Pandemic*, 4 (2005): 1–10.

Dow, Unity. *Far and Beyon'*. Gaborone: Longman Botswana, 2000; Melbourne: Spinifex, 2001.

—— 'How the Global Informs the Local: the Botswana Citizenship Case.' *Health Care for Women International*, 22 (2001): 319–31.

—— '"It Was like Singing in the Wilderness": An Interview with Unity Dow.' By M. J. Daymond and Margaret Lenta. *Kunapipi* 26.2 (2004): 47–60.

Jewkes, Rachel, Jonathan Levin, Nolwazi Mbananga and Debbie Bradshaw. 'Rape of Girls in South Africa.' *Lancet*, 359 (2002): 319–20.

Kitching, Garth. *Bracelet 12–005–35700*. Malvern, SA: umSinsi, 2001.

Mandela, Nelson. 'Closing Address at the 13th International AIDS Conference, Durban, 14 July.' July 14 2000. *ANC Speeches Archive*. Online, 29 August 2007.

Mazibuko, Nokuthula. *In the Fast Lane*. Siyagruva Ser. Claremont, SA: New Africa, 2003.

Mitchell, Claudia and Ann Smith. '"Sick of AIDS": Life, Literacy and South African Youth.' *Culture, Health and Sexuality*, 5–6 (2003): 513–22.

Mwangi, Meja. *The Last Plague*. Peak Library Series Nairobi: East African Educational Publishers, 2000.

Ntsimane, Radikobo. 'Memory Boxes and Zulu Culture.' In Denis, Philippe (ed.) *Never Too Small to Remember: Memory Work and Resilience in Times of AIDS*. Pietermaritzburg, SA: Cluster, 2005. 35–40.

Orford, Margie. *Dancing Queen*. Junior African Writers Series. HIV/AIDS Readers. Oxford: Heineman Educational, 2004.

Rochman, Hazel. Review of *Far and Beyon'*, by Unity Dow. *Booklist*, 1 May 2002: 1518.

van Dijk, Lutz. *Stronger than the Storm*. Trans. Karin Chubb. Young Africa Series (general youth novel series). Cape Town: Maskew Miller Longman, 2000.

—— 'AIDS and South Africa.' *Ulricianum Times*, 11 Mar. 2004, online ed. Online, 20 June 2007.

Florence Orabueze

Speak me to all barren women, she admonished as I strained my ears to hear her faint and dwindling voice. Speak me to all mothers who have only one child in a land and among a people where the value of a woman depends upon her capacity to fill her husband's house with children. Speak me to all women who have a daughter as an only child …. Speak me to all women who forfeited the love and respect of their husbands because they could not fill the dreams of multiple sons to inherit the men when they have joined the ancestors … Speak me to all women who after one daughter, laboured in vain to reverse the misfortune of a womb, dried up in the early hours of creation. (Emenyonu, 1991: 1)

The above quotation points to the fact that the status of womanhood in Africa and in Nigeria, in particular, has been discussed in a number of ways to emphasize the discrimination, gender inequalities, injustice, degradation, humiliation and dehumanization that women reel under. This dying lamentation from Emenyonu's *Tales of our Motherhood* underscores the female situation in Nigeria. This paper takes the analogy a step further as the status of womanhood in the country is looked at from the context of a prison. Sefi Atta's *Everything Good Will Come* is used for critical illustration.

Flora Nwapa's *Efuru* is a pacesetter in debunking the marginalized role and whittled down image of the Nigerian woman in Nigerian male-authored works. And a swipe is taken at the cultural concept of motherhood in the irony-coded novel, *The Joys of Motherhood*. It dawns on the female character, Nnuego, with her several children as she lives and dies a lonely life, that motherhood is a myth and a ploy that gags the freedom of the Nigerian woman (Emecheta, 1980). But in the opinion of a Nigerian poet: 'The fruit that was eaten in the Garden of Eden was one of the unfortunate ones. The woman wanted to be like God, not the woman she was.' (Okoro, 2006 : X).

Evidently, after four decades of feminist writings, the Nigerian woman has made a giant stride in her socio-political and economic standing in the society. She has gone beyond the time when her birth was neither recorded nor celebrated and she was uneducated (Emecheta, 1974). Nevertheless, the new millennium literary artists, like Chimamanda

Ngozi Adichie and Sefi Atta, view her as still reeling under the heavy yoke of dictatorial men, which they parallel with state dictators that brutalize and impoverish the nation and its people.

In Sefi Atta's *Everything Good Will Come*, she points out that despite the constitutional guaranteed rights of the Nigerian woman, she is under the burden of obnoxious native laws and customs that are flagrantly used to violate her rights. She presents a kaleidoscopic view of her relationship in her family, her place of work, at school, in offices, the state and her religion. She still lives in a world where she is caged and Atta draws a nexus between the state and family dictatorship. Unlike Nnuego, her protagonist Enitan believes that true freedom can only come when both men and women discard the webs of silence that ensnare them by raising their voices to be heard in protest and by making sensible choices.

The story has its setting in Lagos within the time frame of Nigeria's dictatorial military and corrupt civilian governments. Atta, like Chimamanda Ngozi Adichie in her *Purple Hibiscus*, uses the first point of view of a dynamic character to narrate the story of the prison world of the Nigerian woman and how her protest gains her freedom. Enitan starts the story from the time she is only seven years old. At that tender age, she sees events, people, situations and actions naively but as she grows up, she interprets them and puts them in their proper perspective. She lives with her middle-class parents in Lagos. She describes the woman's life as a prison with its dos and don'ts and the constant bickering between her parents. She also looks at her life in various educational institutions as another type of incarceration. As she graduates, she works with her father in his office and at the bank, which she sees as another form of imprisonment. Furthermore, she describes the state as a wider prison, which detains people without trial for being critical of the acts and omissions of the governments. Her father is detained and as she goes in search of him, she discovers the horror that female detainees go through in state prisons. She joins a group of women that protests against the incarceration of citizens. Her father and other prisoners are released as they mount pressure on the government. And he promises to narrate to her his traumatic experiences in prison. The novel ends with Enitan's joy for the men's discovery of what it means to be in prison.

Sefi Atta shows through the narrator the burden of the Nigerian woman and what her societal tradition expects of her in the training of her daughters. From the very beginning of the novel, Enitan's mother cooks the family meals and wants her daughter to understudy her, because her custom frowns on any woman who cannot cook for her husband. She is a conservative woman and Enitan's father calls her a 'kitchen martyr'. He intends her daughter to be brought up as a liberated woman. However, as she grows up, Enitan sees the wisdom in her mother's insistence as every woman – wife or mistress – cooks for the man in her life. In far away England, girlfriends cook for their boyfriends. Sheri cooks for her brigadier man-friend, who runs around collecting young girls. Niyi also tells her that despite her education, she is not a 'domesticated woman', because she finds it difficult to run her home. Sheri advises her that no matter her educational qualifications and her level of liberation, she cannot escape from her traditional role as a woman.

Polygamy is another cultural practice that humiliates the Nigerian woman and brings her heartache in her incarceration. The petty jealousies, the viciousness, the intrigues, and the power play in polygamous homes are not left out. Enitan says that apart from her maternal grandfather taking her grandmother's savings to marry a new wife, which results in her own mother's aloofness, her own father's reaction to the wife stems from his insidious experience as a boy from a polygamous home. She says, 'That was why he didn't eat much; that was why he never gave in to my mother's food threats; that was why years later, he still preferred to have an old man in his kitchen' (2005: 154).

Because all the characters in the novel live in a culture that tolerates and eulogizes polygamy, a man can marry as many women as he wishes. Bakare marries two women that look alike. Peter Mukoro, an acclaimed political activist, does not recognize his monogamous marriage under the civil law. Her father likes and admires Mukoro's boldness and calls him a 'man's man'. Niyi also refers to his own monogamous status as a sign of weakness. 'These men', he said, 'I don't know how they do it. I didn't choose to have two families and most days I feel like half a man' (315). Enitan, however, prefers the men who go straight for polygamy to the ones that keep mistresses outside and procreate through them without the knowledge of their families. She is greatly disappointed with the father's choice of having children outside without his family's knowledge, though his staff and friends are fully aware of this.

Moreover, Atta criticizes the customary dictate that motherhood must be the natural and biological quest of every woman. And this has been a recurrent theme in every feminist work. If a woman fails to give her husband a child after several months of marriage, he is encouraged to take on more wives. Enitan's mother loses her husband to other women, because of her inability to give him an heir. A priest puts the situation in its proper perspective:

> In his [Abraham's] culture, bearing children was seen as normal way of life. And as we have seen in the law of inheritance, having an heir in the family is the most cherished prayer a man could say. But as mentioned earlier the heir could be the first son or any of the sons in case of an evolutionary son. (Chidili, 2005: 205)

This quest for a successor may be the reason Enitan's father has to procreate outside in order to have a son who can perpetuate his name and inherit his property. And her parents appreciate this and are worried when in her thirties, she is still unable to bear any child. The mother wants her to follow her to her church for vigils while the father suggests she goes abroad for a thorough medical examination. She experiences unsurpassable joy at the birth of Yimika that she describes her as: 'Like a pearl. I could have licked her!' (323).

The agony of a barren woman is indescribable. This is demonstrated in the symbolic character, Sheri. From the very first time she appears in the novel as an eleven-year-old girl, she has been associated with flowers, and later she is described as a 'scarlet hibiscus' that attracts insects that destroy it. Sheri's beauty attracts the three boys who rape her, and her attempt to abort the unwanted pregnancy results in her barrenness. Her father dispossesses her of her natural mother, and the three errant boys of her virginity and motherhood. Beneath her flamboyant lifestyle, Enitan thinks of her friend's fate: 'Better to be ugly, to be crippled, to be a thief even, than to be barren. ... Marriage would immediately wipe out a sluttish past, but angel or not, a woman had to have a child' (106). But Sefi Atta, like Flora Nwapa in *Efuru* and *One is Enough,* believes that barrenness is not tantamount to the end of a woman. Sheri takes up other projects – catering and running an orphanage, instead of brooding over her situation. These give her independence and tremendous joy.

Atta also takes a swipe at the lack of love in male-female relationships in Nigeria. She presents the marriages in the novel as prisons where the woman endures her imprisonment. Enitan believes that Nigerian men generally do not love their women – be they girlfriends or wives – though they may love their mothers and sisters and strive to protect them. The first stirring of adolescent love Enitan has for Damola is unrequited. While she fantasizes over him, he prefers Sheri to her. She also dates two men in England whose actions never show them as lovers. The first man she loses her virginity to tells her that she is frigid and as dead in bed as other Nigerian women. He doesn't bother to investigate the cause of her frigidity, which is a result of her ingrained memory of Sheri's rape and of a culture that demands that a woman should not be seen to enjoy sex. Springfellow lies that she is his only girlfriend. Her heartthrob, Mike Obi, also dates a younger woman. Sheri's brigadier also does not express any love whatsoever for her.

Even a married woman is not spared this ugly experience. It is only during courtship that she has any semblance of love from the fiancé. After marriage, she is dumped in the house and the man goes out in search of new conquests. Enitan's father is always out of the house attending 'conferences' and there is no sign that other married men in the novel love their wives. Niyi claims that he loves Enitan but the highest affection he shows her is that they hold hands together when they sleep, if they are not quarrelling. Enitan's father showers her with gifts and affection so that the mother complains that he pampers her so that she idolizes him. As the narrator grows up, she sadly recollects: 'At what age was a woman supposed to be celibate? No one ever said. If they caressed themselves, the pleasure they got, they would never say. The thought made me wince. I was twenty when I first saw my father kiss a woman. He did it properly; the way they did it in films. He circled her waist with one hand, bent his knees, straightened up ... I had never seen my mother kiss a man, not even my father' (294). Despite the lack of love from her husband, Enitan says that a woman is more steadfast than a man in her relationships. Clara remembers the sacrifice Peter Mukoro made to ensure she got a university education after she eloped with him. She joins the women's group that petitions the government to release their relations. Enitan's mother's bitterness and resentment of her husband does not deter her from telling her to apologize to her father for calling him a 'liar', because in Yoruba culture, it is a taboo. However, she admonishes her from her own wealth of experiences in marital life that she should: 'Never make sacrifices for a man. By the time you say, look what I've done for you, it is too late. They never remember. And the day you begin to retaliate, they never forget' (177).

Atta also x-rays the widowhood practices that truncate and dehumanize widows and their children, particularly if they are young. She uses the testimony of Mother of Prison to explore this theme. She claims that despite the sacrifices she made for the family, she is not spared the brutality of widowhood. Within twenty-four hours of the man's death, her serene world crashes on her. Her hair is shaved off; she cannot touch her twins; she is forced to stay in a room alone, and she is told to drink the water used in bathing his corpse to prove her innocence that she did not cast any spell on him. Her refusal to do so results in her tragedy.

Also the traditional system of inheritance that disinherits women – daughters and wives – despite constitutional provisions comes under serious condemnation. The constitution guarantees every citizen's right to own a property. However, the Nigerian court shrinks from enforcing these guaranteed rights. It divides a deceased's estate according to whether he lived the traditional or civil way. For instance, when Bakare dies intestate, his brother inherits his property according to the Yoruba custom while he has wives, daughters and sons, who survived him. Enitan views the unjust native law and custom thus: 'Sometimes, a widow couldn't inherit land at all. Even with the progressive customs, widows inherited according to how many children they had, and sons could have double the rights of daughters' (142).

Most African cultures cherish the boy-child above the girl-child as the son perpetuates the family name. And to compensate for the psychological vacuum men feel if they don't have sons, they marry second wives to avoid the indignities their families may be subjected to after their demise. In the Igbo culture, for instance, and in extreme cases, where a man does not have an heir, one of his daughters may be kept in the house to continue the genealogy of the man. She procreates after the traditional rites have been performed. This usually happens if the man loves the wife and does not want to inconvenience her with the presence of a second wife.

> It was Aziagba who solved the problem and saved all of us from slow death. She was willing to remain at home with us to produce male children for her father. After we had performed the nluikwa ceremony, she chose Okonji as a mate. And he was willing to enter the relationship with her. It was a big relief to all of us. (Adimora-Ezeigbo, 1996: 33)

It is in the light of this cultural demand that Sunny intends to bring his son, Debayo, to meet her daughter. He wants him to be identified as part of his family. However, his having children outside his marriage does not deter him from loving Enitan. His act is within the Yoruba culture to have an ideal untainted line of inheritance, though this may be to the chagrin of his family.

Again, Atta scrutinizes the divorce dilemma of the Nigerian woman. A woman that has a job resigns after marriage or at the birth of her first baby to take care of the family. From that point on, she becomes economically dependent on the husband. If she decides to quit the marriage, her culture and the Nigerian court do not recognize that she is entitled to a fair share of the man's assets. Enitan's mother is a chartered secretary before her marriage. She resigns to take care of the family. After several years, she petitions the court for the dissolution of the marriage. Out of the man's vast wealth, he is only willing to part with a duplex. And he finds it difficult to transfer the ownership of the house to her. The court does not recognize the supreme sacrifice she made for the comfort of the family. She is deprived of her daughter and she dies a recluse. Enitan recounts the cause of her death:

> My mother had been dead a day. Going through her medicines later, I discovered a batch which appeared to have been re-dated. I did not know where she'd purchased them, or how long they had expired. I imagined she'd bought them because they were cheaper. (321)

The novelist also directs her searchlight on the unfair treatment of the Nigerian girl in educational institutions at all levels. Enitan discovers that Mike Obi's primary school is ill-equipped. The children are crowded into tiny classrooms; they hawk wares on the streets and motor parks after school and a teenage girl is being brutally flogged by a male teacher, leaving her with tear-stained, red eyes and welts on the back of her legs. She describes the pathetic situation of the African child in this manner:

> The parents beat them out of love .... Teachers beat, neighbours beat. By the time the child turned ten, the adults they knew would have beaten out any cockiness that would develop into wit; any dreaminess that would give birth to creation, any bossiness that could lead to leadership. Only the strong would survive; the rest would spend their lives searching for initiative. This was what it takes to raise an African child, a village of beaters.(135)

Her post-primary school education at Royal College is not different from the primary school. Her father wants her to grow up a liberated woman; yet, he sends her to a secondary school that is exclusively for girls so that she does not grow up like a 'street girl without a home'. She vividly captures the hardship, the mosquito-infested environment and dirty toilets. It is a school where female teachers chaperon them, and their letters are opened and read before they are given to them. Nevertheless, she prefers the school to her home. Intrigues and bickering in homes have driven Nigerian youths to the street. And this is why a Nigerian novelist's character, Jojolo, says: 'For me home was where I found myself. The sky was enough roof for me' (Osanyin, 2000:35). Like Jojolo, Enitan is happy to leave the prison that is her home, but she also discovers that the school is another prison in disguise. She derogatorily describes it:

> The structure of our blocks, three adjacent buildings, each three floors high with long balconies, made me imagine I was living in prison. Walking those balconies, I'd discovered they weren't straight. Some parts dipped and other parts rose a little and whenever I was anxious because of an examination or punishment, I dreamed they had turned to waves and I was trying to ride them. Sometimes, I'd fall off the balconies in my dreams, fall, and never reach the bottom. (55)

After her long sojourn in England, she comes back to Nigeria for a year's study at the Nigerian Law School, Lagos. She finds out that the Nigerian woman is not given her basic freedom, even as a graduate. She says that the authorities are not interested in the improvement of the environment and provision of facilities but to fetter the girls. She describes the Baba that guards the gates of female students as 'the... keeper of graduate vaginas' (88). She describes the bribery and corruption that thrive in the school. And she draws attention to the lack of distinction between the primary, Royal College and the Nigerian Law School. As far as she is concerned, the graduate school is another prison for young women. She says, 'Walking up the stairs, I smelt urine from the toilets and remembered my old school in Lagos. ... The dormitory was like a prison cell: two iron spring beds and four walls sullied by the handprints and head smears of previous inmates' (88).

Atta also highlights the woman's ill treatment in her places of work. Her society expects her to resign from her job to take care of her family. At that point, she loses her economic independence. But if she feels that the man's earning cannot maintain the family, she continues to work, but she may end up being the family's breadwinner. And she has to do that discreetly in order not to tarnish the man's ego. The Mother of Prison says: 'Everything in that house I bought, and I was sending money to my parents in the village, sending money to his parents' (281). However, the wealthy men stop their mistresses or wives from working and provide for them. Sheri's brigadier wants her to stay indoors and not work. And when she opens up an eatery, he insists she must close it. Her refusal to do as he ordered terminates the relationship after a fight. Sheri's stepmothers are also locked up in their purdah, always cooking for the family. Enitan's mother resigns as a secretary to take care of the home. And when she decides to punish her husband by denying him food, she doesn't succeed because the man threatens her with withholding the feeding money. Niyi's mother, a trained nurse, is also at home cooking for her family that one may mistake her for an illiterate woman that does not understand the rudiments of her family members' legal profession. Sheri summarizes this economic-dependence syndrome to Enitan: 'The man is jealous of me. Can you believe it? He is jealous of my success. With all he has. He wants me to have nothing, except what he gives me. He says he will take it back. I said take it! All of it! I did not come to this place naked' (175).

A woman employed in a private company may end up being paid a stipend. This is because the man, whether husband, father or employer, wants to have a hold on her. Enitan's father buys her a car she can drive around the city in, but desists from paying her well. She is paid poor wages like other employees in his chambers.

Enitan says that the experience of the Nigerian woman in public offices is not better than when she works at home or works for a private person. Enitan finds out the harrowing trauma that awaits her: male colleagues push her around, and the bosses sexually harass her if she is attractive. She either resigns from her job or she is sacked if she is pregnant and cannot cope with the rigours of her job. And it dawns on her that men – whether as colleagues, or employers – refuse vehemently to discuss certain issues with women. Her father-in-law keeps silent as a sign of displeasure when she challenges him professionally on a point of law. Her father cannot listen to her when she raises the issues of increment in the salaries and allowances of his staff and the signing of the documents that transfer the ownership of a duplex to the mother. The climax of the situation is seen in Dagogo and Alabi's preferential treatment of Debayo. She narrates of her colleagues' gender-sensitivity in their warm reception and solidarity for him:

> My brother knew everyone in the office. He gave Dagogo and Alabi a manly handshake, before he left *Man mi*, they called him. When I returned to the office I asked Alabi, you know my brother this well? Alabi nodded. He's our paddy. Our paddy – man, Dagogo said. (291)

The novelist also examines the role of religious institutions in her imprisonment. It is through Enitan that the reader glimpses into the exploitative role of Christian and Islamic religions. Islamic injunction is that a Muslim man may marry up to four wives. Bakare and Ibrahim have two wives each who remain in purdah in their compounds. Ibrahim is a strict Muslim who does not talk to women; he insists that his wives and mistress must cover their heads when they go out, which is very occasionally; he also insists his daughters must remain virgins until they go into their arranged marriages. Ironically, though he is a strict Moslem, he collects girls as young as his own daughters. Enitan describes the relationship in the strict Moslem's household as being incestuous to her. Meanwhile, his daughters' closeness to Sheri is because she does not report them to their father, whenever they visit their boyfriends. Also

Sheri's younger stepmother has a boyfriend even in her secluded life.

Christianity, as practised by the Nigerian followers, also leaves a lot to be desired. Enitan as a naive narrator describes these Christians' piety but beneath that description, the reader sees that they are hypocrites that masquerade as martyrs:

> Holy people had to be unhappy or strict, or a mixture of both, I'd decided. My mother and her church friends with their priest with his expression as if he was sniffing something bad. There wasn't a choir mistress I'd seen with a friendly face, and even in our old Anglican church people had generally looked miserable as they prayed (23).

Her mother wears long white gown to her church and gives the impression that she has forsaken material things for the heavenly race. But beneath her outward show of purity lies a hard and unforgiving spirit. The members of her Pentecostal church believe that with their little faith that cannot move a mustard seed, they can heave a mountain. Enitan's mother takes the sick son, Arin, to the church for prayers during a sickle cell anaemia crisis, instead of taking him to the hospital. The other members of her congregation also believe that their adolescent, errant children are possessed by demons and these will be exorcised if they drink spirogyra-filled water, which the pastor deceives them into thinking is holy, healing water. They always burn incense and candles, and cast away imaginary evil spirits, which reside in their neurotic psyche. Their pastor's *modus operandi* is to prey on their neurotic fear of evil spirits, armed robbery, barrenness, death, disease and other dastardly visitations. And with his false and damnable prophecies, he fleeces them of their money and livestock.

Enitan therefore sees Nigerians as religious but ungodly people; a people who are critical but lack introspection. Her mother criticizes the members of her church who complain about her dwindling tithes. She is a woman who is at church more than at home, but she works assiduously to have the husband disbarred after their divorce. As Enitan sees it the Nigerians are a people who pray fervently that their daughters will marry into good families; yet they don't strive to make their own marriages work. Her father disapproves of her marriage to Niyi because he is a divorced Catholic. Meanwhile, he conveniently forgets he has a concubine and children outside his own marriage and that he is also divorced or separated, conditions which go against Christian tenets and Catholic doctrines. Her mother objects to Enitan's marriage because, according to her, madness runs in Niyi's family. One of his aunts is a recluse, but she forgets that she is also reclusive. As a child growing up, Enitan innocently describes a scene in front of her mother's Pentecostal church, which to the mature reader is the epitome of the hypocritical and uncharitable attitudes of the religious. The Good Samaritan's attitude to her neighbour underscores every religious faith, and this is breached in the eleven-year-old girl's account:

> One half-eaten mango on the tree caught my eye. Birds must have nibbled it and now ants are finishing it up. The way they scrambled over the orange flesh reminded me of a beggar I'd seen outside my mother's church, except that his sore was pink and pus oozed out. No one would go near him, not even to give him money which they threw on a dirty potato sack before him. (30–31)

Sefi Atta, like Adichie in her *Purple Hibiscus*, draws a parallel between home and state dictators. Both of them intimidate, subjugate, humiliate, maim and destroy the people entrusted to their care. While the 'mini Idi Amin' in the house brutalizes his family, the state dictator mangles the soul and body of the populace. Kambili, the naive narrator in *Purple Hibiscus,* observes the inhuman treatment of the populace thus: 'In later weeks, when Kevin drove past Ogui Road, there were soldiers at the roadblock near the market, walking around, caressing their long guns' (Adichie, 2004:28).

Atta in *Everything Good Will Come* paints an unsavoury portrait of a state that is on the brink of extinction, because of the deadly stranglehold of irresponsible leadership. Nigeria has been consistently reduced as a beggarly nation despite its abundant natural resources. A historian casts aspersion on the country's oligarchy:

> The Nigerian elite class is not creative. It has its soul in London and New York, while its anus creates havoc in Lagos. It steals the wealth of the nation and transforms it into nothing. By serving foreign interests, our elite class has ensured that Nigerians will remain unable to manage their affairs in the future, thus perpetuating poverty despite the incredible richness of the land. (Taylor, 1990: 155)

In the novel, Enitan narrates the sad story of a people that have been burdened by parasitic leaders. Leaders in Chris L. Wanjala's opinion '… ministers or heads of state whom one cannot write home about and who do not qualify to transact business matters on behalf of their people' (2005: 12). Enitan also sees the state as a prison and vividly describes scenes of violent crime – rape, execution, prostitution, fraud, armed robbery – so that the reader is suffused with haunting memories of these crimes, their perpetrators and victims. It is etched indelibly in his mind that Nigeria is a state where the citizens' guaranteed rights are flagrantly violated with impunity; a state that is run with military decrees and edicts that sack the legislature, abrogate the constitution and oust the jurisdiction of courts; a state where infrastructures are not maintained; a state that is always associated with images of darkness; a state where the citizens have been reduced to stealing, begging, hawking or prostituting; a populace that has been cowed into silence. A people who have witnessed incessant bloody military coups and military men jostle and topple each other in their scramble to loot the wealth of the nation. Enitan describes its devastation in these concrete images that leave the reader shuddering and wondering at the fate of such a nation and its people. A man-made disaster that is worse than natural ones:

Drought, famine and disease. There was no greater disaster on our continent than the few who had control over our resources: oil, diamonds human beings. They would sell anyone to buyers overseas. (302)

Atta does not leave out the relationship between Nigerians abroad and their former colonial mistress. Enitan finds out while studying in England that the colour barrier between the two races is still a reality. Her school mates snub her and make jests of her colour; she is ignored in the office as if she does not exist. While African writers romanticize about the continent, Europeans still regard it as a dark continent. However, David I. Ker, quoting the renowned Nigerian playwright, observes: '... indeed Soyinka has talked about the cannibalistic nature of human civilization' (2003: 5). Another critic observes: 'The past is not an invention, nor is it an intentional over-glorification of Africa. It is a reality and this is what many Western readers fail to appreciate' (Mbabuike, 2005: 27). However, the character Niyi is of the opinion that economic empowerment of the country and its citizens are enough to turn the tide.

Nigeria's notorious prisons do not escape Atta's camera lenses with which she snaps pictures of the inhuman treatment that goes on there. Enitan says that Nigerian prisons are not correctional institutions but are calculated to dehumanize and break the individuals incarcerated there. Minor offenders are locked up with hardened criminals, and the sane share the same prison cells with the insane so that at times the latter murder the former. Minor offences, like loitering during sanitation, are treated as a felony and attract imprisonment instead of a fine. The worst of the leadership is the military that promulgates Decree No. 2 that empowers the state security agents to detain people for years without trial and ousts the jurisdiction of the court to inquire into the cases of the detainees. Political activists, critics and journalists are imprisoned without trial. John Okwoeze Odey eulogizes the effort and sacrifice of Nigerian journalists during those darkest days in the country's history. He calls them the watchdogs of the society whose stars appear in difficult times (2001: 21).

The military perceive critics as opponents and bundle them into prisons where they are detained without trial for several years; most of them unaware of the reasons for their detention; their relations uninformed of their whereabouts and why they are detained; some kept in lonely cells where they either lose their minds, die of infectious diseases or are murdered. And this has been the bane of African leadership, as a reporter narrates: 'Indeed, Taylor had hugely violated the fundamental rights of Liberians during his six-year rule as the president of Liberia. During this period, Taylor arrested and imprisoned thousands considered to be his political enemies' (*Newswatch*, 2006).

Indeed, Atta through Enitan's short incarceration in one of the Nigerian prisons, gives an insight into the deplorable conditions of women prisoners as no other novelist – male or female – before her. She shows that the court spends its time on frivolities, hearing civil suits instead of criminal ones that congest the prisons. The brutal military governments abrogate the rights of the citizens by the suspension of the constitution. With this single act, the constitutional provisions on the rights of a suspect are jettisoned. A suspect may be detained for six years or more instead of being released after twenty-four hours as provided by the constitution; she may not be informed of her offence during and after arrest; she is denied her right to the counsel of her choice and she is kept incommunicado. For instance, Enitan's father is detained without anybody's knowledge of his whereabouts. In detention he is unaware of the major events in his life that have happened during his absence. He is unaware that his divorced wife died; that he has a grandchild and that Fatai is abroad on medical grounds. The character Mother of Prison is also detained for years without trial.

By this graphic description of the denial of the rights of the citizen, Atta achieves one purpose: leaders who subject citizens to violence turn them into brutes. And this is possible because the elite keep silent and hence there is a need for ordinary men and women to raise their voices against oppression.

Enitan makes it clear that the condition of the female prisoners is not different from that of the male. They live in congested prison cells; some do not know their offences; some have been awaiting trial for years. For instance, Mother of Prison has been in prison custody for six years without trial for killing a man who wanted to rape her, in self defence. Enitan shows a sick society where mad women roam the streets and are raped and impregnated by men; in a nation where a married woman cannot obtain an international passport without the consent of her husband. She cannot bail an accused out of police detention because she is a woman in a nation that still allows primitive customary practices to hold sway over its civil law. Atta paints a gory picture of a sick society that gives out a putrefying odour of decay and death. A nation where pregnant women are imprisoned and the sick are uncared for, left to rot and die there. It is a nation that slaughters its young. The conversation between Mother of Prison and Enitan sheds more light on this vicious cycle of a doomed nation and a doomed people.

> 'You have not grown up,' she said. 'You're still a child.' 'I am not responsible for your being here', I said. 'Shame on you. Shame. Bringing another child into the world.' 'I did not arrest myself.' (277)

Atta believes that gender silences in the face of oppression and brutalization are contributory factors to the erection and sustenance of the walls of imprisonment of the individual in the Nigerian society. She shows that silence can be a weapon and a shield, depending on how the individual wants to wield it. She tenaciously believes that silence is no longer golden in the face of oppression and degradation. For instance, Yoruba custom expects a woman to keep silent. She has to be seen and not heard. Enitan's conservative mother teaches her how to cook, stay indoors and scare off wayward friends. The same custom seals a woman's ambition. She cannot aspire to be a president, as no man desires a woman with tall ambitions. Niyi complains that Enitan is not a 'domesticated woman' because she is independent-minded, involved in politics, and wants her voice to be heard, instead of conforming to the stereotyped 'kitchen martyr'. The other men consider her a bad influence on their wives.

Moreover, a married woman is supposed to keep sealed lips over her husband's sexual escapades. Sunny considers Clara Mukoro a disgrace to her family, for informing the press about her husband's bigamist status. Enitan's mother conceals the truth about her father until she grows up to see him for what he is. Enitan reasons about the Nigerian woman's shield of silence over her family: 'Our mothers are wonderful, mostly. They shielded us from the truths about our father, remained in bad marriages to give us a chance' (92). Enitan has always thought the mother a source of the unhappiness in her home. When she discovers that her father has children outside the family, she confronts him with it and he shows no sign of guilt. It dawns on her that this is how he has driven the mother to become a religious fanatic and an embittered recluse. She concludes that the worst men are not those ones that talk or beat their wives, but the so-called decent men, who with their silence ruin the women that live with them. And it is not surprising that as she leaves Niyi's house, the neigh-bourhood can only see, feel and think: 'Everyone is talking about you. They say you left for no reason. He never beat you, never chased. I know he's moody, but he went to work for God's sake. What would you do married to a lazy bugger like mine?' (336).

The same culture that demands silence from a woman does not expect it from a man. From childhood, a boy is trained to be conscious of whom he is. He is brought up to appreciate his manliness. Niyi's cousin who speaks in a high-pitched voice has his manhood slapped on his face. Everybody in the family tells him 'to speak like a man'. It is a show of mas-culinity if a man beats the wife or girlfriend into submission or silence. However, the educated men in the novel feel that verbal altercations and beating of women are beneath them and use silence as a weapon of pun-ishment. Enitan's father's silence drives the mother out of the house. Niyi's silence defeats Enitan so that she decides to pack her bags to avoid her mother's fate, though the neighbourhood chides her. Niyi's father uses this weapon to force the wife to swallow her voice. She never joins in their discussions but she sits, listens and gets thrilled at his ideas and opinions. Niyi and his father ignore her for granting an interview to the 'Oracle'. Niyi uses silence to punish his divorced wife, when she complains that his son refuses to call his stepfather 'daddy'. Enitan describes the bizarre family where this weapon is freely used: 'They had the pride and lack of ambition of a generation that wealth would skip, and ignored each other because they thought it was common to quarrel openly. That was how they settled their differences' (190).

Atta makes it clear that silence is also used as an instrument of complicity and selfishness. Everybody keeps quiet about the exploitation going on in the country. For example, Pierre lives in Niyi's household. In this elitist enclave he is paid peanut wages and he lives in the worst environment with a pit latrine. Niyi keeps silent about the imprisonment of the father-in-law for the selfish reason that he does not want his wife to get involved in case she is imprisoned and loses her pregnancy. Niyi says he is only interested in his family and his family alone. When Sunny's family threatens his wife, saying that he will get another if she does not bear more children for him, he keeps quiet and does not rise to her defence because, secretly, he has already kept a mistress who bears children for him. Nigerians are known to keep silent out of complicity, as political activists are known to keep silent when they are settled with juicy jobs and government appointments. This ugly situation that leaves much to be desired is satirized in Emeka Nwabueze's *Echoes of Madness,* through the character Akamonye:

> Okanume! Come out of that argument. There's no road there. In this modern age, oracles are no longer potent. It's the voice of the man that directs the wisdom of the oracle. As I was saying, I saw Osuofia three nights before he faced the elders to interpret the wisdom of the oracle. I gave him the stipulated amount of money to purchase his voice. (2001: 23)

Gender silences can also be as a result of weakness on the part of the individual. Uncle Fatai, Niyi, Alabi, Dagogo and Debayo keep silent when the nation is burning and at the imprisonment of Sunny. Sunny tells Enitan that Fatai keeps silent 'like a woman'. And Niyi's silence prompts her to ask him: 'What kind of woman are you?' (336). She is frustrated into leaving his house, as she cannot raise her voice in the prison walls of his kitchen and his silent presence. Also the professionals, like the Senior Advocates of Nigeria, keep mute for fear of being detained and the youth keep quiet as their interest is only in making money.

Again silence is used in the novel as a weapon of resentment and/or revenge. Enitan's father ignores his wife at public functions as he resents the calumnies she spreads against him in order to get him disbarred from the legal profession. She keeps silent at his arrest and wants her daughter to stay out of his problem in revenge for his ill treatment of her. Niyi resents his father-in-law's ex-wife and wants Enitan to do the same.

Indeed, Sefi Atta strongly feels it is only the voice of the individual raised in protest against obnoxious native law and custom and draconian leadership that can bring about meaningful change in society. Grace Ameh, who symbolizes the revolutionary spirit in the liberated woman, organizes women to form a pressure group that calls on the government to release their relations from detention. Journalists and political activists raise their voices in protest to free the country from the deadly embrace of the military. The women-prisoners defy the intimidation of Mother of Prison to free Enitan from her verbal and physical abuses. Enitan ignores her husband and father-in-law's silence to fight for her father's freedom and to emancipate the Nigerian woman. She feels that the worst prisoner is not the one at home or in state prison, but the one whose prison is in the mind, that is, one who keeps silent when another is being oppressed or a state is in anarchy:

> Everyone has at least one choice, my father said, whenever I talked about women in home prisons. He was shocked. How could one make a false and simplistic comparison! Likening a handful of kitchen martyrs to people confined in Nigerian prisons. Some prisoners set free would choose to stay on, I argued. My point was about the condition of the mind. (331)

Atta is very honest in her treatment of the plight of the Nigerian woman. She boldly acknowledges the Nigerian woman's complicity and the active role she plays in muffling her voice against an unjust system, unlike other feminist writers before her. A woman loses the right to complain about male domination if she helps to maintain the *status quo ante*. Peni's mother advises her after the husband battered her:

> A little beating from your husband and you run home like a spoilt child. If your mother had run away each time your father had beaten her, would you have been born? ... Tell me why you can't remain quiet in your husband's house like other married women. (Alkali, 2005: 21)

This statement from one of the female characters in Alkali's *The Descendants* tallies with Enitan's opinion that men not to solely blamed for the woman's plight. Enitan reminisces over Alhaja's authoritarian hold on the son's wives. Not only is she instrumental to his abandonment of Sheri's white mother in England, but she intimidates the two African wives. Moreover, Enitan's mother strives very hard to bring her up as a conservative, if not for her father's stiff opposition to that type of training. Sunny's mother suffers the hardship and broken-heartedness involved in a polygamous home, yet she supports and advocates the son to marry a second wife. And this is why a male critic dismisses the rationale behind men's sole responsibility to women's trauma. He queries: 'Who are those that make life difficult for their daughters-in-laws? Are they not women – mothers and sisters who pretend to have better knowledge of women than men?' (Albert, 2002: 67).

Enitan also believes it is pretentious for any woman to complain about a man's economic marginalization if she willingly decides to depend solely on a man. Sheri, for instance, is a trained teacher, but she decides to become the brigadier's mistress, instead of working. She erroneously feels that her beauty can sustain her. Then she learns otherwise: 'Prettiness could encourage people to treat a woman like a doll, to be played with, tossed around, fingered, dismembered, and discarded. Prettiness could also make a woman to be lazy.... Now she was a kitchen martyr, and may well have forgotten how to flaunt her mind' (109). Enitan's mother could also have taken the bull by the horns when the sickly son died, she could have gone out to get a job, but she decided to lock herself up in her house, go to her Pentecostal church and nurse a deep grudge against the husband.

So we see that the Nigerian woman can be a contributory factor to her own imprisonment. Enitan's mother is aware that her husband likes her to look beautiful and he provides everything to ensure that. With the birth of Arin and his subsequent illness, she finds it difficult to look pretty for the husband's admiration. After the son's death, instead of picking up the broken pieces of her life, she lapses into nagging, wearing a sullen face and exorcising imaginary devils, all of which drives the husband into the waiting arms of other women. Enitan recalls, 'My mother once had thirty three bottles of perfume on her dressing table, before she started wearing those church gowns smelling of bleach and starch' (179). Enitan's father used to boast to her that the wife used to be the prettiest, the best dancer and she had the tiniest waist.

Atta feels that women are both victim and victimizer contributing as they do to the heartache of others. Sheri goes out with Ibrahim, knowing full well that he has a family; some go out with their girlfriends' fathers for money. Sunny's mistress must be aware he is married; yet, she has four children for him. Peter Mukoro's second wife knows he is already married with children. These are women who want to identify with the rich and the powerful men. When Mike tells Enitan he is an artist to impress her on their first meeting, she thinks: 'Most women I knew would sprint from an artist. It meant that they might have to dabble with poverty and poverty always cleared people's eyes in Lagos' (87). She sums it up in her statement that no man has any affair or relationship with himself.

Furthermore, women are always afraid and uncomfortable with other women, who have their own minds and are liberated. They do all they can to bring them down to their lowly level, where they will huddle together and complain that men oppress and subjugate them. Bono and Kemp opine, 'Emancipated women have only become further isolated within institutions and in the eyes of public opinion. Not only do they continue to suffer the age old lack of respect and support of the "males", they also now have to contend with the parallel lack of solidarity from feminism' (1991: 294). In *Everything Good Will Come*, women are jealous and afraid of Sheri because of her beauty and independent mind. She is seen as a street woman and an object of their gossip. After her rape, everybody blames her and overlooks the boys that committed the dastardly act that ruined her life. Enitan is also labelled a feminist, a hotheaded person because she raises her voice to be heard.

The reader will note that Sefi Atta has succeeded in creating male characters that are not stereotyped as they can be in women's fiction. They are neither charlatans nor dummies nor spineless men. There is some objectivity in their portrayal. These are men one sees everyday in one's life. Sunny, for example, is not as devilish as the resentful wife would want the reader to believe. It is evident that Sunny once loved her and still loves the daughter, but he is a more realistic person than the wife. As soon as he discovers that both of them are sickle cell carriers, he swings into action. He gets a mistress to bear children that will be free of the sickness. He keeps his affair outside his family, remembering what he suffered as a child in a polygamous home. In fact, some other men would have married a second wife as the family suggested, but he resisted that.

Another well depicted character, despite his failings, is Mike Obi. He would have made a better husband to Enitan than Niyi. He has a deep insight into people and actions. He helps Enitan to get reconciled with the mother and to appreciate her despite her weaknesses. He is also very gentle. He cooks for her and bathes her after their lovemaking:

> The last person who washed me was Bisi, our house girl. I was nine. 'Spread your lecks' she would say, and I would spread them hating her sawing motions. But Mike washed me with the gentlest motions, like a mother washing her baby. I felt sure that my fear was like any other fear, like the fear of a dog bite, or of fires or of heights, or death. I was certain I would never be ashamed again. (137)

Mike's bathing of Enitan after their lovemaking, therefore, is a symbolic act of cleansing. After the bath, she is purified of her culturally oriented fear of sex, as an unclean act for women and a therapeutic treatment for the psychological trauma she suffered after Sheri's rape at the beach as a teenager. Before this bath, she washed herself after sex with men. But after it, she stops the act. Mike also helps her to have a more healthy sexual relationship with the husband when she married.

Conclusion

Sefi Atta in *Everything Good Will Come* shows that the Nigerian woman actually lives in a prison, but by her acts and omissions she helps in its building and sustenance. The walls of her prison will crack and crumble, if she willingly raises her voice against obnoxious cultural and religious practices, antiquated legislation, and the inimical acts of home and state dictators. It is only by raising her voice in protest that she can gain her freedom, her family's and the entire country's. And to achieve this feat she needs the complementary voice of men, because it is very evident that silence in either gender is no longer golden.

WORKS CITED

Adichie, Chimamanda Ngozi. *Purple Hibiscus*. Lagos: Farafina, 2004.

Adimora-Ezeigbo, Akachi. *The Last of The Strong Ones*. Lagos: Vista Books, 1996.

Albert, Isaac. 'Rethinking the Impact of Patriarchy on Feminist Epistemology and Methodology in Nigeria' in Ukhun, Christopher. (ed.) *Critical Gender Discourse in Africa*. Ibadan: Hope Publications, 2002: 59–78.

Akali, Zaynab. *The Descendants*. Zaria: Tamaza, 2005.

Atta, Sefi. *Everything Good Will Come*. Lagos: Farafina, 2005.

Bono, Paola, and Kemp, Sandra. *Italian Feminist Thought: A Reader*. Massachusetts: Blackwell, 1991.

Chidili, Bartholomew. *Provocative Essays on The Practices of Religion and Culture in African Society*. Jos: Fab Anieh Nigeria Limited, 2005.

Emecheta, Buchi. *Second Class Citizen*. London: Fontana, 1974.

— *The Joys of Motherhood*. London: Heinemann, 1980.

Emenyonu, Ernest. *Tales of our Motherland*. Ibadan: Heinemann, 1999.

Ker, David. *The African Novel and The Modernist Tradition*. Ibadan: Mosuro Publishers, 2003: 25–35.

Mbabuike, Michael. 'The Reception of Chinua Achebe in the United States of America' in Opata, Damian et al. (eds) *The Eagle in Ascendance*, Ibadan: Heinemann, 2005.

Nwabueze, Emeka. *Echoes of Madness*. Enugu: ABIC Books, 2001.

Odey, John. *The Anti-Corruption Crusade: The Saga of a Crippled Giant*. Enugu: Snaap Press Ltd, 2001.

Okoro, Fidelis. 'Preface' to *Bleeding Heart Breaks*. Enugu: El' Demak, 2006.

Osanyin, Bode. *The Noble Mistress*. Lagos: Longman Nigeria, PLC. 2000.

Taylor, Quintard. *The Making of the Modern World: A History of the Twentieth Century*. Iowa: Kendall Hunt Publishing Company, 1990.

Wanjala, Chris. L. 'Foreword' in Onochie, Selina. et al. (eds) *Imagination of Poets: An Anthology of African Poems*. Port Harcourt: Penpower Communication Company, 2005.

Newswatch Magazine Editorial: 'The Flight into Trouble'. Lagos: Newswatch Communications Limited, April 10, 2006.

┌───┐
Manufacturing Skin
for Somalia's History:
Nuruddin Farah's Deep Hurt
in *Links*
└───┘

Tej N. Dhar

Nuruddin Farah wrote in 1988 that the overall theme of his novels is 'truth versus untruth' and his aim in writing them is to 'put down on paper, for posterity's sake, the true history of a nation' (Farah 1988: 1599). Although Farah's fictional style has changed over time, he has held on steadfastly to his involvement with the Somali nation and its social and political history. His Dictatorship trilogy is a searing critique of the repressive regime of Syed Barre, in which he exposes the untruth of the official truth and its baneful effect on ordinary lives. Though some critics have noticed a change in his concerns in the Blood and Sun trilogy, because *Maps* marks a shift from what Derek Wright calls 'political geography to psycho-physiology, from powerscape to mindscape' (1990 33), it still remains true that Farah intertwines the dilemmas of individual lives with serious concerns of identity, loyalty, and nationhood in its novels, which provides an extra edge of complexity to them. Some other critics, in fact, consider the last novel of the trilogy, *Secrets*, to be Farah's *Things Fall Apart* (Alidou and Mazrui 2000: 122–8).

In *Links*, the political condition of Somalia and its effect on individual lives take the centre-stage. In a way, it is a continuation of what Farah started in *Secrets*, which is set during the start of the civil war in the country. In his 'Author's Note' to *Links,* he writes that the novel is a work of fiction 'set against the background of actual events that took place in Mogadiscio', for which he read extensively, spoke to scores of people, scrutinized a host of documents, but 'covered all borrowings with skin of my own manufacture' (2004: 335). This essay discusses the nature and purpose of Farah's involvement with the history of his country, its mode of fictional representation in *Links*, and the techniques used by him for the purpose. In a large measure, these distinguish him from many contemporary African writers.

It would not be an exaggeration to say that for Farah Somalia is both an obsession and the source of his creativity. He has consistently maintained that 'you can never write effective fiction unless it is based on your country where you understand intimately people's behaviour and ways of existence' (Jonas 1987: 60). The chequered history of Somalia and its legacy of blighted institutions have been adequately documented in learned essays and historical works (for example, in Ali Jimale Ahmed, and I.M. Lewis). *Links* provides an acute dramatization of an aspect of this history, about the civil war in Somalia, the pain and suffering that it brought in its wake, and the scars that it left on the psyche of its hapless people.

Since African writers' involvement with history has been widely recognized and commented upon, most commonly within post-colonial and postmodernist frames, it would be helpful to distinguish Farah's approach to it from that of his contemporaries like Chinua Achebe and Ngũgĩ wa Thiong'o. Unlike them, Farah did not write about the distant past of his country, to produce novelistic narratives that contest imperialist historiography, and to demonstrate, like Achebe, for example, that Africa did not have a disfigured past. Instead he wrote about the social and political history of his own time, contesting different varieties of nationalist historiographies that were being popularized by the rulers of his country to keep themselves in power. In this, Farah virtually accepted what Soyinka urged writers to do in the 1960s: 'The African writer needs an urgent release from the fascination of the past' (1988: 19). Soyinka considered it the best way in which the African writer could play the role expected of him: 'The artist has always functioned in African society as the record of the mores and experiences of his society and as the voice of his vision in his own time. It is time for him to respond to this essence of himself' (20). And Farah does exactly that.

Farah's call of conscience, reflected in his desire to engage himself with his present, has virtually shaped his career as a writer and defined the contours of his fictional world. His enthusiastic response to the revolutionary government of Syed Barre turned sour soon after a play by him was rejected by his government as 'scandalously revolutionary' and the serialization of his Somali novel was officially stopped (Wright 1994: 12). When the publication of *A Naked Needle* prevented him from returning to his country, he 'changed from being a homeward-bound traveler, in transit, to an exile, and became the proverbial hunchback who must get used to his misfortunes' (Farah 2000: 58). Though physically absent from his country, Farah believes that 'I am not absent spiritually nor am I exiled from my own people who, to the best of my knowledge, have a high respect for the principles by which I stand... (Jaggi 1981: 183). It is his principled stand on affairs within his country and his continuous search for truth about it that makes him into an intellectual in the mould of Edward Said, 'a spirit in opposition, rather than in accommodation' (Said 1994: xv). He has continued writing relentlessly and steadfastly, in spite of knowing full well that 'combining politics and writing is a lonely business' (Farah 2000: 59) or what Said calls a 'lonely condition' (xv).

Farah's exile is 'an actual condition' as well as a 'metaphorical condition' (Said 1994: 39): he is not only physically out of his country but also in a state that Said defines in a metaphysical sense as one of 'restlessness, movement, constantly being unsettled, and unsettling others' (39). Farah converts his disadvantaged position of an exile into one of strength. He uses his physical exile to clarify his perspective on his country: 'I think I have learned a lot more about Somalia by questioning myself and my country from afar' (Jonas 1987: 60). It also brings him other gains: freedom from meeting home-bound obligations, familial loyalties, and the dread of censorship. To make up for his physical absence from Somalia, he lives as close to it as possible by living in Africa and not in Western metropolitan centres, where most of the exiles flourish. His metaphorical condition provides him the motive force for his creativity, for his ceaseless engagement with his country's history. This is clear from the way he describes his creative process: 'Fiction is part recreation, part imagination, and I suppose part sensitivity. But you have to know what to re-create, and the experience of Africa helps me consolidate my knowledge of the situation, as well as what I already carry within me' (Jaggi 1989: 187).

Farah's condition of exile – both actual and metaphorical – is vital for understanding the nature of his engagement with Somalian history in general, and in *Links* in particular, and also for the manner in which he handles it. Except for a short visit to Mogadiscio in 1996, Farah has been in exile for decades. Since his fiction bears a strong imprint of exilic consciousness, it is important that we understand it in its true perspective, for writers like Achebe have expressed their misgivings about 'the advertisement of expatriation and exile as intrinsically desirable goals for the writers' (96). This is because the condition of exile creates a special role for memory in the creative process, which has serious implications for writers' engagement with history. It can be understood in its fullness by comparing Farah with another exile Salman Rushdie, who has written approvingly about him (1991: 201–2). Both are exiles, but of a different kind. Farah was pushed into exile, but Rushdie went into exile voluntarily. For Rushdie, his country turns into an 'imaginary homeland', but for Farah it is the 'country of his imagination'. Because Rushdie has to work hard to recreate his country, he gets caught up in the process of recreation; the narrative space of both *Midnight's Children* and *Shame* is dominated by the problem of history-writing, which brings his fiction within the ambit of postmodern style. Farah has no such problems; everything about his country is vivid and clear to him. Rushdie's effort is characterized by a kind of playfulness, which though enjoyable is also disconcerting, for it seriously questions the very existence of history and its epistemological value. Towards the end of a very striking passage in *Midnight's Children*, the narrator, almost exasperatingly, says that 'what actually happened is less important than what the author can manage to persuade his audience to believe' (Rushdie 1981: 263). Far from being an expression of unease, it is one of authorial arrogance. Farah has no such problems; neither of perception nor of writing about his country, for there are no faded margins in his memory. It is active and enabling: 'Memory is active when you are in exile, and it calls at the awkwardest hour, like a baby waking up its parents at the crack of dawn' (Jonas 1987: 60).

Farah's recreation of the history of his country is characterized by acute seriousness. He sees clearly the brutality and inhumanity of its rulers and their perverted thinking: how during Barre's time Somalia turned into a 'badly written play' (Farah 2000: 79), and how after his exit 'the anachronistic sentiments of clannism' (Farah 2000: 5) created a climate of 'thuggery, horror, and decapitation' and drenched it in 'a miasma of sorrow' (Farah 2000: 9). Because of the clarity of his vision, he finds the realistic mode adequate for his purpose, but Rushdie finds realism inadequate and drapes his narratives in cloaks of fantasy. Quite understandably, Rushdie at one point gave up on his country and said that 'Literature has little or nothing to do with a writer's home address' (Achebe 105). But Farah's ties with his country have withstood the test of time. In *Links,* his involvement with his country's history is as vigorous as it was in his first trilogy.

For a proper understanding of Farah's treatment of history in *Links,* it is also necessary to know about his mode of recreation in the perspective of how novelists deal with history. Quite often, this is misunderstood, because the novelists' work is judged either by equating it with that of professional historians or simply considered inferior to theirs. A perceptive observation by Nadine Gordimer helps us see the difference: 'If you want to read the facts of the retreat from Moscow in 1815, you may read a history book; if you want to know what war is like and how people of a certain time and background dealt with it as their personal situation, you must read *War and Peace*' (1996: 20–21).

Gordimer's observation clarifies the fact that the novelist's approach to history is different from that of the historian, though one has to admit that over time, there has been a steady expansion in the range, depth, and variety of the subject matter of history, as well as in the art of history-writing, which is largely because of the influence of novelists on historians. For many, however, the novelist's concern with history is reflected in his interest in the past that is removed from the present by a considerable gap of time. This is evident in the formulations of a number of theoreticians, right from Manzoni to the present century, and is reflected in the currency of the term historical novel, which, in my view, has not only proved an unstable category but is also inadequate because it is limiting and inhibiting. Margaret Laurence aptly states that 'all fiction is written about the past' (1978: 15), implying that the novelist's concern with the past does not tie him down to any chronologically determined depth; he is not bound by any periodized view of time, which the historians may find convenient, even necessary. Degrees of pastness are quite flexible for him, and may vary between events or happenings that have just passed, or a period that stretches to the limits of one's memory, or about the remote past. The novelist is also not bound by any sequential patterns of linearity that a large majority of historians observe with meticulous consistency. Novelists can jump time, disrupt chronology, and treat the actual in diverse ways. They can write about it directly or through disguise; inter- rogate or problematize it, or treat it obliquely through the modes of allegory and satire. One of the most valuable ways in which the novelists deal with the actual is to dramatize it and convert it into what Milan Kundera calls the 'illustration of a historical situation, the description of a society at a given moment, a novelized historiography' (1988: 36).

I emphasize this variety in the novelist's use of history because assess- ments have quite often ignored this vital aspect of his art, though novelists have been doing these things right from the time the novel came into its own in the West. Critics have often set up unfair and false standards for judging the novelist's effort by comparing it with the work of professional historians. James Ogude, for example, writes on Ngũgĩ's novels to correct the failure of the existing criticism to 'locate Ngũgĩ's texts within the contested terrain of Kenya's historiography', in the context of the current debates on history and fiction, but by stating that 'Ultimately, the explanatory power or even the epistemological useful- ness of literature depends on how close it approximates the historical truth which is its ultimate referent' (3), he sets up an erroneous standard for judging Ngũgĩ's effort. For he implies that there is a 'historical truth' out there, set up obviously by the historians – firm, solid, fixed, and immutable – and a novel that claims to deal with history has to conform to it. Even professional historians would shy away from this kind of certitude, for they too believe that there are several versions of the so- called historical truth.

When Farah writes that *Links* is 'set against the background of actual events that took place in Mogadiscio', he does not imply that these events are meant merely to provide an environment in which characters come to life, a prop for writing a novel in verisimilar mode. If that were so, then the novel would not be about the history of Somalia, and the characters would have been shown busy living their private lives. But that does not happen in the novel, for they are inextricably embroiled in the civil war. Compelled to live under its dark shadow, it impinges on their lives. Some make sense of it by interrogating it; some try to defy it, and some others take advantage of it. In short, the novel illustrates what it means to live in a country that has been torn apart by civil war, the result both of its decadent institutions and the collapse of a tyrannical political system.

Links is organized around Jeebleh's visit to the city where he was removed from a prison soon after the country's takeover by the warlords, and then packed off to the U.S. Now he is back in the strife-torn city, fully aware of the grave risk to his person. Almost at the very beginning of the novel, during his meetings with people, we get to know that he has come to visit the grave of his mother, who had died in suspicious circumstances during his absence from the country. But Jeebleh does not think of his mother's death only as a matter for private grief, but as a kind of symbolic event, representing, as it were, the deaths of all those people who perished as a result of the siege of the country by its warlords. That is why his mission is 'to locate his mother's story in the context of the bigger national narrative' (2003: 29). This helps us to connect it with the other stated reason for his visit. Since he had been forced out of the country without getting a chance to talk to his friend and co-prisoner Bile, he wants to have an 'air-cleaning session with Bile about their unfinished business' (28).

Thus we see that though Jeebleh's visit, which he undertakes against the express wishes of his wife and daughters, has an ostensible purpose, the movement of the narrative clarifies that his visit is also propelled by a deep urge to renew his links with his fellow Somalians. This is suggested in the epigraphs of the novel as well, particularly the one from Freud, which reads: 'The individual leads in actual fact a double life, one in which he is an end to himself and another in which he is a link in a chain which he serves against his will or at least independently of his will.' The lines effectively bring out the force of this link, for it defies reason and stresses the deep instinctual bond that connects people; it is a kind of atavistic desire of individuals to stay in touch with their people in solidarity even in the face of adversity or grave danger. The title of the novel, too, stresses this connection.

The moment we understand this link and its binding force, we see Jeebleh for what he is: not only a character in his own right but also Farah's persona. His actual journey into Somalia translates into Farah's imaginative journey into his country: to be with his people to share in their plight; an expression of his solidarity with them in their hour of trial. While talking with Shanta, his childhood friend, Jeebleh mentions to her a book by Shirin Ramzanali Fazel, which he likes because it points to 'the gaps in the world's knowledge about Somalia', is 'unlike many books by authors with clan-sharpened axes to grind', and is also a 'book about the civil war from a Somali perspective' (226). These characteristics are equally applicable to *Links,* too, for it attempts to show what war has done to the Somalis, is critical of what has been happening, and does not uphold the rightness of any of the contending factions. If Shirin's book is the result of her deep hurt, so is *Links* the result of the deep hurt of Farah, for 'when you are deeply hurt, you return to the memories you've been raised on, to make sense of what's happening' (226). Almost all the happenings related to the civil war are unfolded in a tone of righteous indignation; everything hateful about it is condemned unequivocally.

The depth and intensity of Farah's hurt is also reflected in the fact that within days of his stay in the city, Jeebleh's involvement with his country extends beyond his stated purpose. After experiencing the rot that has set in, he feels that he has not only to locate his mother's grave but also to 'give a hand in recovering Raasta [who symbolizes peace] and her companion from their captors; and recruit Dajaal to exact vengeance on Caloosha [an active agent of disruptive politics]' (133). He chooses to do so even though it is fraught with new dangers, mainly because justice demands it. This is clear from what he says to his friend Seamus: 'I'm now part of the story, in that I've taken sides, and made choices that might put my life in danger' (215). When he is about to leave, he is happy and satisfied to have done all that he should to renew his links with his people. This comes out clearly in the Epilogue to the novel: 'Jeebleh assured himself that he loved his friends enough and that they loved him. He knew that they would visit one another, welcome one another into their homes, and into their stories. He and his friends were forever linked through the chains of the stories they shared' (334).

Once we accept the centrality of Jeebleh in the narrative design of the novel, as its central consciousness, in the Jamesian sense, or as a focalizer, in the language of narratology, we get a clear access to the kind of skin that Farah manufactures, as he makes him the main source of our seeing, knowing, and understanding things. Jeebleh's stated motive in the early parts of the narrative provides a basis for the novel's constituent events, which are essential for the onward progression of the plot. The novel also builds into it many supplementary events which, strictly speaking, are not essential for the plot, but considerably enlarge its meaning. The narrative also provides for a number of paratexts – allusions to books, brief quotes from writers, parables, myths, folk stories – which enrich its texture and its overall meaning.

The novel has also a third-person narrator, invariably a more reliable focalizer than any other character in a narrative, but most of the time he functions like a Hemingway narrator, who performs the bare minimal tasks of setting up the narrative. These include the sketching of locations for the characters to interact with each other, and describing them for the readers before they get involved with Jeebleh. The latter strategy helps Farah to build into the main narrative the smaller narratives of Bile, his sister Shanta and her husband, and his friend Seamus, so that we know them sufficiently before they interact with Jeebleh. Though there is a personal edge to their stories, Jeebleh meets them as people who live under the shadow of the civil war.

The centrality of Jeebleh is established in the two opening pages of the novel. When he lands at a 'desolate airstrip' and not at the expected airport, and when instead of uniformed service staff he meets 'loiterers … out to get what they could, through fair or foul means' (3), Farah makes us see that Somalia has degenerated into chaotic lawlessness, and thus prepares us for the nature of events to follow. It also sets the tone of the narrative by suggesting that things have reached a point in his country where the line between fair and foul has been blurred for ever. On this very page, the narrator lets Jeebleh take command just after the few opening lines; and on the very next page there is an explicit mention of what Jeebleh is meant to do: 'Jeebleh observed...'; 'Jeebleh saw...'; and 'Jeebleh thought ...' (4). So like a roving eye, Jeebleh sees and observes, and also thinks about and reacts to the things around him in the city of Mogadiscio, which paradigmatically stands for the whole country. The nature of what he sees is also suggested by the epigraphs from Dante's Inferno: 'the suffering city', of 'eternal pain', where people are 'lost' because they lack 'the good of the intellect' (1). Since the city's character remains the same throughout the narrative, Farah persists with epigraphs from the Inferno for all its four parts and the Epilogue.

Soon after Jeebleh gets off the plane, the picture of chaos and confusion is filled with details. The country is in the grip of gun culture, for it is 'ruled to ruin by gunrunners', who represent different parties of the civil war, which is actually 'a civil anarchy in which one might die at the hands of an armed youth because one belonged to a different clan family from his' (10). Brash and loud in their manner, the youth take potshots at innocent citizens; in the airport, they kill a small boy without any qualms. Very soon, Jeebleh sees them everywhere: in his hotel, where they have been stationed to keep watch on his activities; on the roads, where they monitor the movement of travellers and exact money from them for their masters, and even in graveyards, where they push him into submission. All the time they remind him that the country is in the grip of clan rivalry, where people are linked to each other not by the human bonds of shared love and affection but by clan affiliations. Time and again, he hears that in Somalia people have 'no friends, but clans'.

Through Jeebleh, Farah makes us see the sorrow and misery of the city ravaged by war. Take this passage:

> A poet might have described Somalia as a ship caught in a great storm without the guiding hand of a wise captain. Another might have portrayed the land as laid to waste, abandoned, the women widowed, the children orphaned, and the sick untended. A third might have depicted it as a tragic country ransacked by madmen driven by insatiable hunger for more wealth and limitless power. So many lives pointlessly cut short, so much futile violence. (15)

Farah is so deeply hurt by what he sees that one voice is not adequate to articulate it; multiple voices are needed for the purpose. Even these prove inadequate. As Jeebleh moves into other parts of the city, its nightmarish quality is repeatedly brought to our attention. At one point, he finds the city beyond recognition: the houses are 'gutted; the windows were bashed in ... a city vandalized, taken over by rogues who were out to rob whatever they could lay their hands on, and who left destruction in their wake' (35).

The effect of such descriptions is heightened by Farah's use of animal imagery of the kind that is traditionally associated with demonic worlds.

Most of the time Jeebleh sees only ugly and predatory animals, who feed on dead bodies and waste: vultures, crows, marabous. In the Yemini quarter of the city, goats are

> forced to feed on pebbles; there were no shrubs, and the grass and the cacti were dry. The cows Jeebleh saw chewed away at discarded shoes. ... The dogs looked rabid and were so skinny you could see their protruding ribs. ... There were waste dumps every few hundred metres or so, where vultures, marabous, and the odd crow were having a go at the pickings. Jeebleh felt he had arrived in an area just devastated by wildfire, which had reduced it to spectral ruins. (133)

Jeebleh's friend Seamus too thinks that 'Somalia was a home of grief, a ship with no master that was floundering in a windstorm' (193). The entire city is covered with 'the pervasive smell of excrement and the rotten odor of waste' (200). Jeebleh rightly concludes that in such a state one could not 'expect an iota of human kindness from a community existing daily with so much putrefaction' (201).

Jeebleh not only observes and sees, but also reflects on what he finds around him. The technique employed by Farah for this is to relate what he sees in the present to the city's past, when things were different. The past invoked is nothing like the ideal city of the Bible, or like the ancient regime, a strategy generally employed by satirists for creating a standard with which to castigate what is ugly and unpleasant, but the actual historical past of Somalia that Jeebleh knew as a young man, whose fitful glimpses we get through his troubled consciousness. This not only helps us to see Somalia's present in a historical perspective but also heightens its nightmarish character. Right in the opening paragraph of the novel, the unruly behaviour of the loiterers at the airport is contrasted with the happy crowds that would throng such places in the past: 'He [Jeebleh] knew that Somalis were of the habit of throwing *despedida* parties to bid their departing dear ones farewell, and of joyously and noisily welcoming them in droves at airports and bus depots when they returned from a trip' (3). The chaos and noise of the place, and the danger lurking in the movement of the loiterers, is in strong contrast to the pleasant merriment of the bygone times.

While waiting to be taken to his hotel, Jeebleh remembers the city when it was 'so peaceful he could take a stroll at any hour of the day or night without being mugged, or harassed in any way' (14). Ruefully, he also remembers his visits to places in long-gone days, when the 'people of his country were at peace with themselves, comfortable in themselves, happy with who they were' (14). He keeps on getting these flashes as he moves around the city during his waking hours, and sometimes in his dreams, too. In all of them, we see Mogadiscio as a city that 'was orderly, clean, peaceable, a city with integrity and a life of its own, a lovely metropolis with beaches, cafes, restaurants, late-night movies. It may have been poor, but at least there was dignity to that poverty, and no one was in any hurry to plunder or destroy what they couldn't have' (35).

Aside from making us see the city through Jeebleh's roving eye, Farah also makes us understand the reason for such a sorry state of the country. Details about the civil war – its nature and its effect – are woven into the narrative through intense dramatization, in which Jeebleh talks with people who support and speak for it and also the ones who oppose it and work to ameliorate its evil effects. Jeebleh's encounters with the warring parties provide an insight into their positions, credos, beliefs, and their modes of operation. This also provides for a great deal of discussion and debate in the narrative. The major characters that are against the war are well-read people: they know several languages, are familiar with different cultures of the world, and are intellectuals like Farah, but sufficiently individualized as beings in their own right.

Jeebleh's first brush with the civil war takes place right in the opening scene of the novel, when he arrives in the city to see people all around him with guns, learns about the kidnapping of Raasta and Makka, and experiences first-hand the overall atmosphere of menace. The reception he gets there is determined by his clan affiliation. Af-Lawe, a shady product of the war between warlords, arranges for his transportation to the northern part of the city only because of his affinity with a particular clan. For several days, his life is virtually dictated by an invisible hand; he also finds that he is under constant watch. When the impact of clan affiliation sinks into him, he gets bad dreams; in one of them, he sees himself fighting with Caloosha, the security advisor of the Strongman North. Later, he also learns how people like Af-Lawe use the conditions of war to serve their selfish interests. He runs the business of trading in dead bodies behind the philanthropic cover of an NGO, lives in a villa that has been deserted by its rightful occupants, and is dangerously unpredictable because of his shifty and mysterious manner.

Jeebleh gets details about the cause of the civil war when he gets into a vehicle with an army Major with whom he travels part of the way to his hotel. The Major is critical of the Strongman South and his attempt to establish an all-inclusive government based on reconciliation because 'no one is able to rule over a people if they're prepared to fight. We're ready to kill; we're ready to die until our ancestral territories are back in our lands' (27). Like his clan-mates, he is fully convinced that he is fighting for 'a worthy cause, the recovery of our territory. We're fighting against our oppressors, who're morally evil, reprehensively blameworthy, every one of them. I see Strongman South as evil for wanting to impose his wicked will on our people' (28).

Even though Jeebleh tries his best to avoid meeting his clan elders, he cannot escape their sharp eye. With the help of their spies, who keep a constant watch on him, they force their presence on him, and we get to know the demands they make on people, especially the ones from the affluent West. They speak of their ties with him by reminding him that they are from his mother's side. But Jeebleh remembers with sadness how the very same people treated his mother badly when she was forced to be a single mother and a widow, forcing her to fend for himself. In spite of this, Jeebleh treats them with respect, offers them tea, listens to them with patience, but keeps on remembering that 'clan elders were self-serving men, high on selective memory and devoid of dignity' (128). When they ask him for money to help them fight their enemy, he tells them that he will send them money only after reaching home, which they take as an insult. When they are gone, he is shocked to find that everybody looks at him with disapproval. Frightful words attack him: 'He who alienates his clan family is dead' (132). When he luckily escapes being attacked, because of his absence from his room, Jeebleh moves into the southern part of the city, to stay with Bile and his other friends, though they are from a different clan.

Jeebleh does not meet the warlords, only their minions, like Af-Lawe and Caloosha. As an unhealthy representative of war-mongers, he is drawn repulsively: 'Caloosha's distended belly was filled with sentiments of war and wickedness, which was why he looked so ugly, and so unhealthy. Attrition retarded his brain, evil dulled his imagination, did not sharpen it' (102). A slight encouragement from Jeebleh makes him recount his evil deeds with glee, the worst being the pure fabrication of the story about his mother. When Jeebleh goes to meet Caloosha's mother's housekeeper with his clan people, it does not take him long to find that she is a fraud; when he is taken to see his mother's grave, he finds instantly that it was not the one he was looking for, because it did not look as Shanta had told him. When the people accompanying him notice his doubt and hesitation, they force him to bend before the grave by prodding him with a gun, which nearly kills him.

Brutalities caused by the war are also woven into the main narrative through the shorter narratives of Bile's long solitary confinement, and its impact on the lives of Shanta and her husband, Seasmus's narrative of his losses and sufferings in Ireland, which were as senseless and disruptive as they are in Somalia, because of which he considers it the 'Ireland of my exiled neurosis' (216). His confrontations with people on both sides of the clans confirm how risky life has become in Somalia. He narrowly escapes getting killed on two occasions.

It is significant that Jeebleh's experiences and what he learns from others are not presented as just clinical details. We have already seen that Farah's attitude towards what is presented in the novel is suggested by the epigraphs from Dante's Inferno as well as by Jeebleh's frequent comparisons of the present with what it was like in the past. But he does not stop at that. From time to time, Jeebleh comments severely on what he sees. On his way to see Bile with his trusted man Dajaal, he is reminded of Virgil's words related to people slaughtered 'in one another's blood', and forces a grim reflection: 'He would like to know whether, in this civil war, both those violated and the violators suffered from a huge deficiency – the inability to remain in touch with their inner selves or to remember who they were before the slaughter began' (70). The words clearly suggest that war is a senseless and soulless exercise.

Jeebleh had learnt about the dangers of clannism in his youth from his mother, who always encouraged him to be his own man. Remembering her words in the context of his new experiences reinforces his attitude towards clannism: '...beware of your clansmen. They'll prove to be your worst enemies, and they are more likely than not to stab you in broad daylight if you choose to have nothing to do with them' (96).

Consistently, Jeebleh's reflective consciousness broods over the incapacity of human beings to see each other's view, to reach a compromise, and to understand how so much of suffering could have been avoided. The saddest part of this is their insensitivity to the destructive outcome of their actions, which comes in the way of their experiencing grief: 'I don't know if it is possible to have a good, clean grief when people have no idea how big a loss they have suffered, and when each individual continues denying his or her own part in the collapse' (167).

Since the American incursion formed a part of the actuality of the civil war, it is understandable that it figures in Jeebleh's conversation with people. Though he had read about it in his home in the U.S., and also remembered its TV images, the people who speak to him tell him the truth about it as historical witnesses. Interestingly, Farah makes Seamus the first to express his misgivings about the generally held position 'of Yankees as "good angels" come on a humanitarian mission, to perform God's work here' (260), which is a faint echo of the rhetoric of old colonial times. Seamus has an interesting explanation for their failure, which confirms this: 'they saw everything in black and white, had no understanding and no respect for other cultures, and were short on imagination' (260). In fact, he equated their failure in Somalia with their failure in the Gulf, against Iraq, for in both cases, wars had been converted into TV shows. Dajaal too condemns the Americans, though they were welcomed in the beginning. It is because soon afterwards, they arrested people for no reason, 'humiliated and intimidated' them, and acted clumsily. He narrates to him the shameful scene in which his granddaughter was blown away in a helicopter uprush of air and reduced to a vegetable. When Jeebleh goes to see the girl and her mother, the latter tells him about the inhuman behaviour of the soldiers; they simply gloated over her misfortune. And Jeebleh agrees with Seamus and sympathizes with Dajaal.

It is also significant that Dajaal has a different estimate of the soldiers, the Marines, and their officers. The officers were 'arrogant' and 'loony' (267); because of their ineptitude they sent contradictory messages to the warlords and actually contributed towards prolonging the war. The soldiers seemed to be lost, as if they were fighting the war unwillingly: 'I felt as though each of them was alone in his fear, like a child left in pitch-darkness of a strange room by parents who were enjoying themselves elsewhere.... I imagined them questioning in their own minds the explanations put out by military spokesman at Pentagon on briefings' (267). Dajaal seems to show that most of these incursions are officially sponsored and the public at large does not approve of them. Since Jeebleh accepts it quietly, we have every reason to believe that Farah too shares the same view.

Thus we see that though Jeebleh's visit is occasioned by his desire to pay respect to his mother's memory by creating a small memorial near her grave, in which he is eventually helped by Seamus, and to get to know all the details about Bile's imprisonment and his life after that, which he has dedicated to treat people affected by war, his presence in the novel is used by Farah to give us a complete picture of what Somalia was like during the war. By mixing with people, talking with them, and helping the ones who were not even touched by others because of their belief in taboos, he brings out clearly the absurdity of the civil war and the misery and misfortune it caused to Somalia and its people. The novel thus dramatizes a significant part of its unfortunate history in its fullness as only fiction can.

WORKS CITED

Achebe, Chinua. *Home and Exile*. 2000; New York: Anchor Books, 2001.

Ahmed, Ali Jimale, ed. *The Invention of Somalia*. Lawrenceville, NJ: The Red Sea Press, 1995.

Alidou, Ousseina D. and Alamin M. Mazrui. '*Secrets*: Farah's *Things Fall Apart*.' *Research in African Literatures*, 31, 1 (Spring 2000): 122–8.

Farah, Nuruddin. *Links*. 2003: New York: Riverhead Books, 2004.

—— *Yesterday, Tomorrow: Voices from the Somali Diaspora*. London and New York: Cassell, 2000.

—— 'Why I Write?' *Third World Quarterly*, 10, 4 (1988): 1591–9.

Gordimer, Nadine. *Writing and Being*. 1995; Cambridge, Massachusetts: Harvard University Press, 1996.

Jaggi, Maya. 'A Combination of Gifts: An Interview with Nuruddin Farah.' *Third World Quarterly*, 11, 3 (July 1989); 171–87.

Jonas, Maggie. 'Farah – Living in a Country of the Mind.' *New African* (December 1987): 60–61.

Kundera, Milan. *The Art of the Novel*. Trans. Linda Asher. 1986; London: Faber and Faber, 1988.

Laurence, Margaret. 'Ivory Tower or Grassroots?: The Novelist as a Socio-Political Being.' *A Political Art: Essays and Images in Honour of George Woodcock*, Ed. William H. New. Vancouver: The University of British Columbia Press, 1978.

Lewis, I. M. *A Modern History of Somalia*. 4th Edition. Oxford: James Currey, 2002.

Ogude, James. *Ngũgĩ's Novels and African History: Narrating the Nation*. London: Pluto Press, 1999.

Rushdie, Salman. 'Nuruddin Farah,' *Imaginary Homelands: Essays and Criticism 1981-1991*. New Delhi: Penguin Viking India, 1991: 201–2.

—— *Midnight's Children*. London: Jonathan Cape, 1981.

Said, Edward. *Representations of the Intellectual*. London: Vintage, 1994.

Soyinka, Wole. 'The Writer in a Modern African State.' *Art, Dialogue and Outrage: Essays on Literature and Culture*. Ibadan: New Horn Press, 1988: 15–20.

Wright, Derek. *The Novels of Nuruddin Farah*. Bayreuth: Bayreuth University, 1994.

—— 'Somali Powerscapes: Mapping Farah's Fiction.' *Research in African Literatures*, 21.2 (Summer 1990): 21–34.

Ada Uzoamaka Azodo

> *Unhu*, that profound knowledge of being, quietly and not flamboyantly; the
> grasp of life and of how to preserve and accentuate life's eternal interweaving
> that we southern Africans are famed for, and what others call '*ubuntu*'.
> – Tsitsi Dangarembga. *The Book of Not*, 102–3

To liberate a person to bond with other persons in an organic community,
society needs to balance unique individual desires and social ideals. This
article will explore this idea, through the examination of the relationship
between a person and the community, that is, between the individual and
society, as well as the ethical notions of good and evil, right and wrong,
and responsibility for one's actions. How does a person relate to the
community metaphysically and socially? Does the reality of the individual person have primacy over the reality of the community? Does the
communal social order erase the concept of the individual in thought and
practice? Is the individual secondary to the community? Indeed, how can
a community or society develop an ethic of humanity free of social
inequities and injustices?

These are some of the conceptual issues that Tsitsi Dangarembga's
second novel, *The Book of Not* (2006), in full *The Book of Not* [Stopping
the Time], appears to raise, and which I shall focus on in this study,
employing the Zimbabwean *unhu* principle of personhood. The maxim
'thou shall not' applies here, and aptly describes, 'both a moving story of
a girl's coming of age and a compelling narrative of the devastating human
loss involved in the colonization of one culture by another.' As in her
award-winning seminal novel, *Nervous Conditions* (1988), the reader again
encounters Tambudzai Sigauke and her cousin Nyasha. The era is the 1970s
post-war Zimbabwe, but the new nation is still segregated in practice and
remains racist. However, the novel's swing between the particular and the
general makes it possible to expand the immediate problems from the
nation to humankind and the fundamental problems of the individual to
her or his relationship with other persons in the community.

Around 1977, Dangarembga interrupted her studies in medicine at
Cambridge University, England, returned to Zimbabwe, and enrolled in

the psychology department of the University of Zimbabwe. She became involved with a theatre group, the Drama Club of the university. She wrote three plays, *She No Longer Weeps*, *The Lost of the Soil*, and *The Third One*, at a time when Zimbabwean writers were still all men. After graduation, and working as a teacher, in 1985 Tsitsi wrote a prize-winning short story, 'The Letter,' for a literary competition organized by the Swedish International Development Authority (SIDA), later published it in the anthology, *Whispering Land* (1985). In 1988, she published *Nervous Conditions*, followed in 1992 by a film, *Neria*, and a fictional work *Everyone's Child*, produced as a film in 1996. In 2002, she produced another film, *Ivory*.

Both her novels, *Nervous Conditions* and *The Book of Not*, continue the serialization of the life and experiences of the pair Tambudzai Sigauke and her cousin Nyasha, among other recurring characteristics, and especially Tambu's pursuit of education, in order to better herself and have a bright future that would in turn help her to contribute to her community as an adult citizen.

Indeed, Zimbabwean independence in 1980 (after several years of guerrilla warfare by the black population against the white minority Rhodesian government) irrevocably changed the Zimbabwean novel. Gone was the usual acrimonious Rhodesian discourse, racist venom and innuendos. Instead new themes emerged on the war of liberation from all backgrounds and women writers began to exert a forceful impact and influence at home and abroad. They include Nozipo Mareira, Yvonne Vera and Tsitsi Dangarembga. Dangarembga and Mareira were the most remarkable but different from Yvonne Vera in a number of ways. Whereas Vera was prolific with five novels before her death in 2005, Dangarembga has published only two novels, her second novel coming full seventeen years after her debut. The reason appears to be her foray into short story writing, training in film at the *Deutsche Film und Fernseh Akademie*, and later production of films.

As an African novelist, Dangarembga can best be categorized as a modern writer. In her first novel, she deals with the colonial past, the anarchy, despair and disorder of the nation, and in the second she indicts the post-war present of instability, racism, and oppression. The author shows concern and therefore conscious experimentation in conveying the historic past and present of the nation, seen in the alienation, isolation, and disintegration of the principal characters. And, it is not by an act of chance, but of careful calculation, that the author draws a parallel between French existentialists and the white girls doing drugs at the Ladies College of The Sacred Heart high school (*The Book of Not*, 124). From the angle of portraying a mirror of individual and collective turmoil under oppression, Dangarembga compares well with her predecessors of the modernist tradition in African literature, such as Mariama Bâ, Aminata Sow Fall, Gabriel Okara, Ama Ata Aidoo, Ayi Kwei Armah,

Chinua Achebe, and Ngũgĩ wa Thiong'o (Ker 1997: 1–15), the last two of whom she confesses to have been influenced by. More specifically, I am inclined to insert her, not in the postcolonial tradition as Elizabeth Willey and Jeannette Treiber have done in *Emerging Perspectives on Tsitsi Dangarembga: Negotiating the Postcolonial* (2005), but rather in David I. Ker's communal perspective of the modernist tradition in the African novel (1997: 125–85). From a communal perspective, then, the principal character of The *Book of Not* remains an integral part of the community, despite her ordeals, never carrying her rebellion to the point of wanting to sever all ties with the nation. One could go as far as to say that at a certain point, the protagonist merges with the author, becoming the author-narrator, whose intention all along is that of being at once participant and observer.

Thus, in this article, I will examine the benefits of resurrecting the Zimbabwean principle of *unhu* and applying it to the national problems of the post-war era, in order to see how an ethic of humanity can return to a nation now inhabited by different races, skin colours, and cultures. Perhaps, through *unhu*, the nation could be reunified under one umbrella of cooperation, solidarity, reciprocity, among many other values, morals and morality. There is a concern for social healing of all persons in the new Zimbabwean society, irrespective of race and skin colour and the side they fought on during the hostilities. For individuals to survive and achieve their full potential, thus moving the nation forward, there must be a move from turmoil and struggle to triumph, that is to say, individual and collective triumph that expands to attain a human brotherhood and sisterhood.

In his internet essay on the person and community in African thought Kwame Gyekye grapples with the intellectual questions on the metaphysical and moral status of a person:

> The existence of a social structure is an outstanding, in fact, a necessary feature of every human society. A social structure is evolved not only to give effect to certain conceptions of human nature, but also to provide a framework for both the realization of the potentials, goals and hopes of the individual members of the society and the continuous existence and survival of the society. The type of social structure or arrangement evolved by a particular society seems to reflect – and be influenced by – the public conceptions of personhood held in the society. These conceptions are articulated in the critical analyses and arguments of its intellectuals. (1)

Metaphysically, he seeks to understand if a person in human society is so self-complete in his or her individuality that he or she does not depend on other persons in the society to realize her or his potential. First, who has ontological supremacy or priority over the other, the individual person or the community? Put differently, is a person a communal being, given his or her essential relationship with other persons in the human society? Consequently, some issues arise. What fundamental rights does the individual person possess, which may not be overridden as the situation warrants in the interest of the community? Second, with regard to duties what role(s) should a person play with regard to the interests of self and of others in the community? Third, is there room for the existence and appreciation of collective good in the affairs of the individual person in the community or society? (ibid).

These questions touch on the moral ideals that this article will explore. The study will seek to establish what is expected of a person, and how such an individual must respond to others in a particular period of history.

In Shona thinking, there is a certain human connectedness, which makes it incumbent on all to behave with humanity towards other people in the community. This is because, according to the *unhu* philosophy, one is (exists) only because others exist in the community. A person actualizes, becomes human, only through other persons she or he touches. A universal bond connects all persons to other persons. This connectedness can also be abused when employed with other conflicting ethical views or ideologies. Thus, the idea here is that the human space that connects all human beings is elastic, and so expandable and contractible, depending on individual or group understanding or interpretation of its meaning. Therefore, the connecting space between human beings can be at once good for some individuals and evil or bad for other individuals. It is from this point of view that the added difficulty of firmly grasping this concept of communal living takes relevance.

Not surprisingly, different Southern African nations and cultures have different names for this communal principle that the Shona call *unhu*. For the Chewa it is *umunthu*, *umundu* for the Yawo, *bunhu* for the Tsonga, *botho* for the Sotho or Tswana, *umuntu* for the Zulu, *vhutu* for the Venda, and *ubuntu* for the Ndebele and Xhosa. According to Desmond Tutu:

> A person with *ubuntu* is open and available to others, affirming of others, does not feel threatened that others are able and good, for he or she has a proper self-assurance that comes from knowing that he or she belongs in a greater whole and is diminished when others are humiliated or diminished, when others are tortured or oppressed. (1999)

Nonetheless, no matter the nation or culture, the fundamental meaning of moral obligation to care for the other as a human being just like oneself remains the same (Nussbaum 2003: 2; Koster 1996: 111). One shows feelings of citizenship and reciprocity towards the other, just because one cares for the other's human dignity and humanity. In that way, one contributes towards community building with justice, equity, and mutual caring. From this angle of vision, *unhu* is a person affirming his or her individuality, through caring for others. As Sindave and Liebenberg have also rightly described this principle, 'a person is a person through other persons' (2000: 38). Equally illuminating is Nelson Mandela's illustration of one's humanity towards another embedded in the principle, when he says:

> A traveller through our country would stop at a village, and he didn't have to ask for food or for water. Once he stops, the people give him food, entertain him. That is one aspect of ubuntu but it has various aspects. (1994)

One can infer that some of the other aspects not mentioned would include things like the taboo to address an elder person by his or her first name, the respect a daughter-in-law owes her parents-in-law, and above all, the recognition of connectedness and reciprocity under the human condition, seen in the greetings throughout the day in form of inquiry after the health of the interlocutor:

Morning
'*Mangwani marara sei?*'   (Good Morning?)
'*Ndarara kana mararawo.*'   (I slept well, if you slept well.)

Lunch time
'*Marara sei?*'   (How has your day been?)
'*Ndarara kana mararawo.*'   (My day has been good, if your day has
    been good).
    (Tambulasi and Kayuni 2005: 148)

In sum, *unhu* is a philosophical notion that obliges everyone in the community or society to behave in a humane way towards the other for the common good. This is clearly elaborated in the novel :

> Comfort and useful, a contradiction in terms? Not at all, if you were one with the community. Besides, useful jobs did not only bring comforts to be spread amongst yourself and your family. They were useful in a sense beyond you, for when you were good at your useful job; you inspired others to work hard so they could take up useful jobs later on too. You only had to look at Babamukuru. He had inspired me to be hardworking and useful. Perhaps one day I would inspire someone else to be hardworking and useful too. We could end up with a nation of inspiring useful hardworking people, like the British and the Americans, and all the other Europeans who were guiding us and helping us in our struggle. So being good at a useful job was quite different from being useful at a useless job like prostitution or politics where no one benefited. (*The Book of Not*, 2006: 102–3)

Tambudzai Sigauke's awareness and execution of the *unhu* principle follows her psychological itinerary, from childhood in the village homestead with parents, Mai and Jeremiah, and at the Mission with the extended family, her maternal uncle and principal of the mission school, Babamukuru, his wife Maiguru, and cousin, Nyasa, through her biracial (minority black and majority white) tenure at the Ladies College of the Sacred Heart, and finally to her job as a copywriter with an all-white advertising agency. From stage to stage, Tambu matures from a state of delusion, to that of awareness, allowing the principle of *unhu* to guide her thoughts and actions, although at the end her hopes for the future would be dashed by white racist practices, an experience that makes her doubt that the nation could be saved, could survive, if individual hopes and aspirations are constantly allowed to disintegrate to mere personal calamities. Awakened to the endemic nature of social inequities and injustices that mar the nation, Tambu believes that human society is bad, and that change can only occur through people working collectively to change the status quo.

The Book of Not opens with the disciplining of collaborators with the Rhodesian forces by Big Brothers, members of the African guerrilla forces, engaged in a nationalist struggle against the dominant white minority. Netsai, Tambu's younger sister is involved as a collaborator with the enemy, and so is Babamukuru, her maternal uncle, for sending his niece (Tambu) to a European school reputed to be better than the ones that the Zimbabwean indigenes attend. As the older sister at sixteen years of age, Tambu agonizes, regretting her powerlessness to defend her younger sister one of whose legs is blown off by a bomb: 'I was her sister, her elder sister. By that position, I was required to perform the act that would protect her. How miserable I was, for nothing lay in my power, so that both the powerlessness and the misery frustrated' (3). The same feeling of helplessness and powerlessness recurs in the case of her mother, Mai, who faints at the sight of violence meted out to her daughter: 'I was the older girl, the oldest child now two brothers had died. I was expected to perform appropriate action' (4). The same feelings are also there in the uncle's case, this inability to stop such an act of humiliation, violence, and injustice against her benefactor; he gets thoroughly beaten, not for collaboration with the enemy, but rather for breaking with the black community and desiring white education for his niece. Tambu is torn between playing moral roles imposed on her by tradition and her loyalty with her people. She is passive, not active, as is her sense of *unhu* at this material time. But, all that will change as she approaches her senior year in college. As she puts it, it is the contradictions and human complexities at the girls' high school that help her to resuscitate her *unhu*.

At college, then, Tambu embraces education with vigour, so that in the future of the new nation of Zimbabwe, she would be in an advantageous position to use skills acquired for her survival, and also for the betterment of society. Having resurrected her *unhu*, she now apologizes when she hurts a fellow student, and humbly and reverently accepts merited punishment for misbehavior or perceived misbehaviour (103):

> Ruminating on this – the amount of *unhu* I possessed and how to show this to people – kept me very occupied. I often, therefore, walked all the way from assembly to class, or from class to library without knowing how I'd come from one place to the other. I was often so sunk in myself I frequently did not notice anything or anyone. (104)

Moreover, her meditations on *unhu* require her to avoid any misdeed that would earn her a black dot against her name on the library notice board, for the existential truth, she argues, is that you become what people perceive you essentially to be:

> The idea of the mark was bad enough, but what made it worse was everybody could see you had one. That meant everybody could see what kind of person other people thought you were. *Tirip kana makadini wo*! I am well if you are right too! That was the greeting we gave to each other, first heard on Mai's back when it was nothing more than a great buzzing booming confusion of utterance. That greeting went round the land like a blanket that covered and kept warm, a fabulous protection from fate. Everything was reciprocal and so were we; we all knew it, so said it every day in our greetings. This meant that what people saw you as being was a large part of what you were! (65)

Tambu's declared focus is to excel at the 'O' levels and go on the honor roll, and in that way distinguish herself as a person:

> Then people would know who I was, a person to be reckoned with and respected, not a receptacle of contempt like the gardeners, maids, cook boys and terrorists. So she looked forward to the prize giving day for her name in honor roll. (114)

Yet life at the girls' college is rife with racism and discrimination against the six black students all huddled up in the African dormitory constructed for four. Tambu says:

> You came to a school where you frequently had to pinch yourself to see if you really existed. Then (…) you quite often wished you didn't. So you ducked away to avoid meeting a group of people. That's when you found out how you were going to manage after all, when you'd almost given up hope, to bring people to admire and respect you. Life could be like that, in the end, with all pieces dovetailing in together and becoming beautiful! I had an aim in life. Now life was good! (114)

On the issue of conflict of individual desire with community expectations, specifically in regard to three white students rusticated for smoking dope on school grounds, Tambu has this to say: 'They must have been too full of themselves, and didn't drugs contribute to wild delusions – girls thinking they could do anything anywhere, no matter what anyone else stipulated, and get away with it without any consequences!' (123). She cannot understand their utter disregard of the principle of *unhu*, which in this case is flouting the school rules, for *unhu* only allows strong-headedness only when it benefits other people, as the following Shona greeting implies: '"How are you?" "I am well if you are well too!" That is how people with *unhu* greeted each other' (123).

However, Tambu has an intrinsic problem with the expulsion of the girls, who defend themselves by citing the earlier cases of French existentialist philosophers, people gifted with exceptional intelligence, who needed to smoke dope to help themselves. If dope exists in nature, the girls seem to argue, it must be because it is put there by God for a purpose. Then, why spoil someone's life, just because she or he partakes of an element in nature that God must have put there for the purpose of uplifting human intelligence? Tambu concludes that there is an apparent loss of *unhu*, when it is 'a characteristic that was so essential to becoming a person – which the girls faced because they were expelled' (124). Something appears wrong, she continues, since everybody has to be well for a given subject to be well:

> *Unhu* meant other people shouldn't lose it; it was like being well everyone should be. The unfortunate smokers had made a mistake, which meant they'd already lost a good bit of *unhu*. Now people were making sure they lost more, instead of helping them to retrieve it. If it was blood, would people do that? You might as well leave the blood vessels to empty, if you weren't going to staunch people's *unhu*. I kept feeling sorry for the girls. (124)

This argument, at the gut human level, has nothing racist about it. Tambu has a feeling of solidarity with the expelled girls, and this despite the racism that she and the other African girls are victims of at the school (125–32). Worse, although she comes up at the top of her class for the 'O' levels, yet the prize for best performance goes to a white girl, Tracey Stevenson, who did not even come second in ranking, because the rules were changed to accommodate her (162). Before then, Tambu had been tabled by the headmistress for using the good toilet in the school building reserved for white students, when she was expected to run back to the dormitory for African students to relieve herself. Later, the principal sent back a note to her uncle accusing her of having a complex. Tambu would say this later of these experiences: 'Those incidents embarrassed me so much that I disowned my actions and treated them as aberrations' (164).

Still, Tambu makes up her mind to shine at the 'A' levels, putting disappointment and victimization completely behind her. With hope in the future, she bends back down to hard work. Yet she is not allowed to attend classes with the white girls at the boys' high school. Someone, a volunteer student, brings back her notes for her to copy. This student also explains the lessons to her as much as she could. Needless to say that Tambu gets depressed. She confesses her abjection: 'It is hard to stand upon the foundations you are born with in order to look forward, when that support is bombarded by all that is around until what remains firm and upright is hidden beneath rubble and ruins (164). With reference to *unhu* she adds:

> The thing about *unhu* was that you couldn't go against the grain on your own. You weren't a clan, a people with a poem of praise, or a boast of what petrified enemies. *Unhu* required an elder aunt, or a *saltwira* – someone you were related to not by blood but by absolute respect, liking and understanding – to go forward to the authorities in order to present your case, showing that what disturbed you was not the flighty whim of one badly brought-up individual. What *unhu* prescribed to me who was moving against the larger current was to come to one's senses, realise the sovereignty of the group and work to make up for the disappointment. (164)

Tambu is disillusioned, given all the oppression and discrimination by the white school authorities and the white students against her and the other African girls. Tambu could no longer justify community service helping the Rhodesian soldiers. She stops knitting and dumps her unfinished materials in the dustbin, but not without agonizing that she is giving in to evil. According to a general rule of wisdom, she says, one should: 'Love your neighbor as yourself! I am well if you are well also!' (166). To add salt to injury, her 'A' levels are despicable: Ds and E and an O in mathematics, (187–9).

It is now time to enter the workaday world, since she cannot go forward academically or enter one of the big professional schools in medicine as her uncle expected. According to this uncle, Babamukuru: 'You will have to not want too much, Tambudzai. Even if you qualify for university with what you have, you will not qualify for a decent profession' (193).

Finding a desirable job is not easy for Tambudzai, as she goes from being a clerk in an establishment, to becoming a temporary teacher of very dull black children, whom nonetheless she influences, raising them a step higher than she found them (194). Eventually, she lands a job in ZimAir advertising agency as copy writer. But, the discrimination and racism from high school continues in the work world. Worse, she works in an establishment in which her high school arch rival is director of operations. As Tambu goes to work in the morning, she laments the changed times, when the rich keep their riches to themselves, whereas before they were ready to share with others, who then sought to emulate them and become like them too, so that the poor and lowly also raised their standards of living:

> If you were rich, you did not have to fear as there was nothing wrong. You were merely made; for all wealth did, as my reflections on *unhu* had predicted, was make the person. This knowledge fuelled the citizens' quest for money. Craving for the signs of possession encroached, much as my cousin Nyasha's craving for food when she was bulimic, until the city's residents craved excess, calling it comfort. (210)

Tambu unwittingly becomes a role model for the young secretary Pedzi, who aspires to complete her 'O' levels, and later goes on to obtain her 'A' levels also. Seeing, in her parlance, 'Sisi Tambu', gave her the impetus to forge ahead to improve her life.

But, the work at the agency is so dishonest that Tambu wonders if she would ever fit in the new nation: 'Oh, was I ever going to function in the new Zimbabwe, if I couldn't go to the necessary lengths, stop letting people put their names to what in the end was mine!' (200). Not only is she made to edit the senior editor's work at this agency; she is also obliged to keep the editor's name on the edited work. In the end, she is compelled to cede her laudable advertising statement to a white man, Dick, just because it is not proper that she should present it to the community. That is the straw that breaks the camel's back. Tambu resigns from the agency, to save her human dignity. She resolves that the promises she made to herself and providence, to carry 'forward with me the good and human, the *unhu* of my life', no longer makes sense. Now that it is about her personal survival in society, she sees no conflict with any interpretation of *unhu*:

> As it was, I had not considered *unhu* at all, only my own calamities, since the contested days at the convent. So this evening I walked emptily to the room I would soon vacate, wondering what future there was for me, a new Zimbabwean. (246)

Conclusion

Metaphysically speaking, how should a person relate to the new and modern Zimbabwean society? First, there is an ontological bond between the individual and the community, and neither is secondary to the other. It is the society that defines the person by its attitude and behaviour towards such a person, yet the person has an intrinsic quality that may or may not be trampled upon, without the effect of compromising the integrity of the composition of the community. Put differently, a person is a person, although this personhood can also be acquired, in which case the society defines the person. One can infer that Tambu is who she is, although she is constantly fashioned and constructed by her experiences throughout childhood, through adolescence to maturity.

Then again, can a person fail in the quest to distinguish herself in this modern Zimbabwe? Going by the example of Tambu again, it would seem so, since against all odds, she fails in her life quest to get a good education, get a good job, in order to make a comfortable living and be useful to society at the same time. The inimitable forces of racism and nepotism at school and at the work place would not allow her to distinguish herself and make her mark on society beyond the rudimentary level, influencing the few people that come her way in her daily activities. Clearly, when a person fails in her or his acquisition of personhood, it could be due to wrongful application of *unhu* by the generality of people in the society.

Socially speaking, is an individual denigrated, diminished by the metaphysical notion of *unhu*, according to which a person and community are one and the same? Who should be held responsible when an individual fails? Did Tambu fail due to some innate failing to meet prescribed standards, or is the society that privileges one group against another at fault? Is Tambu guilty of abandoning her homestead and seeking to enter the European world, a world which is not accepting of her kin, at least not at the time she was there?

Then again, what is the status of the individual person in the body politic of modern Zimbabwe? Clearly, a person seeks to distinguish himself or herself in what she or he does best, in order to claim the agency to affirm himself or herself as a human being in the community. Such a person feels the potential for originality is possible only in the society in communion with other citizens (Gyekye, 'Person and Community in African Thought', 2). From this point of view, Tambu fails, because she is ahead of her society that is not yet rid of racism. It would seem that her mother is right, for consistently she mocked her daughter's presumptuousness, borne out of innocence and inexperience. Tambu says after she quits her job: 'There was no longer a place for me with my relatives at the mission,' and continues, 'I could not go back to the homestead where Netsai hopped unspeakably on a single limb, and where Mai would laugh at me daily' (246). It is a despicable situation that crushes the individual and spells social injustices and inequities in the land, because yardsticks for measuring success and excellence are faulty. Although all individual members of the society are perceived as equal under the law, yet the majority do not abide by the foundational rule of loving your neighbor as yourself.

This study has sought to establish the Zimbabwean *unhu* philosophy as the panacea for the metaphysical and social ills of the modern nation. By following the trajectory of the heroine, Tambudzai Sigauke, I have explored the concept of personhood in the community, arriving at the conclusion that a person may be ontologically complete as a human being yet socially wanting, due to extraneous circumstances of discrimination, racism, oppression, etc., factors which rear their ugly heads when everyone in the community is not abiding by the lofty ethics of *unhu*, a principle of values, morals, and morality. Such notions as right and wrong, evil and good, and responsibility for one's actions take their relevance from this angle of vision.

A person's aptitudes, hard work, qualifications and talents are not enough to affirm his or her person, given its impossibility in a society full of persons of so many divergent aspirations and needs. All depends on the willingness and goodwill of the other persons to assist in the individual's quest for excellence or recognition.

Society remains important, nonetheless, for all human becoming, because the individual cannot exist gainfully outside the community. This point tends to diminish the importance and self-sufficiency of the individual person, because it places emphasis on the collective action as a group, interdependence and human solidarity. To circumvent this social ill, focus should be on providing a social structure that promotes self-fulfillment and realization of potentials, cravings, and aspirations for all individuals, essentially because, according to *unhu*, 'I am well if you are well also.' Put differently, the common good determines the good of each individual. Because individual success is intrinsically linked to a person's identity with the group, any failing on the part of the group to live up to the dictates of *unhu* spells disaster for the individual. Hence in a situation where the person, now an organic whole with the community, is ripped away, stripped of his or her place in the moral fabric of society, due to discrimination or other forms of oppression, the individual suffers isolation from the group, and the community stands condemned as an invalid social structure.

In the end, there is no antithesis between the person and the community. True, individual needs and desires to be met contribute to social conflicts, yet the notion of the common good requires one to be guided in working towards the common good. By extension, this implies assuming one's responsibility or agency to fight institutional ills and to reestablish the values of society embedded in *unhu*. One does not give up, but rather struggles to achieve, to compete with oppositional concepts, stances, and practices. In modern Zimbabwe, it is through this philosophical perspective on the nature of human society that the worldview of *unhu* would most assist social reintegration and regeneration. The *Book of Not* lives up to the injunction 'thou shalt not' stop the time, for the time is now, not later.

WORKS CITED

Dangarembga, Tsitsi. 'The Letter'. In: *Whispering Land: An Anthology of Short Stories by African Women*, published by SIDA, 1985.

—— *Everyone's Child*. Produced by Media for Development Trust, Zimbabwe, 1996.

—— *The Book of Not: a sequel to Nervous Conditions*. Oxfordshire: Ayebia Clarke Publishing, 2006.

Gyekye, Kwame. 'Person and Community in African Thought.'
http://www.home.concepts-ict.nl/~kimmerle/frameTest9.htm

—— 'Person and Community in African Thought.' Chapter V.
http://www.crvp.org/book/Series02/II-1/chapter_v.htm

Kerr, David I. *The African Novel and the Modernist Tradition*. New York: Peter Lang, 1997.

Koster, J.D. 'Managing the Transformation'. In *Citizen Participation in Local Government*. I Bekker. ed. Pretoria: J.L. van Schaik Publishers, 1996: 99–118.

Mandela, Nelson. *A Long Walk to Freedom: The Autobiography of Nelson Mandela*. New York: Little Brown and Company, 1994.

McWilliams, Sally. 'Tsitsi Dangarembga's *Nervous Conditions*.' *World Literature Today*, 31.1.1991.

Menkiti, Ifeanyi A. 'Person and Community in African Traditional Thought.' In: Richard A. Wright. Ed. *African Philosophy: An Introduction*. Maryland: Lanham Press, 1984.

Nussbaum, B. *African Culture and Ubuntu: Reflections of a South African in America*. World Business Academy 17, no. 1, 3003.

Parekh, Pushpa Naidu, and Siga Fatima Jagne. 'An Interview with Tsitsi Dangarembga.' In: *Postcolonial African Writers*, 1998. (Also in *Novel*, 26.3.1993).

Primorac, Ranka. 'Blood on the Sand: Yvonne Vera's *Butterfly Burning* and the Zimbabwean Tradition'. In: Nasta, Susheila. Ed. *Wasafiri: Africa 05*. No. 46, winter 2005: 11–16.

Sindave, J. and Lienberg, I. *Reconstruction and the Reciprocal Order: The Philosophy and Practice of Ubuntu and Democracy in African Society*. Politeia 19, no. 3, 2000: 31–46.

Tambulasi, Richard, and Happy Kayuni. 'Can African Feet Divorce Western Shoes? The Case of *Ubuntu* and Democratic Good Governance in Malawi.' *Nordic Journal of African Studies* 14 (2), 2005: 147–61.

Tutu, Desmond. *No Future without Forgiveness*. London: Rider Press, 1999.
Wikipedia. 'Ubuntu(ideology)'. http://en.wikipedia.org/wiki/Ubuntu
Willey, Ann Elizabeth, and Jeannette Treiber. *Emerging Perspectives on Tsitsi Dangarembga: Negotiating the Postcolonial*. Trenton, N. J.: Africa World Press, 2002.

'Coming to America':
Ike Oguine's *A Squatter's Tale*
& the Nigerian/African Immigrant's Narrative

Christopher Okonkwo

For many of the Nigerian immigrants of my generation that I knew, coming to America was not so positively transformative. Many of these immigrants were people with middle class backgrounds and sensibilities – lawyers, doctors, university teachers, or the children of these – who were forced to lead a working class and marginal existence upon arrival in America. Immigration was therefore for them, at least initially, a fall in status and the experience was to some extent embittering. And many of them carried, at least initially, [a] sense of injury.   – Ike Oguine, private interview

Beneath its satiric humour, intermittent narrative levity, and its delusively uncomplicated plot, Ike Oguine's novelistic debut *A Squatter's Tale* (2000) emerges as a serious, deftly conceived project that has only recently begun to elicit a welcome, rigorous critical inquiry.[1] The hitherto scarcity of scholarly attention to the work was rather unfortunate, given the currency of its ancillary thesis of globalization,[2] as well as our perennial, transcontinental and often charged conversations on the interlocked subjects of immigration, nation, nationality, religion, class, gender, identity, subjectivity, race and power. Most momentous, however, is that the novel does not just emphasize the important but largely under-fictionalized topic of a first-generation, postcolonial African immigrant's experience in the United States. It also evokes, concomitantly, the dynamics of power relations between centre(s) and border(s), between, as it were, grand 'master' narratives and (subversive) 'peripheral' stories/texts. In inscribing the issue of contemporary African immigration to the United States as its overarching agenda, and moreover in its relatively recent publication, *A Squatter's Tale* gains literary citizenship with twentieth-century American (immigrant) letters, its ethnic minority discourses and, most significantly, Africa's new novels.

The novel is the protagonist Obiora's (Obi's) first-person and self-reflexive narration of his experiences and later inner growth as an (African) immigrant in 1990s US and the watershed events in his home country that precipitated his adventurous translocation. In what follows, I hope to examine Oguine's mobilization of Obi's situation and tale as a periscope to contextualize and synthesize the peculiar exigencies of immigration. Oguine empathetically captures the complex of disorienting tensions that emanate as the (African) immigrant, in this instance the Nigerian,[3] dislocated from his familiar homeland and now straddling borders, attempts to negotiate personal, social, economic, cultural and psychological quandaries, to reject subalternity and ultimately assume a viable even if integrative subjectivity and identity in America. But then he must navigate those competing impulses and imperatives without compromising his sense of self, goals, priorities, home and family. With its authorial-cum-narrator's messages targeted toward multiple demographics, the novel also insinuates inseparably the inevitable and permanent interdependency of 'host' and 'guest', of America's mainstream structures and occupants of its fringes, in human, political, and narrative/textual terms. Near the story's end, Obi, a former banker and the novel's implied author (see 34, 197) reflects on his interesting first-year journeys in 'America' at which time he lived 'at the margins' (196), like his unmarried, fifty-year-old maternal uncle, Uncle Happiness, who 'for all the time he had spent in this country . . . had, in a sense, never arrived in America' (138). As Obi wills his life toward a new and more promising direction, he poignantly observes, 'although I would always be in a sense apart from it, always be more Nigerian than American, I also had to strive for a place inside it; I had to find a way to be both apart from and part of this vast country' (196).

A key assertion indicative of an introspective and maturing consciousness, indeed a young man really searching in his liminality for his place and identity in the host nation's schema, Obi's resolve above does more than echo Rina Benmayor and Andor Skotnes' insights. Both scholars have rightly commented on how 'contemporary global migration [disrupts] static conceptions of identity, challenging notions of cultural homogeneity, essentialism, and stereotype' (9). Obi's sentiments convey as well the ambivalences but equally the countervailing, ardent dreams of especially many 'Third World' immigrants in the United States. These are people whose pigmentations, human presence, polyglot sagas and accents have for decades permeated America's cities, enriched its lore and register, and helped disarticulate dominant white hold on the nation's destiny, identity, literature, and history – a case made most persuasively by the recent, monumental election of Barack Obama, the biracial child of a Kenyan immigrant father and a white American mother, as the nation's first African-American president.

Twentieth-century United States history brims with sociological studies and imaginative literature on America's new-arrivals. It is replete with the often arresting accounts of people who, crossing and narrowing by road, sea and air the world's geographical distances and socio-cultural separations, have come to America in search of a better life. As James M. Jasper states correctly, it is these newcomers who 'have sustained both the dream and the nightmare of American mythology. They were the ones who, able to compare the new land with the old, created an "American" identity at a time when the native-born were more likely to think of themselves as Virginians or Yankees rather than as Americans' (11).

Whereas the lives of the US's foreign-born and their descendants, most notably those from Europe, Asia, the Caribbean island-nations and South America, have been extensively studied, the equally engrossing odysseys of thousands of post-World War II African immigrants, called and lured *also* by liberty's Statue to America, have still to attract comparable devotion in published fiction, particularly. For reasons about which one could only speculate, African novelists generally seem to have overlooked, perhaps are uninterested in, or are inadequately equipped to treat knowledgeably and commercially successfully this current and fascinating aspect of African peoples' free-willed encounter with the 'New World'. Because this dearth simply has been too protracted and glaring to be critically ignored, the appearance of Ike Oguine's *A Squatter's Tale* in 2000 becomes all the more a significant literary moment especially for the huge Igbo citizenry in the United States and for African fiction in general. I see it as a publication and thematic event in light of, for instance, Africans' long history of forced migration to the Americas, the documented [pre-September 11, 2001] upsurge in African immigrant population in the United States, and the fact that Nigerians do not only far outnumber any other African immigrant group in the US today (Arthur 2), they also have contributed remarkably and positively to the nation's socio-cultural, intellectual, political and economic life.

To suggest, as part of this preliminary remark, that the African novel has yet to treat substantively and quantitatively the issue of recent African immigration to the United States is not to prescribe, imperially, to the novelists. Any such directive would be resisted and futile anyway because, as Chinua Achebe famously insists, 'no self-respecting writer will [and should] take dictation from his audience' ('Novelist' 42). To comment on that thematic lacuna is not to extrapolate that African authors, some of who are students, professionals, exiles, expatriates, legal residents and/or naturalized citizens in the Occident, have totally ignored the themes of (e)migration in their works. Sure, since its formal inception over half a century ago the modern African novel, along with the pedagogy, theories and criticism on it, has overwhelmingly and understandably emphasized the nuances of African peoples' lives *on* the African continent. And this is mainly because, as an Igbo proverb axiomatizes, '*Onye ulo ya na-agba oku, anagh achu oke*': A person whose house is burning does not neglect it to pursue escaping rodents. Even as we begin the twenty-first century, much of Africa remains at crossroads. It makes perfect sense therefore that the fiction writers should prioritize the continent's internal struggles and triumphs. This explains Achebe's remark in *Home and Exile* that, notwithstanding his long residency in the US, he would not write a novel on America because, he reasons, 'America has enough novelists writing about her, and Nigeria too few' (96–7). That's a fact.

Achebe may, in fact, not want to write about the United States. But he and several other African diaspora intelligentsia appreciate fully the impact that migration has had on Africa's history, on Africans spatially uprooted, dispersed, and consequently de-eased from their physical, cultural, and spiritual homelands.

Oguine pays attention to the novel's architectonics and also sustains our interest through his brilliant characterization of the story's witty hero. The story proper is set in Nigeria and the United States, in Lagos and Oakland, California, specifically, and at the time of Governor Pete Wilson's infamous Proposition 187. Oguine strategizes this split setting, Obi's shifting physical residencies, his emotional and monologic migrations between Oakland and Lagos. As the story maps its hero's fortunes, it also through his spacial and narratological driftages subjectifies the other African and Asian immigrants, some of whom Oguine 'deliberately typecast to reflect a cross section of varied responses to the experience of immigration' (private interview).

As Obi responds to his immigrant ordeals, Oguine enjoins us to reflect on some of the work's integral, major questions. For instance, who are some of these fictive Nigerians emigrating to the United States in the 1990s and what push factors instigate their westward departures? How do they upon arrival see *that* America they 'saw' and heard so much about at home, (thanks partly to the global reaches and power of television, magazines, and Hollywood films) is different from American reality? How do they react to America's often interpenetrating politics of race, ethnicity, nationality, religion, class and gender? What does it mean, in the text, to be an unmarried and recent Nigerian female immigrant? And very important, is there a cost associated in the homeland with failure in America? In short, what does 'coming to America', to invoke Eddie Murphy's blockbuster comedy of the same title, mean to Obi and his fellow sojourners? Oguine filters the above and other questions through Obi's experiences and narrative consciousness, the latter witty, ironically detached, cynical, critical, polemical, sometimes sardonic, chauvinistic, openly disaffected but resolute.

The narrative opens with a scintillating teaser, a funny scenario that situates the story's umbrella paradox. Narrative flashback to eighteen years ago, when Obi was ten, introduces us to Uncle Happiness. Named fittingly, the ebullient Uncle Happiness visits Nigeria from 'America', his first such return in eighteen years. Like an impressed and impressionable traveller returning home from God's Own Country, he brings Christmas gifts, primed with hyperbolic fantasies of America's majesty and affluence. Uncle Happiness utopializes America as, among other things, an Eden with mini-town malls, thirty-lane highways, and distaste for old cars (5). In America, Uncle Happiness guarantees, not only do people throw away food but also from New York's Empire State Building 'you could see what is going on in the moon . . . [and in] Canada and Mexico' (5). Uncle Happiness insists that his nephew, whom he calls 'Obi the Giant! Only a tiny ant yesterday!' (6), must come to America. Obi must come and he, Uncle Happiness, would make a way for him. But no sooner does Obi land in America eighteen years later than his disillusioning introduction to paradise begins. Obi realizes immediately that he hardly has a permanent residence in Oakland. Spatially and emotionally in-between as is an agonist ogbanje-abiku, he squats from place to place, as Uncle Happiness and his (Obi's) friends from home, Kurubo the Hook and Ego, all disappoint him. Even worse, Uncle Happiness contributes in quite stunning ways to Obi's nightmarish initiation when he defrauds him (26–28). Quickly for Obi, Edenic 'America', signified in Oakland, emerges as a thorny garden, not exactly the 'El Dorado [or] Gold Mountain' of immigrant imagination (Muller 2).

That Obi as an aggressive and imaginative newcomer to America undergoes his share of the thorny realities of immigration is clear. One soon starts to wonder, however, why early on he appears overly irritable, confrontational, embittered, strident and smug. Should he not, as a now-rootless 'third world' African 'native', genuflect for living in 'First World' America where he enjoys many civil liberties, metropolitan infrastructure, and other socio-economic conveniences unavailable to him uniformly and also inequitably distributed among his country's ethnic groups, back home? Why does he swagger and, upon that, exude a sense of hurt, knowing that having overstayed his visa he now resides in America 'illegally'? Why sneer at humility, considering that he is from the (in)famous 1990s 'Nigeria' , a nation from which, as he himself concedes and as Adichie's 'The American Embassy' depicts so powerfully, many in his generation were trying to escape by all plots conceivable?

The novel attributes Obi's initial disaffection and his emigration to Nigeria's 1990s socio-economic and political eruptions. Gilbert H. Muller has noted that 'As postcolonial societies experience political disruptions that send millions of exiles on journeys to America from the nearest and farthest shores of the Third World – the Caribbean, Asia, the Middle East, Africa – the fiction depicting this global turbulence reflects the multicultural diversity characterizing postmodern literature, with novelists and short story writers viewing immigration through the filter of race and ethnicity' (14). Oguine sifts the immigrant's discontents through the critical introspections of a dislodged Igbo-Nigerian in the US. He suggests that if Obi is displeased, haughty and disdainful of nearly everything and everybody it is in part because he is literally both a product and victim of Nigeria's 1990s nadirs.

Obi appears sour, unfulfilled and unappreciative of the reasons of his ostensible personal and social losses. As the narrative affirms the 1990s Nigerian generation to which he belongs lost serious existential time, economic ground, and social lustre upon leaving home and emigrating in droves to European countries and even South Africa, with the hope of securing transit visas from there to the destination extraordinaire: America. Many of Obi's frustrated peers, at great personal and financial expense, strategized their ways into the US, where they must at best start over. Obi recalls also his father's unsavory experience with insidious ministerial power and his family's subsequent economic adversity – a situation that underscores the precariousness of Nigeria's middle-class. Obi rants about Nigeria's widespread 'putrefaction', desperation and greed (104), echoing the Ghanaian society of Ayi Kwei Armah's *The Beautyful Ones Are Not Born*. In addition, the veritable historical moment Obi recounts as the 'latest military government's pseudo-market economic policies' (67) encouraged in 1990s Nigeria the formation of many teething banks and some dubious private investment companies whose crash affected many unwary citizen-investors, depicted in the character, Chief Sawa. Prior to his emigration, Obi, enabled mainly by Sawa's huge investment, had risen to a lucrative executive position with Baobab Trust Finance House (BTF), a fictional model of such upstart but folded financial investment establishments in Lagos. In America he and his fellow Nigerian sojourners must begin a new life, as they endure the expectations and indignities of survival overseas.

John A. Arthur has noted that to survive in America new arrivals must 'learn the expectations of American culture if they are to survive and adapt to life in their new country' (30). He adds, however, that African immigrants' efforts to do that are stymied by 'discriminatory practices designed to exclude them from mainstream society' (70-73). Extending that finding, Flore Zephir posits in her study, *Haitian Immigrants in Black America*, that unlike White Americans of European descent who because of their colour can de-emphasize their ethnicity and assimilate fluidly in the dominant White community, non-Whites and blacks especially cannot do so because '[t]heir imposed racial identity . . . in many ways [over]determine[s] their residential, employment, and class locations' (19). They cannot, as 'Others' marked by pigment, culture and inflection, quite melt in(to) that mythical Americanization salad-bowl. 'Being a "migrant"', Benmayor and Skotnes contend, 'is often the dominant culture's negative strike against foreigners' (8).

The above statements, particularly the problem of 'branding', marginalization and exclusion, bespeak strikingly the individual as well as the collective socio-cultural and economic difficulties facing Oguine's foreigners (52–8). Take, for example, Ego's experience with the colour line. 'Marked' by her foreignness, Ego, a Nigerian woman, is alienated, ridiculed and effaced in the predominantly white community where she lives with her husband, Doctor Ezendu. An Asian girl Obi meets in Cody's Bookstore in Berkeley rebuffs his seduction overtures because of his Nigerian/'African' accent (46–7). It then occurs to Obi that 'the often hilarious efforts of some of my fellow immigrant countrymen and women to sound American had nothing to do with affectation; it was a matter of survival – to many American ears,' he adds, 'a foreign accent was off-putting, like a bad smell' (47).

As the African immigrant who 'still has an accent' knows empirically, the issue of our purported 'exotic' native cadences can sometimes do more than bedevil or ruin dating chances. And it does not matter many native-born's gendered and sometimes patronizing fetishization of African tonality or, even, the African immigrant's suave, interracial marriage, advanced education, academic or professional profile, proficiencies in English language, and eventual citizenship and acquisition of an American passport. In a society that venerates and models Western ontology, where it shocks, saddens and even angers some native-born to be told that they, too, like 'the rest of us' – to echo part of Chinweizu's book title – do indeed 'have an accent' or various American regional timbres sometimes tasking to unaccustomed foreign ears, having an 'African' intonation could be a serious impediment. A 'crippl[ing] leg', as Obi calls it (48), it could, like the glass ceiling, hinder one's educational, professional, cultural, political and/or economic advancement. Little wonder, then, Mr. Cassidy's unsuccessful mimesis of what Obi sees as the 'rhythm of African American English' (27). Worse still, mostly menial jobs are available to many new Nigerian/African immigrants, their college education notwithstanding. Maina, the Kenyan, thinks and dreams big, but has achieved little. And through the Chinese immigrant Fung's multiple and recurrent troubles, Oguine emphasizes Fung's humanity and also challenges mainstream America's stereotyping conflation and affirmation of Asians as business and computer geniuses, indeed the nation's model ethnic minority – not those 'African laggards' (60). Obi shows that as America's 'other' non-Caucasian immigrants, Asians, *too*, are dispossessed and by no means totally inoculated against those societal markings, occlusions, denials, slights, and hostilities couched in Arthur and Zephir's elucidations earlier.

Obi's and the other characters' collective experiences therefore translate migration as cause of economic, familial, cultural and psychological straits. Migration destabilizes relationships, particularly when families and/or friends are geo-physically separated and their communication becomes as brief, infrequent, inconsistent and expensive as are the immigrant's occasional, logistics-heavy, and temporary visits to the homeland. During such separations, it could also test spousal marital and sexual fidelity. In the novel, Obi's Lagos girlfriend Robo, who in his absence from Nigeria functions briefly as a surrogate narrator reporting on the homeland part of the story, can no longer bear his absence. She breaks up their fourteen-year-old friendship (by mail), marries another man, and leaves Obi devastated. While Robo's engrafted letter and Obi's subsequent desolation enable Oguine to historicize the relationship, they highlight more pointedly the human bond severely jeopardized by the often pathetic contingencies of immigration. And as evident in the recent, truly chilling but previously sparse reports of a spike in fatal marital violence, specifically of Nigerian men killing their Nigerian wives in the US, the pressures exerted on immigrants/immigrant couples could be tremendous, costly, and permanently scarring. Migration muddles memories, desires, and cultural affiliation. It inflicts a Nyasha-impasse as when, reminiscent of Nyasha's debilitating identity dilemma in Tsitsi Dangaremgba's *Nervous Conditions*, the American-born and -educated teenage child of Igbo parents resident in the US struggles, most times unsuccessfully, to arbitrate his/her performances of parental and Igbo cultural expectations *and* his/her constellar subjectivity as an English-speaking-Igbo-Nigerian-African-American.

At various narrative moments Obi succeeds in exciting pathos for his predicament as one of the casualties of Nigeria's 1990s crisis points. Oguine implies that as we commiserate, however, we must not fail to query Obi's indiscretions, chauvinism, cynicism and rage. Obi's own revelations clearly implicate him and Phillip, his BTF boss, as some of the scriptwriters and actors in the nation's 1990s theater of pain and nihilism presented in the novel. Aggravated by Nigeria's political instability and the military dictatorships' fiscal policies at the time, the pervasive ethical devolution accelerated the nation's nightmarish decade. Those conditions, Obi indicates, spiraled to the swift exodus of many Nigerians to western nations.

Further, if for Oguine 'Obi represents the moral corruption of my generation' (private interview), then Oguine firmly roots genuine nation-building in sites other than leadership, politics, and economy. He pragmatically (re)situates it in self-restraint, in individual citizens' as well as every epoch's routine exercise of collective civic and just responsibilities. In other words, for Oguine, material acquisitiveness, hedonism, angst, and misapplied genius 'failed' Nigeria as Nigeria's unspeakable 1990s autocracies in turn betrayed and thwarted the country's human and intellectual capital. Oguine implies that this mutual complicity and culpability must not be expunged from the nation's and this generation's metanarratives. We must not dissemble it, even as Obi's peers, understandably desperate but without staying back to help restore their nation to health, abandon ship and head for safety in paradise's 'greener' pastures and subterfuge. We recall here Mongo Beti's scathing satire *The Poor Christ of Bomba* and that unforgettable scenario of the French colonial missionary Father Drumont – 'Jesus Christ' himself (3) – hurriedly deserting his flock and the child-narrator Denis without waiting to rectify the stunning syphilis infestation that he helped originate among the Tala brides in the sixa' (167–206). In and from their distant, 'safe', but interstitial spaces in Drumont's ex-imperial Europe and, in this case, neo-imperialistic US, some of Obi's fellow (post)colonials not only denounce the West but also, oddly, disavow their motherland in that tone of grievance that Obi evinces.

In his polyfunction in the story, Obi as a decentered and thus 'mobile' first-person narrator also takes us into the domestic and public spaces of some of his fellow Nigerians in America. His movements among them debunk the myth of immigrant monolithicism as the author also exposes immigrant contradictions and prejudice. Of interest are two Nigerians: Andrew, the non-reactionary born-again Christian and 'property of the church' under white pastor Tim (38–9) and Ezendu, the medical doctor. Politically ambitious, class-obsessed, and aligned with the Republican Party's conservatism (134), Ezendu endorses Governor Pete Wilson's Proposition 187. He attacks illegal immigration and professes ultimate faith in America's capacity to toughen weaklings and make them men. Quite interesting also, Andrew (29-30) and Ezendu (126–7) demean African Americans, exemplifying, as it were, Obi's haunting observation that 'The African immigrant sometimes exhibits as much bitterness towards his African-American cousins as do the worst white racists' (29-30). We must not miss the irony, however, that Andrew chooses a 'back seat' in the predominantly white church he attends (38–9) and Ezendu himself complains of being the victim of racism and prejudice. Ezendu's experience buttresses what African Americans especially have known all along, namely, that in the United States black people's attainment of higher education and middle-class status does not insulate them from racial bigotry.

Ensuing from two black/African men, Andrew's and more so Ezendu's racial and class sentiments enact, on the one hand, part of that black middle-class bourgeois attitude that E. Franklin Frazier lambasts in *The Black Bourgeoisie*. They evoke, on the other hand, the hypocrisies of some African Diaspora immigrants to America. Although they are in ways beneficiaries of the African American liberation struggle and cultural experience, some of the newcomers sometimes seek, as John A. Arthur posits, to accentuate their foreignness [and nationalities] because of the derogatory associations of the identity 'black' in America (4). Arthur adds that 'The cultural barriers and the social and economic differences sepa-rating the Africans and the African-Americans [are] sometimes the cause of simmering hostility and misunderstanding between them. Sharing a common physical characteristic of skin colour [as Obi does with the African-American character Mahamood (60–1)] has not ensured cultural and economic unity between African immigrants and American-born blacks' (77–8). But in under-treating that issue of race and intra-racial discord, Oguine misses an opportunity to complicate that dimension of African and African-American relationship in the United States. Nevertheless, Obi's recognition and appreciation of black American women's diversity and beauty, as well as African-American cultural pro-duction, technically invalidate the imports of Andrew's and Ezendu's

attitudes toward black Americans. Obi's racial and gendered consciousness is extended also in his meeting and later relationship with Vivian,
another of the novel's Igbo immigrants.

Vivian's meeting with Obi reveals further his chauvinism, insecurities,
selfishness and maturing consciousness, but more important, it continues
Oguine's exposure of the experiences of the novel's other Nigerian immigrants. Through that meeting, Oguine introspects on the plight and perse-
verance of the young, unmarried Nigerian woman immigrant in the
United States. Smart, beautiful, ambitious, hardworking, compassionate,
lonely, emotionally vulnerable but strong, Vivian must mediate her
personal and career goals *and* the many financial needs of family
members at home. Vivian's statement to Obi that 'I am depressed sometimes and miss home but I'm also very happy to live in America' (160)
articulates the tightrope many foreign-born face. Their appreciation of
new and greater economic opportunities is often dampened by the psy-
chosocial impact of familial and cultural separation.

Vivian's slow presence in Obi's life is, however, mutually regenerative
for both of them. Positioned in the text professionally and symbolically as
a 'nurse', she would help him control some of the pressures of immigration. Similarly, his sympathy and audience help her voice and claim her
story of trauma and gender oppression in Nigeria. Further, their socializa-
tion and later intimacy help recharge her latent sensuality and sexuality.
In Obi's concession that 'There's nothing in this world as wonderful as a
kind-hearted woman' (198) – such as Vivian who implicitly forgives his
cruelty and insults as he 'acted out the tragedy of [his] heartbreak' by
Robo (192) – Oguine unmasks Obi's bravado and alludes to his growing
wisdom. Oguine suggests, nevertheless, that a healthy male-female
friendship or companionship could help ease the psychic and emotional
tightness the (Nigerian) immigrant experiences because of his or her
strenuous drive to succeed in America for both oneself and loved ones at
home.

America's constraints notwithstanding, the immigrant believes that
the nation generally rewards industry. Along with knowledge of the huge
cost at home for one who 'fails' abroad, this belief serves as a powerful
check against lethargy and contentment. Thus, the immigrant works
triple-hard. However, Oguine mistrusts the sometimes narrow definitions of 'achievement' that motivate some immigrants' absorbing quests
for 'success'. He recognizes, nonetheless, that the purposeful Nigerian
immigrant in America cannot afford to 'fail' without replicating Uncle
Happiness's or the persona Nebraska Man's fates. A racially/ethnically
indeterminate figure who 'fails' in America but returns to Nigeria where
he waxes and remixes dubious epics of his feats in America, Nebraska
Man embodies putatively for Lagosians of Obi's generation the cautionary pitfalls, pain, and stigma of an unsuccessful pilgrimage, especially to
America (194–6). He is an aborted personal performance, a signifier also

of the 1990s generation's pastiche formation, its (dis)continuities, and arrested growth. As a metaphor, Nebraska Man raises the question: How does one confess to family and friends at home, in a society that measures 'success' largely materially, that one had the fortune of going to 'America' but returned home 'empty-handed'? How *does* one begin such a narrative?

Obi hands us both Nebraska Man's and Uncle Happiness' missteps and misfortunes, especially, as sites of instruction and also ponders the reasons some immigrants struggle perennially and/or fail to 'make it'. Obi estimates that some who fail are perhaps groping for a sense of meaningful direction; they may lack the calibre of educational, professional, and social competencies required by host society, its economy, and the times; or they are involved in regressive activities. But if, Oguine implies, Obi grew up in and survived 'Lagos', Nigeria – with its not incomparable urbanity, modernity, racial, ethnic, religious, linguistic and cultural plurality, its cosmopolitanism, intensity, chaos, infamy, prejudices, hostilities, creativities and potential – he should with time make it in Oakland and elsewhere in America. To forge ahead and avoid Nebraska Man's or Uncle Happiness' failings, Obi knows he must confront his melancholia, moderate his cynicism, and find a way to mediate productively his inevitable global citizenship, indeed his hyphenated experiences as an 'Igbo-Nigerian-African-American'. For him, it starts with finding both Vivian and his uncle.

In reconnecting with Vivian and Uncle Happiness, Obi apprehends more the significance of family. In his union with Vivian, Obi sees reason for hope and renewal, culminated in his reconciliation with his Uncle Happiness at the story's denouement. In its overtones of penitence and celebration, the novel's end is not quite 'an end', but rather a milestone. It is the point of (new) beginning, particularly for Obi – in his crisscrossing subject-locations as a human being: son, nephew, self, protagonist, an Igbo man, Nigerian, African immigrant, postcolonial subject, cultural hybrid, friend, lover, and storyteller/novelist. In its cyclical structure – the story begins and rounds off with a harmonious 'family reunion' *and* Uncle Happiness' musical 'performances' – the plot in its mobility 'travels' or 'migrates' back. It journeys back, but towards a calming fatalism (199), towards freshness, hope, wholeness, home and, most important, family.

Beginning and 'closing' the story with hilarious musical moments which could be said to frame, integrate, 'encircle', 'embrace' and hence 'soothe' those vexations of immigration Obi shares 'inside' the novel, Oguine alludes to the therapeutic power of music and laughter. He intimates their inherent capacity to 'check', 'contain' and hence alleviate life's 'internal' stresses. In our intense quest to achieve, we must find time to laugh at ourselves and the world (196), and also see the universe around us:

> America was all around me [Obi says], immense, indifferent, frightening, but
> also incredibly varied, challenging and . . . still full of opportunities. Though
> inside it, I had remained at the margins – for the previous year I really hadn't
> been living in America but in a sort of halfway country, a sort of satellite life
> outside the life that went on, tenuously linked to the American way of life by
> work and common currency, shops and television. Now, though I would always
> be in a sense apart from it, always be more Nigerian than American, I also had to
> strive for a place inside it; I had to find a way to be both apart from and part of
> this vast country. (196)

Perceptible in the above resolve, however, is the unvoiced reality that
Obi is yet another (Nigerian/African) immigrant unconsciously readying
himself for the possibility of protracted, voluntary exile – in America.

But as we prepare to depart Obi's narrative stage and bid him farewell
and God speed in America, we must pause for one last revelation that
seems to be the novel's subscripted 'epilogue'. It is my considered view
that, all along, *A Squatter's Tale* has also been dramatizing cleverly the
unsettled power positioning and (inter)play between host nation and
immigrant, center and border, self and other, and between 'master'-narra-
tives and (marginal)ized counter-hegemonic discourses or 'texts'. In this
dynamic, as it were, the novel inverts real power, investing it in the
perimeter.

Oguine stages that power interplay formally, in the novel's construction
and textuality, more specifically in the allegory of Obi's narratological
positioning relative to the other immigrants. To immigrants generally,
America is 'host' nation and its soil, its land, the living 'space'. In a similar
vein, Obi's narrative *and* the material pages on which it is inscribed
together function as 'host/master text or country' for not only the *other*
'foreigners' (Uncle Happiness, Andrew, Ego, Ezendu, Maina, Fung, and
Vivian) but also their migration experiences, stories and implicitly 'texts'.
A Squatter's Tale doubles then as 'narrative/text' *and* 'nation'. In placing
these 'other' characters' experiences as 'sub' plots in the whole tale, in
locating them as 'peripheral' narratives/'texts' in the mainstream of Obi's
metaphoric 'master' or centring narrative, Oguine intimates the 'ancillary'
situatedness of those 'other' texts and their owners' marginality. We notice
that, as the novel's 'legitimate', 'legitimized' and thus 'authorized' voice,
its *first*-person narrator, Obi as 'mainstream' voice 'speaks for' *and* 'about'
the other characters at various discursive moments. Just as a 'warehouse'
job (48) enables the immigrants to earn a meager salary while it simultaneously 'stores', delimits, controls and frustrates their potentials, Obi's larger
and self-authored master-story dually 'contains' the stories of 'his fellow'
immigrants. In other words, it subsumes and circumscribes even as it also
occasionally allows the other characters room to 'act', 'recall' and 'talk' in
their own 'voices', as opposed to narratological 'reported' speech and
action. As implied author, owner, and hence controller of *A Squatter's Tale*
and its main/ central story, Obi, the titular squatter, determines not only
when and where but also how much narrative and discursive time and

space the other characters' experiences are granted within the/his master-text's external, territorial boundaries (that is, the perimeter of the novel's material/physical pages) as well as within its internal borders (or the novel's chapters and episodes).

We cannot, however, ignore one important point relative to the fore-going power play. Just as mainstream America's master-tales are incom-plete without the accompanying, complicating, indispensable and resistive dramas of the nation's border-line 'other' subjects, Obi's own centre-stream account, his 'master' narrativization and historicization of self, in short his novel as (host) nation, would be severely lacking without 'the other' characters' stories. His account/novel would be short, literally and otherwise. It would lack full identity, context, authorial credibility, social relevance, character diversity, and thematic strength. And most important, it would not be as interesting without the energies and intrigues contributed by such contrastive figures as the conflicted Dr Ezendu, 'Mr. Cassidy – who help[s] people', Kurubo the Hook, Maina the disgruntled dreamer and womanizer, Vivian and, of course, Uncle Happiness. These 'peripheral' characters in part constitute elementally the indivisible events of the novel's thematic and narrative possibility, a major fact Oguine underscores by granting Uncle Happiness formidable presence and agency at the narrative's beginning and end. The fact that most, if not all, of the other immigrants were *already* in America years before Obi's recent arrival is also quite significant. It is undeniable that some of them initially help show him the way and also twist it, introducing him to the collective sights, sounds, and spaces of 'America'. Evidently, then, as Gilbert H. Muller points out, 'the margin modifies the main-stream' (3), or is in fact indispensable to its existence, both literally and literarily.

In *A Squatter's Tale*, Oguine has written a thoughtful, postmodernist novel, one self-referentially conscious of its own existence, context, creation and audiences. As the novel, through author and narrator, speaks more directly to the (African) immigrant population and experience in America, it also addresses other constituencies. It engages postcolonial Africa, Nigeria's 1990s leadership and generation, structures of power in mainstream United States and their intricate relationship to those on the edges, whether human or text. Obi's story unravels ultimately as an African character's growth into greater knowledge of self, others, and the world. In this respect, *A Squatter's Tale* becomes arguably an immigrant bildungsroman, joining those black 'coming of age' narratives Geta LeSeur chronicles in *Ten is the Age of Darkness*. Now joined by the more recent voices of Chris Abani, Chimamanda Ngozi Adichie, and Sefi Atta, Oguine invites us to commemorate the experiences of those Igbo, Nigerians, and Africans whose coming-to-America stories are truly worthy of complex fictional representation. Oguine's novel not only grants permanent (narrative) residency to but also legitimizes the humanity, stories and cases of those who, while negotiating the complexity of their new nationalities, ethnicities, and subjectivities in the embattled cleavages between the US's margins and its centres, help make possible the nation's 'First World' image-claims and also render less insular its constructions and performances of history, identity and power.

NOTES

1   See, for instance, these recent essays: Kwadwo Osei-Nyame 'Toward the Decolonization of African Postcolonial Theory: The Example of Kwame Appiah's *In My Father's House* vis-à-vis Ama Ata Aidoo's *Our Sister Killjoy*, Helon Habila's *Waiting for an Angel*, and Ike Oguine's *A Squatter's Tale*' (2008); Obi Nwakanma, 'Metonymic Eruptions: Igbo Novelists, the Narrative of the Nation, and New Developments in the Contemporary Nigerian Novel' (2008), and Nana Wilson-Tagoe, 'Re-thinking Nation and Narrative in a Global Era: Recent African Writing' (2005).
2   Nana Wilson-Tagoe (2005) discusses *A Squatter's Tale* in the context of globalization.
3   Of interest in recent imaginative adaptation of Nigerian nationals' emigration to both Europe and the US is the Nigerian home movie industry Nollywood's exploration of the theme in various films.

WORKS CITED

Achebe, Chinua. *Things Fall Apart* (1958) New York: Anchor Books, 1994.
—— 'The Novelist as Teacher'. *Hopes and Impediments: Selected Essays*. New York: Doubleday, 1989.
—— *Home and Exile*. Oxford: Oxford University Press, 2000.
Adichie, Chimamanda Ngozi. *Purple Hibiscus*. Chapel Hill: Algonquin Books, 2003.
—— 'New Husband'. *The Iowa Review* 33. 1 (Spring 2003): 53–66.
—— 'The American Embassy'. *Prism International* (Spring 2002): 22–29.
—— 'You in America'. (2001) *Discovering Home: A selection of writings from the 2002 Caine Prize for African Writing* (Bellevue: Jacana, 2003): 27–34.
Aidoo, Ama Ata, *The Dilemma of a Ghost*. London: Longman, 1965.
Armah, Ayi Kwei. *The Beautyful Ones Are Not Yet Born* (1969). Florence: Heinemann, 1988.
Arthur, John A. *Invisible Sojourners: African Immigrant Diaspora in the United States*. Westport: Praeger, 2000.
Atta, Sefi. *Everything Good Will Come*. Northampton, M.A: Interlink, 2005.
Benmayor, Rina and Andor Skotnes, 'Some Reflections on Migration and Identity'. In Benmayor and Skotnes, eds. *International Yearbook of Oral History and Life Stories Vol, III: Migration and Identity*. Oxford: Oxford University Press, 1994: 1–18.
Bugul, Ken. *The Abandoned Baobab: The Autobiography of a Senegalese Woman*. Chicago: Lawrence Hill Books, 1991.
Chinweizu. *The West and the rest of us: white predators, Black slavers, and the African elite*. New York: Random House, 1975.
Dangaremgba, Tsitsi. *Nervous Conditions*. Seattle: Seal Press, 1988.
Frazier, E. Franklin. *Black Bourgeoisie: The Rise of a New Middle Class in the United States*. New York: Collier Books, 1962.
Jasper, James M. *Restless Nation: Starting Over in America*. Chicago: The University of Chicago Press, 2000.
Kotun, Debo. *Àbíkú*. Pasadena: Nepotist Books, 1998.

Kramer, Judith R. *The American Minority Community*. New York: Thomas Y. Crowell Company, 1970.

LeSeur, Geta. *Ten is the Age of Darkness: The Black Bildungsroman*. Columbia: The University of Missouri Press, 1995.

Mathabane, Mark. *Kaffir Boy in America: An Encounter with Apartheid*. New York: Charles Scribner's Sons, 1989.

Mortimer, Mildred. *Journeys Through the French African Novel*. Portsmouth: Heinemann, 1990.

Muller, Gilbert H. *New Strangers in Paradise: The Immigrant Experience and Contemporary American Fiction*. Kentucky: The University of Kentucky Press, 1999.

Nwakanma, Obi. 'Metonymic Eruptions: Igbo Novelists, the Narrative of the Nation, and New Developments in the Contemporary Nigerian Novel'. *Research in African Literatures* 39. 2 (Summer 2008): 1-14.

Nwokogba, Isaac. *America Here I Come: A Spiritual Journey*. Ist Book Library, 2001.

Oguine, Ike. *A Squatter's Tale*. Oxford: Heinemann, 2000.

—— Personal (email) interview. (May 28, 2002).

Onyeama, Dillibe. *John Bull's Nigger*. London: Freisin Press. 1974.

Osei-Nyame, Kwadwo. 'Toward the Decolonization of African Postcolonial Theory: The Example of Kwame Appiah's *In My Father's House* vis-à-vis Ama Ata Aidoo's *Our Sister Killjoy*, Helon Habila *Waiting for an Angel*, and Ike Oguine's *A Squatter's Tale*'. *Matatu: A Journal for African Culture and Society* 36 (2008): 71–92.

Soyinka, Wole. 'Telephone Conversation'. Gerald Moore and Ulli Beier, eds. *Modern Poetry from Africa*. Baltimore: Penguin Books, 1966.

Stoller, Paul. *Jaguar: A Story of Africans in America*. Chicago: The University of Chicago Press, 1999.

Ugwu-Oju, Dympna. *What Will My Mother Say?: A Tribal African Girl Comes of Age in America*. Chicago: Bonus Books, 1995.

Wamba, Philippe. *Kinship: A Family's Journey in Africa and America*. New York: Dutton, 1999.

Wilson-Tagoe, Nana. 'Re-thinking Nation and Narrative in a Global Era: Recent African Writing'. *African Literature Today* 25. New Directions in African Literature (2005): 94–108.

Zephir, Flore. *Haitian Immigrants in Black America: A Sociological and Sociolinguistic Portrait*. Westport: Connecticut, 1996.

Charles E. Nnolim

> A voice in Rama was heard. Lamentation and great
> mourning; Rachael bewailing her children and
> would not be comforted, because they are not.
> (Matthew 2:18, Douay)

I suggested in an earlier publication that African literature in the twentieth century was not happy. It was lachrymal: it was a literature of lamentation.[2] I suggest further in this study that Chimamanda Adichie's *Half of a Yellow Sun* is a carry-over from the twentieth century. *Half of a Yellow Sun* is a weeping novel, a novel about what happened to the Igbo of Nigeria at a certain point in their history. The world created by Adichie is one of betrayal, death, conflict and loss. The Igbo were victims, also, of the residual shenanigans and schemings of British imperial policy in Nigeria.

It is a historical novel, going by its four major divisions. The historical novel broadly reconstructs a series of historical events and the spirit of a past age. In these historical events personages and characters are introduced who participate in actual historical events and move among actual personages from history. The fictional characters interacting with actual historical personages, through their actions give expression to the impact which the historical events have upon people living through them, with the result that a picture of a bygone age is created in personal and immediate terms.

The responsibility of the historical novelist is to give a truthful picture of the age he or she describes and to establish a historical context. This is the kind of picture well-known historical novelists like Sir Walter Scott created in *Ivanhoe,* Charles Dickens in *A Tale of Two Cities* and Leo Tolstoy in *War and Peace.* In Africa we have Thomas Mofolo's *Shaka,* Peter Abrahams' *Wild Conquest,* and Sol T. Plaatje's *Mhudi* although Mofolo's *Shaka* and Plaatje's *Mhudi* were first written in the vernacular and later translated into English. The classic historical novels like Scott's *Waverley* (which recreates the Jacobite rebellion of 1745), Leo Tolstoy's

War and Peace (which recounts Napoleon's invasion of Russia in 1812) and Peter Abrahams' *Wild Conquest* (which recreates the famous *Great Trek* undertaken by the Boers of Cape Colony, South Africa (1835–1838) – these bear similar affinities to Adichie's *Half of a Yellow Sun,* which recreates the Nigeria–Biafra conflict (1967–1970). The Boers undertook the Great Trek to preserve their own identity and chosen way of life just as the Igbo declared their own independence to protect themselves from the wanton massacres of the Igbo in the North and harassment in other parts of Nigeria. The antecedents to these massacres will not be pursued in this study, since most of us are still living witnesses to the events that preceded the massacres. In the long run, *Half of a Yellow Sun* is a historical novel. After all, it is a novel about the Nigerian civil war with the attendant horrors of massacres, mass starvation and battle-field vicissitudes.

A good work of art must not only invite comments and criticism: it must compel both. Adichie's *Half of a Yellow Sun* compels criticism. The world she creates is one of robust life-style, robust sexuality, and robust human relationships often frustrated by historical forces far larger than individuals could cope with. Educated Igbo men and women who had planned a life of middle-class leisure and comfort, had their lives shattered by the Nzeogwu coup (1966) and its terrible aftermath of dislocations, deprivations, and war.

The idyllic environment created by the University of Nigeria at Nsukka gathered intellectuals around a tranquil world of parties, tennis, cocktails, and booze. And it is with families enjoying themselves that Chimamanda Adichie started, before the scattering and the picking up of what was left of their lives. It is said that after a war, it is no longer who was *right* but who was *left.*

Adichie began this novel by leaving behind us the preoccupation of African women writers in the twentieth century: Feminism. The women she creates were no longer there to carry foo-foo and soup to men discussing 'Important Matters'. They had been empowered by education so that at Odenigbo's parties, they held their own among world-class intellectuals, like Odenigbo, Dr. Patel, Professor Ezeka, and Professor Lehman. The two central female characters, Olanna and Kainene had been educated abroad and Lara Adebayo was no push-over. The women we encountered shared complete equality with their male counterparts.

Olanna's live-in relationship with Odenigbo was ideal, to the end, and Kainene's live-in white lover, Richard Churchill was dominated by Kainene. In fact, he was always tagged on to her and was unsure of himself. At first, for Olanna, marriage was out of the question even though Odenigbo proposed several times. She later caved in because of the fragility and uncertainties of the war situation. It was Richard who began to address himself as the fiancé, sometimes, as the husband of Kainene, although it seems Kainene would, even to the end when she went missing, have none of it. No woman in *Half of a Yellow Sun* even suffered from the disabilities that invited the unwelcome sobriquets that smelt like a bad odour around twentieth-century feminists: castration complex or penis envy. We are in a new world of completely emancipated women even if Edna Whaler and Alice Njokanma suffered at the hands of unfeeling men. The narrative voice had told the reader that she (Olanna) once told him (Odenigbo):

> That she did not have that fabled female longing to give birth, and her mother had called her *abnormal* until Kainene said she didn't have it either. (104)

We have moved far from the inordinate quest for children by African women in the works of Flora Nwapa and Buchi Emecheta in the twentieth century with the ironic paradox: 'If you don't have them, the longing for them will kill you; and if you have them, the caring for them will kill you.'

Rather, Chief Ozobia's two daughters Olanna and Kainene, highly educated and independent-minded, disdained marriage and chose relationships with men as live-in lovers, refusing marriage in the conventional sense. Refusing repeated marriage proposals from Odenigbo, Olanna had argued that:

> They were too happy, precariously so, and she wanted to guard that bond; she feared that marriage would flatten it to a prosaic partnership. (52)

Olanna does marry Odenigbo eventually during the dislocations caused by the endangered stability of things during the war, because of the fragile existence in a war situation. But Kainene never did accept marriage to Richard till she disappeared. In *Half of a Yellow Sun* feminism as an ideology is behind us. The major female characters were empowered before the novel opens, through higher education.

The novel deals with human relationships. And it is among the robust relationships mentioned earlier that we discover infidelities and betrayals. But this later. There are four strands in the tale that Adichie weaves:

a) The story of Odenigbo and Olanna;
b) The story of Kainene and Richard;
c) The story of Ugwu and Odenigbo/Olanna; and
d) The story of the civil conflict.

And it is around these strands that the major themes of the novel revolve.

The theme of betrayal looms large in the novel. It is the key point in this fascinating work. Odenigbo betrays Olanna by sleeping with Amala, a village girl who bears him a baby girl. Olanna betrays Odenigbo and her twin sister Kainene by sleeping with Richard Churchill. Richard betrays Kainene by sleeping with Olanna. Northerners betray their Igbo neighbours and friends by killing them in an orgy of massacres.

Biafra betrays Nigeria by its act of secession, and the Nigerian Government betrays the Igbo living in the North by refusing to intervene in the massacres of unarmed Igbo and by refusing to prosecute or punish the rampaging Northerners guilty of the crimes. The Yoruba betray the Igbo by harassing and even killing the Igbo living among them in Lagos. And inside Biafra stories of saboteurs, real or imagined, are rampant. On a minor note, Olanna's father betrays his wife by keeping a mistress, for which Olanna plucks up courage to rebuke him; and Susan, Richard's chaperone who works at the British Council, betrays her friend by sleeping with her husband. Each is unfaithful in those fateful days of war, struggle, and domestic peace.

Half of Yellow Sun is a sad story of monumental loss for the Igbo objectively rendered. The dream that was Biafra was lost on the battlefield. That dream was further lost in the thousands of lives lost in the battlefield and through starvation. The losses were both national and individual. Olanna lost Kainene, her twin sister, and her parents could not get over it.

For some artistic balance, the scenes of betrayal discussed above are attenuated by pockets of fidelity and loyalty. Ugwu's loyalty and even love for Odenigbo and Olanna remains steadfast to the very end, even after his battle-field experience where he earned the sobriquet 'Target destroyer' through his courage. Returning to the Odenigbos and resuming his position as 'houseboy' beats the imagination. Harrison equally returns to Richard and Kainene. Equally uplifting is Mohammed's risking of his life to protect Olanna during the Kano massacres.

To assuage hurts, some of the characters who hurt or betray others abase themselves before those they hurt through confessions. Olanna confesses to Odenigbo that she slept with Richard. Richard is forced by circumstances to confess to Kainene that he slept with Olanna who equally confesses to Kainene who exclaimed that some offences were unforgivable, and in her rage burnt Richard's manuscript: *The Basket of Hands*.

Overwhelming loss etches all the corners of *Half of a Yellow Sun*. In fact it is a landslide of remembered losses: as major characters try to gather the splintered shards of their broken lives. Odenigbo loses his mother. Ugwu loses his own mother also as he hears of the death of Eberechi killed during shelling.

Richard feels the loss of Kainene deeply, his live-in lover who gets lost in the attack trade. Prominent personages like professors Okeoma and Ekwenugo do not survive the war, not to speak of the vexed issue of abandoned property of the Igbo and all their investments and money in Nigeria which made the slogan of 'No victor, no vanquished', seem a mere charade.

The horrors of the Nigerian civil war evoked world-wide passions. Publishers Mark Press undertook to expose those horrors. I said earlier that African literature in the twentieth century was lachrymal, a weeping literature, a literature of lamentation. *Half of a Yellow Sun* becomes a spill-over, a carry-over of this sad phenomenon into the twenty-first century, but with a different hue. In the twentieth century, it was over what European enslavers and imperialists and operators of the apartheid system inflicted on Africans. In *Half of a Yellow Sun,* it is now about what fellow Africans are inflicting on their brothers and sisters. *Ex Africa semper aliquid novi.* And the current orgy of blood-letting in Darfur is still with us.

Even though the Biafran National Anthem, sung to the tune of the *Finlandia* had prematurely anticipated. 'The victory we won over might and wrong', it was not yet *Uhuru.* The Biafra ordeal as I earlier said, excited world-wide passions. Julius Nyerere, President of Tanzania, in recognizing Biafra said among other things:

> When more than twelve million people are convinced that they are rejected and that there is no longer any basis for unity between them and other groups of people that unity has ceased to exist. You cannot kill thousands of people and keep killing more in the name of Unity. There is no unity between the dead and those who killed them. And there is no unity in slavery and domination.[3]

President Houphouët-Boigny of Ivory Coast harped on the same point, stressing:

> We cannot admit as to ourselves that it (unity) should be his grave. We say yes to peace and through peace; unity in love and through brotherhood. We say no to unity in war and through war, or unity in hatred. Unity is for the living and not for the dead.[4]

The above were passionate utterances provoked by the horrors embedded in the Biafran ordeal. Vistas of those horrors found themselves in *Half of a Yellow Sun.* Will the reader ever forget the pathos in the woman carrying the severed head of her daughter in a calabash with the beautiful braids on her head? Who will ever forget Richard's servant, Ikejide, running even after his head was severed by shrapnel after a bombing raid, and kept running headless until he crashed down the street?

The stunning thing about *Half of a Yellow Sun* is the author's objective rendering of these horrors, devoid of emotional outcries by a daughter of Biafra. The impartiality, the refusal to take sides, the absence of judgemental stance or apportioning blame is part of the greatness of this novel.

Certain characters in *Half of a Yellow Sun* are disguised but identifiable, making the novel read like a *roman a clef.* The poet-reading personage Okeoma is identifiable as Christopher Okigbo. Professor Ezeka arrested in his house after the cessation of hostilities is probably Professor Kalu Ezera, and the finance minister Chief Okonji can be no other than Chief Okotie-Ebo, the corrupt minister of finance in the first republic, killed during the Nzeogwu coup.

In sum, there are no saints in *Half of a Yellow Sun,* only fallible human beings. Ugwu, Odenigbo's 'my good man' takes part in a gang rape in his soldiering days. The pastors we encounter show no uplifting behaviour as 'Men of God'. And there is the maid Chinyere, sneaking across the fence at night to have quick sex with Ugwu, no words exchanged. There were no sacred cows either. Ojukwu himself, Head of the embattled State of Biafra was said to be openly having affairs with other men's wives.

> The only saboteurs we have are the ones Ojukwu invented so he can lock up his opponents and the men whose wives he wants. Did I ever tell you about the Onitsha man who bought up all of the cement we had in the factory shortly after the refugees starting (sic) coming back. Ojukwu is having an affair with the man's wife and has just had the man arrested for nothing. (313)

In one of the humorous scenes in the novel, we see the prayer warrior, Pastor Ambrose, dashing off after he is discovered by Olanna spying on her as she takes a bath in the early morning haze. She calls after him:

> 'Pastor Ambrose', she called out, and he dashed off, 'You are not ashamed of yourself? If only you would spend your time praying for somebody to come and tell me what happened to Ugwu instead of spying on a married woman taking a bath'. (383)

Another man of God, this time a celibate Catholic Priest, Rev. Father Marcel, is taken down a peg. He had impregnated a refuge girl, Urenwa, taking advantage of her hunger and destitution. Kainene had been shocked as she blurted out:

> He fucks most of them before he gives them the crayfish that I slave to get here. (398)

The portrayal of Richard Churchill's character is one of the achievements of this work. This white man, a British man who speaks Igbo and calls himself a Biafran, is unique, and his portrayal points to new directions in the depiction of white characters in African literature. We are used to seeing white men as haughty, snobbish, above board and among the ruling class, either as district officers, commanders in the military elite or governors who are oppressors that belong to the ruling class. But Richard is ordinary or even less than ordinary. He is unsure of himself. Susan chaperones him at parties organized by fellow white men where he is nervous and uncomfortable. He is an appendage and even in his relationship with Kainene he is worse than an appendage as she dominates every aspect of his life, refusing his proposals of marriage. In bed he can hardly perform, being forced to ask Igbo houseboys to find him local herbs for sexual enhancement.

In the character of Richard, the character of the white man as ordinary, fallible human being in African literature is beginning to emerge. This image of a British man in our midst, lacking the haughty, supercilious attitude with which white men are associated in our literatures, is a clear departure from the norm. He is willing to fully integrate himself with the Biafran cause, eager to marry and settle down with Kainene, our daughter. He is a cipher in the presence of Igbo world-class intellectuals like Okeoma, Odenigbo, and Ezeka, playing second fiddle in his relationships with Susan or Kainene, moving in first with Susan, and later with Kainene. The image of the white man as even worse than we are is fully fleshed out in a recent work *Unbridled* by Jude Dibia[5]. African literature has come of age! Chimamanda Adichie's narrative style in *Half of a Yellow Sun* is captivating. Before the end of each chapter, she advances her story by surprising the reader with new information, a combination of O. Henry's technique in the short story genre and what Joseph Conrad calls *progression d'effet* – putting down nothing that does not advance the story. Adichie's detachment, her avoidance of maudlin sentimentality in narrative passages that depict the many brutalities inflicted on her fellow Igbo brothers and sisters during the internecine fratricidal conflict, points to her maturity as a young writer. Chimamanda Adichie amazes.

NOTES

1   Chimamanda Adichie. *Half of a Yellow Sun*. Lagos, Farafina, 2006.
2   Charles E. Nnolim, 'African literature in the twenty-first century: Challenges to writers and critics'. *African Literature Today,* Vol. 25. (2006).
3   Document recognizing Biafra (1968)
4   Document recognizing Biafra (1968)
5   Jude Diabia *Unbridled*. Lagos, Blacksands Books, 2007.

Reviews

Edited by James Gibbs

Helon Habila, *Measuring Time*
London: Hamish Hamilton, 2007, 384 pp., £16.99
ISBN 1-4352-8281-7 / 978-1-4532-8281-0

Measuring Time represents an unequivocal affirmation of the pre-eminent position of the intellectual/historian, especially when set beside the politician and the professional fighter. At another level, it stands as an author's expression of his unbroken pact with his community of origin.

Helon Habila's first novel, *Waiting for an Angel*, was set in Lagos, in the context of a military dictatorship, with the story narrated by a socially conscious journalist who abandons his studies at the university when his room-mate succumbs to acute psychotic depression. In *Measuring Time*, Habila travels inland, far into the North Eastern part of the country, setting the novel in Keti, a small community located, as stated in the novel, in Gombe State. Keti is no doubt fictitious, but it is not difficult to establish a relationship between it and the author's place of birth: Kaltungo, a minority, predominantly Christian, community in Gombe State. Kaltungo people are poor, often subject to the vagaries of weather, and, like most of the other minority groups in Nigeria, marginalised. Habila makes clear his passionate commitment to these people in *Measuring Time*, affirming his faith in their abilities to re-invent themselves as time and circumstances demand. The novel recounts in detail the people's arrival in their current place of habitation, records how they displaced the original inhabitants of the land, and how, following the arrival of European colonialists and Christian missionaries, they experienced dislocation themselves.

Mamo, the elder of a set of twins, serves as the voice of this community. He stumbles on his vocation when he discovers *A Brief History of the Peoples of Keti* written by an American, the first Christian missionary to arrive in Keti. Mamo is persuaded by his girl friend, Zara, to review the book. His observations turn him into a local hero, and he is commissioned to write a biography of the reigning traditional ruler.

Mamo and his twin brother, La Mamo, had spent their early adolescence thinking of how to achieve fame. Together with their cousin, Asabar, they plan to run away from the village in order to pursue careers as soldiers. But

Mamo, who suffers from sickle cell disease, experiences a crisis at the very moment of their departure and has to stay behind. In the end, only La Mamo becomes a soldier, a mercenary, participating in wars in Libya, Mali and Liberia. When he returns home after fifteen years, he has become totally disillusioned about war, seeing it as an expression of the bestiality embodied in humanity, and insisting that only wars of liberation are justifiable. This aspect of his new conviction prompts him lead an invasion of the palace by the village people on the day after his return to Keti. He is killed in the engagement.

Habila designs *Measuring Time* as a huge irony. Mamo, the hero, inherited his mother's blood disease. And, as is well known, children with sickle cell anemia are often weak and many die before they reach twenty. His twin brother, on the other hand, is very strong and healthy. He excels in physical activities, but he dies at the age of thirty-one. Asabar becomes a politician, but after being shot in the spine during an election riot he is left confined to a wheelchair, and he becomes an alcoholic. Ironically, only Mamo, the sickler, survives. He lives to write the history of Keti people and the biographies of every major character that the reader encounters in the novel.

Measuring Time can be read as an elaboration of a point made by Chinua Achebe. In *Anthills of the Savannah* (1987), Achebe first lines up three major professionals: the soldier, the politician and the story-teller, and having emphasised the indispensability of each of them, then argues that the story-teller deserves the 'eagle feather' among the three. He justifies this view with a simple statement: 'it is the story that outlives the sound of war – drums and the exploits of brave fighters.' Habila seems to concur with this, and reserves pride of place in his new work for the character who devotes his time to rendering an account of his people's struggles.

Structurally *Measuring Time* is a straightforward narration. The story revolves mainly around Mamo, the protagonist, and it is through him that we meet other characters, hear what they say and see what they do. The presentation follows a conventional linear pattern with hardly any attempt at making the organisation complex or convoluted. Once, La Mamo's letter takes readers away to Liberia, making them witness the horrors of the war that took place there. But, as soon as this ends, readers are transported back to the rural environment of Keti, the main geographical setting of the novel.

The simplicity of the plot is not in itself a drawback, especially since the novel meditates on a number of ideas and issues, including the world and its ironies, the processes of history and its real makers, the dynamics of cultural encounters, the nature of wars, religion and the logic of pluralism. Of course, not all of Habila's conclusions on these issues can be considered profound, but forcing readers to look afresh and ruminate on matters that they might otherwise have been taking for granted is salutary in itself. It is certainly valuable to provoke debate, force agreements or deepen disagreements.

The pages of Habila's new work are full of tragic incidents. Misfortunes, disasters, deaths and violence are very common, and one keeps on reading, concerned, as it were, for the life of the protagonist. It is a great relief, on reaching the end, to see Mamo setting out to re-connect with Zara, his love. With *Measuring Time*, Habila consolidates his position as an eminent member of the new generation of African writers.

Wumi Raji,
Obafemi Awolowo University, Ile Ife, Nigeria
(It has been pointed out that Habila's premise that one identical twin might be a sickler and the other not is unsound. JG)

Ama Ata Aidoo ed., *African Love Stories: an Anthology*
Oxford: Ayebia Clarke, 2006, 249 pp., £10.99; ISBN 0-9547023-6-0

Twenty-one love stories by African women, ranging from romantic fantasy to sharp social critique, from introspective meditation to hilarious anecdote, with, at the back, a useful section featuring biographical notes on the authors.

And what an impressive bunch they are: seriously well-educated women with seriously well-qualified professional lives. Obliquely, the biographical section does much to demonstrate why historically there has been an under-representation of women's voices in African fiction. Faced with the challenge of dealing with critical issues of education and development, a writer, conscious that her education represents a huge investment of her country's resources, may well find it difficult to justify, even to herself, spending time writing about 'frivolous' subjects such as love and relationships. Eminent Ghanaian author Ama Ata Aidoo makes this point in her introduction to this volume. At the same time, she stresses the ultimate seriousness of writing about love, which is, according to her, one of the three great concerns of literature.

There are didactic and non-didactic stories, stories that have a serious intent and others that are playful, if not rather naughty. Main characters range from young girls to older women and while there is often a strong identification of 'Point Of View' character with the authorial voice, it is refreshing when at times this authorial voice indulges in bad behaviour (all too rare in fiction written by women generally).

Although certainly of interest to the general reader, these stories have been written by a very small cadre of educated African women, and will be particularly rewarding to readers who also belong to this select company. It's an aspect of our lives we hardly ever see represented: recognizable, domestic, personal, messy, full of ambivalences. I particularly enjoyed reading about the African man as object of desire, without any of that pesky 'othering' that's usually part of the portrayal.

Most of the stories are contemporary, and in a way they are almost acts of translation, because implicit in almost every one is an explanation of one set of assumptions – let's say those that come with a Western education - in the light of another set – let's say those indigenous to the writer's country of origin. But it is fascinating that the direction of translation between these two positions is not fixed: and the authors themselves tend to waver, constantly, dynamically, between each position. This tendency is at its most slyly deadpan in Rounke Coker's 'Ojo and the Armed Robbers':

> I walked just down the road to Tunde and Felicity's, where I found them trying to use the phone. What other terrible thing could have happened to induce them to try something so futile? 'I was trying to call the police!' explained British-born Felicity.

In this respect, Tomi Adeaga ('Marriage and Other Impediments') records her family's attitude to her marriage to a German in full awareness that a Western audience may find it surprising. In a way, the story is an act of witnessing from one part of her life to another, setting down the beloved familiar on the same terms as the new adopted life, drawing out the parallels, demanding the same respect.

Different readers will pick their own favourites out of this rich anthology. For me, Doreen Baingana's 'Tropical Fish', poignant, painful, understated, echoes with an awareness of problematic relations between men and women that extends well beyond the post-colonial context in which the story is fixed. 'Jambula Tree' (Monica Arak de Nyeko) poetically relates a longing for something so culturally unacceptable it can scarcely be defined, let alone elaborated on. Stylistically innovative and radically condensed, 'Three [Love] Stories in Brackets' reflects on the absence of material records from which to reconstruct women's lives in past times.

Folake Shoga
Independent artist, Bristol
('Jambula Tree' won the 2007 Caine Prize for African writing; 'Tropical Fish' was short-listed for the same prize in 2005. JG)

Tsitsi Dangaremgba, *The Book of Not*
Oxford: Ayebia Clarke Publishing, 2006, 250 pp., £9.99; ISBN 0-9547023-7-9

The Book of Not follows the protagonist, Tambudzai Sigauke, from secondary school as a scholarship girl (one of the 'African quota' of only six girls) in what was then Rhodesia's most prestigious girls' school through to her young, independent adulthood. The backdrop to this progress is the liberation struggle for Zimbabwe, *chimurenga*. The story begins with a shockingly violent incident, and ends with a long-awaited act of self-determination.

The Book of Not resumes Tambudzai's story from *Nervous Conditions*, Dangaremgba's acclaimed previous volume. However, the focus of the story has changed: whereas before, Tambudzai's own struggle is with home, family and background, here she is exposed to an insidious daily racism during her immersion in the white-dominated world, and her struggle is as much with herself as with external circumstances. Progress to secondary school should bring material advantage to the village girl but due to constant undermining, slights and exploitation, it does not deliver on its promise. This is a hard story to read, not least because of Tambu's acquiescence in her situation.

One is surprised, in the light of events depicted, that white Zimbabweans have survived the rage their actions induced. Nevertheless, within the narrative, nothing is uncomplicated: events, motivations, reactions, interactions, and Tambudzai's loyalties are all painfully divided. 'The white man, hit it on the head to make it run' sing the freedom fighters in the bush. 'It was all too much for me, so I just stood watching her, arms folded, rigid and taking care to be aloof.' This is Tambudzai's response, and it represents her emotional position for most of the book. She has an instinctive recoil from the violent struggle, which is seen to strike terribly but chaotically, like a force of nature, ferocious, crippling whatever is in its way. Yet she is left disarmed in the face of the racism she must encounter; and her only strategy – to work hard, be clever and be successful – renders her particularly vulnerable to exploitation.

As a piece of storytelling, *The Book of Not* is wonderfully written, and so masterfully put together that its internal structure (the stylistic and metaphorical reiteration of its major themes) is not easily apparent. Flashes of dry wit and wordplay ease the reader through Tambudzai's rather inhospitable internal world with the force of direct speech. She describes a work colleague: 'A man with biceps as big as her beauty would without moving a muscle be labelled a bully.' The game the writer is playing here, referencing African orality by way of Middle English alliterative rhythms, demonstrates her highly skilful writing technique as much as it does her polymath approach. She wears her learning lightly, constructing a detailed local reality anchored to the universal by the breadth of her frame of reference.

The narrative is generally more restrained than in *Nervous Conditions* and it is a painful restraint, implying perhaps feelings almost too difficult to control. The characterisation, though vivid and deft, is schematic, indicative of Tambudzai's truncated subjectivity: her feelings are so repressed that all her relationships are reduced to a series of anxious tics. However this means that those she interacts with never come to independent life as characters. Her little sister, Netsai, stalks physically crippled through Tambudzai's consciousness like a figment, not a person. However, on reflection we can see that Tambudzai herself is just as unquiet, and spiritually just as crippled.

This is the second part of an intended trilogy, and the significance of Dangaremgba's literary contribution is not in dispute. Neither is its quality. I feel, though, that it is impossible to enter sympathetically into the world of *The Book of Not* without having read *Nervous Conditions* to fill in the emotional deficit. In addition to the vivid but one-dimensional depiction of secondary characters, Dangaremgba writes here with a sort of coldness, a dislocation from the material. The strongest emotion expressed is a tamped-down, meticulously recorded, fearful resentment. We scarcely know the narrator's feelings apart from a sort of sequential anticipatory dread. She is caught up in an obsessive-compulsive calculation of strategic moves, trying to keep herself safe, or at least, temporarily free from attack.

What is one to make of this coldness, this withdrawal from emotion? The narrative maintains an unsettling objectivity as the protagonist negotiates one humiliation after another – the refreshing rage of *Nervous Conditions* seems to be absent from this stage of Tambudzai's life. Even characters who should be objects of hatred to her (the white characters, for example) receive not direct criticism, but a dispassionate evaluation. Meanwhile Tambu continues to try to cultivate *ubuntu* (according to the glossary, 'no direct translation: a philosophy of being...based on the essence of the person'). A feeling of dread builds in the reader, echoing the steadily accumulating fears Tambu acquires in her progress towards adulthood. One wishes, more and more, for an act of potent rebellion from this girl, equal in violence to that which starts the novel. She seems to have no comforts – not home, not family, not friendships – apart from her own cleverness, and even that proves an ambivalent blessing. She exists in a state of paralysis – a state of 'Not', I suppose, countering the external denial of her rights with a rigorous internal denial of feeling as described in the first chapter, 'deliberately not feeling too many hates and rages and despairs to enumerate.' One act of defiance ends the book without which it would have been a very grim read indeed.

Folake Shoga
Independent artist, Bristol

(Desmond Tutu and Nelson Mandela are among those who have provided definitions for *ubuntu* that has been linked with the Zulu maxim: *umuntu ngumuntu ngabantu* that has been translated as 'a person is a person through (other) persons'. JG)

Marilyn Heward Mills, *Cloth Girl*
London: Time Warner Books, 2006, 467 pp., £14.99; (hbk), ISBN: 0-316-73188-9

Marilyn Heward Mills's meticulously researched first novel is set in colonial Ghana in the 1930s and 1940s. The novel fills out the biographies of real historical figures, adding fictional domestic scenarios, relationships and conversations to the known facts about their lives. Key members of the African elite – particularly the lawyer Robert Bannerman and his circle of influential male friends – are fleshed out by Mills as they enter the political race towards decolonisation. In fact, such men become all-too-carnal in the case of Lawyer Bannerman, who is represented as a promiscuous patriarch whose 'roving eye' secures him the women of his choice as mistresses and wives.

Heward Mills is not, however, primarily interested in the big men of Ghanaian history. Preoccupied instead with the question of women's marital freedom in different cultures, the novel adds two women to Ghanaian history, one African, one European. The stories of the illiterate 'cloth girl', Matilda Quartey, and the alcoholic, perpetually bored Audrey Turton, are inserted into the larger narrative of the country's colonial encounter. In spite of their divergent backgrounds and characters, both Matilda and Audrey find themselves in similar domestic situations, unhappily married to unsuitable husbands and facing problems with the gender ideologies imposed on them by their families and friends. Through these two contrasting heroines, the novel debates the advantages and disadvantages of being a 'European woman' or a 'West African woman' in the colonial society of the 1930s and 1940s.

Focussing on the most intimate details of the women's married lives, including sexual desire and childbirth, the novel follows the two heroines as they experience similar dilemmas about whether or not to leave their husbands. Testing 'African' ideals of womanhood against 'European' gender codes, the author shows both women to be similarly constrained. Ultimately, however, their marital choices are shown to be different, determined by the responsibilities brought to bear by their cultures.

At one level, *Cloth Girl* is a love story is centred on the life of Matilda, the intelligent but apolitical 'cloth girl', who reluctantly becomes the second wife to Robert Bannerman, but falls in love with somebody else. At another level, *Cloth Girl* is part of a Ghanaian literary tradition stretching back at least to the 1880s: in becoming Bannerman's second wife, Matilda enters a familiar canon of literature in which the question of polygyny is debated in fiction. *Cloth Girl* takes a strong position in this debate. As the unwilling bride to an older man, and as junior wife in a polygynous marriage, Matilda is shown to be in an impossible position. For the duration of the novel, she is taunted by Bannerman's malicious first wife, the 'frock lady', Julie, who is an unchanging and spiteful character. Nevertheless, Matilda remains obedient: she is the angel in the house who makes the best of her difficult marriage, cooks food for the family, and cares for the children of the household. In this aspect of the novel, the author utilises a popular Ghanaian storyline whereby polygynous marriage is debated through the contrast of a 'bad' wife with a 'good' wife: most often in popular literature, the 'baddie' is the seductive young good-time girl brought in as the mistress or second wife to the loyal senior wife. Mills inverts the line-up without altering the convention.

Both heroines are realised with the same degree of sympathy and complexity in this detailed historical novel. Julie, however, is a stock figure whose place in the narrative is simply to illustrate the pitfalls of polygyny for women. Locally published Ghanaian literature remains preoccupied with issues of marital fidelity and polygyny: the latter debate is conveniently resolved in *Cloth Girl* by the elimination – and not before time – of the evil-spirited, foul-mouthed senior wife, who wears a brand new Western-style dress every day, puts salt into food cooked by Matilda to make it unpalatable, and continuously taunts her poor co-wife in public, without shame. I rather liked Julie's foul-mouthed commentaries, but that is to read against the grain of the novel, which dramatises the injustices and indignities of polgyny for the junior wife.

From its title onwards, *Cloth Girl* maintains the contrast between the cloth girl and the frock lady. As a result, the novel is strongly didactic at all stages of its development. Nevertheless, Heward Mills presents such powerful and convincing character portraits that these ideological polarisations are absorbed into the subtle, well-plotted narrative. The novel contains strong traces of *Jane Eyre*, with Matilda as the West African Jane whose Rochester suffers a debilitating accident; it also has scenes reminiscent of *A Passage to India*, showing colonial society in its tea-sipping glory and the rape of a young white wife (although the assailants this time are low-class white ruffians). Above all, this is a detailed, well-realised narrative about the range of choices available to women in late-colonial society.

Stephanie Newell,
English Department, University of Sussex

Ngũgĩ wa Thiong'o, *Wizard of the Crow*
London: Vintage, 2007, 768 pp., £8.99; ISBN 1-84655-034-3 / 9781846550348 (UK edition)

Wizard of the Crow, Ngũgĩ wa Thiongo'o's recent magnificent novel courageously attempts in his own words to 'sum up Africa of the twentieth century in the context of global forces of world history'.

Ngũgĩ creates a fictitious country, the 'Free Republic of Aburiria', to play out the struggles of a people under the yoke of a monstrous leader whose inflated ego causes him bodily to expand, belching noxious gas to the point of self-explosion. Corruption is everywhere, the west toys with the leader like a needy child dishing out rewards and penalties depending on which way the economic wind blows and on its own strategic interests. Better the despot you know. ... A once fertile land is laid to waste and the people suffer terribly.

The leader of Aburiria is sick; he has many problems. The women of the country do not know their place, including his wife who he has had to lock up. There is an outbreak of queuing as a rumour spreads that a new venture, The Marching to Heaven Tower, might result in jobs for the masses of unemployed. The Tower will be taller than Babel and will succeed where Babel failed. It will connect Aburiria with outer space and is a gift from a grateful nation to its ruler. The only problem is it needs funding from the west through the Global Bank and they are being fickle. They have invested millions in the leader in his fight against the subversive elements in his society and have even praised him for the ruthless slaughter of the communists, and they are now demanding that he prove the benefits to his people of this visionary tower. With the imminent arrival of a delegation from the

Bank the queues might be misinterpreted as a sign of protest. When his birthday celebrations are disrupted by snakes creating panic, the ruler knows he must act to quell the opposition forces he suspects are responsible for releasing the snakes.

Magnificent storyteller that he is Ngũgĩ creates a web of intrigue around this tragicomic despot's attempts to stay in power. The tyrant is aided and abetted by his two sycophantic ministers one of whom has modified his eyes and the other his ears to be able to serve more efficiently. The stench of money and corruption in the ruling party vies with the stench of garbage in the streets. Most of those in power suffer from 'white-ache'. A tree is discovered that grows dollars only to be consumed by an infestation of insatiable white termites. The innocent and the guilty end up as food for the crocodiles in the Red River. This is a place of palpable evil.

That good survives at all is a miracle but survive it does in the form of Kamiti and Nyawira who together create both the myth and the reality of the *Wizard of the Crow*. Kamiti is a university graduate and his initial desire is to withdraw from the world and live as a hermit in the forest. He wants to learn the secrets of the ancestors, study the traditional methods of healing and tap into the rich seam of knowledge that underpins the spirit of Africa. His is 'the ministry of wounded souls'. Nyawira is the materialist, a political activist who is working undercover in the Movement for the Voice of the People. She lives in the midst of the city patiently educating the people and, through persistent acts of defiance, undermining those in power. Hers is 'the ministry of wounded bodies'. All the calamities that beset the Republic of Aburiria are eventually blamed on the wizard of the crow. The narrative of the book traces the fortunes of these two as they duck and dive trying to outwit the massed forces of the government who are out to destroy them. Nyawira's courage, her refusal to give up the struggle and her eventual union with Kamiti give us both a symbol of the resilience of a people in the face of oppression and also a fragile hope.

This is a wonderful book. Tragic and beautiful by turns it is also tremendously funny. Anyone who wants to understand the forces at work in and on Africa over the last century should read it. The story of the 'Free Republic of Aburiria' echoes the history of many, too many, African countries emerging from colonialism through independence into what Ngũgĩ calls the 'corporonialism' of global capital. Translated from Gikuyu there are obvious references to Ngũgĩ's native Kenya and the fate of writers and intellectuals who challenge the state in the novel all too closely mirrors his own experiences. But the book is a statement about Africa. It resonates beyond Kenya to all the despotic regimes and their supporters around the globe that blighted the continent in the twentieth century, and those that remain in the twenty-first.

Jane Collins
Reader in Theatre at Wimbledon College of Art,
University of the Arts, London

Chris Abani, *Becoming Abigail*
New York: Akashic Books, 2005, 121 pp., $11.95, pbk. ISBN 1- 888451-94-7

Chris Abani's sixth book and first novella is the harrowing tale of a young woman who suffers sexual abuse in childhood, falls into prostitution as a teenager, and fights back. It is a coming-of-age story of the most horrifying sort. At the same time it is a beautifully rendered narrative about belonging, madness, and the extent and limitations of the human will to survive.

Becoming Abigail is written in the third person through the fragmented thoughts of its protagonist, Abigail, who sits, one evening, on the edge of an ancient Egyptian Sphinx above the river Thames, toying with matches and cigarettes, remembering the 'now' of her life in England and the 'then' of her past life in Nigeria. Travelling back and forth in time, *now* and *then* serve as chapter headings for this 121-page novella. The author sets the scene so that at the very beginning a reader learns that Abigail is named after her mother who died in childbirth and that her father cannot cope with the loss of his wife. In childhood Abigail mourns her mother through bizarre rituals such as dressing up dead birds in bits of her mother's wedding gown. She also marks her own body, at first with ink but later with fire and needles in acts of self-mutilation. As a teenager Abigail is vulnerable to the vagaries of her own mind (sane or insane one cannot be sure). She becomes the victim of sexual abuse by others, from one uncle in particular who will take her away from her home in Nigeria to England where his abuse knows no limits. These are the grim facts of a story that in any other author's hands might have fallen into the sensational or faltered from the sheer weight of its horror. This has not happened with Abani's *Becoming Abigail*.

From the outset, the reader is gripped by the power of the writing. The language is magical, reminiscent of much of the author's earlier work (in particular, *Daphne's Lot)*. Take, for example, the description of a necklace with its large amber pendant depicted as a blob of honey melting on dirty ice, or the likening of night to a new banknote. Even the layout of the words on the page is well crafted, like notes on sheet music evoking the exact tempo of emotions to be conveyed. Here prose, poetry and music are rolled into one. It is undeniably masterly, yet at times the writing appears almost too self-consciously crafted and this hinders rather than helps to convey certain images. Such is the case when Abigail holds the only man she has ever truly loved, her one glimmer of hope, and we read of her 'cupping his big face between her small hands, a pair of rare, black butterflies sitting on an outcrop of chalk.'

Between the lines of prose-poetry-music lurk deliberate ambiguities and questions. How much of what Abigail says is true or invented? Abani writes that '[Abigail] wasn't always able to tell how much she was inventing and how much was real,' and the reader also has difficulties. The novella is also filled with references to maps and to Abigail's keen searching of them through the course of her tormented life. What exactly does *becoming Abigail* mean? Is it to become 'independent and fierce' like her mother, or to remain perpetually lost, orphaned and out of place? Perhaps, in the most tragic of senses, it is to become like her father who cannot cope with life.

The story grips from the start and doesn't let go – it is simply told, yet hauntingly full of questions, just as quietly shocking in its ending as it is in its beginning. It leaves its mark on the reader in the same way that marks are left on Abigail's body. This is not a story easily forgotten.

Sarah Ladipo Manyika
English Department, San Francisco State University

Chris Dunton, *Boxing and Other Stories*
Lesotho: Institute of South African Studies, 2005, 96 pp., £11.95;
ISBN 9789991131405
Tunde Fatunde, *Shattered Calabash*
trans. Jamary Molumeli, introduction by Chris Dunton, Lesotho: Institute of
Southern African Studies, 2005, 64pp., £11.95; ISBN 9789991131399
Both available from the African Books Collective
See http://www.africanbookscollective.com/books/boxing-and-other-stories

Chris Dunton is professor of English at the National University of Lesotho and has extensive scholarly publications to his name as a critic of African literature. He is thus perhaps better known as an academic than as a writer of short stories. However, there is a wonderful tone of detachment combined with an eye for physical detail in all of the eight stories in this volume that makes them exceptionally fine and vivid, really suiting the style to the form. The reader is perhaps wrongfooted by the cover illustration, which leads one to expect a homoerotic content which is in fact almost entirely absent from the stories, the one exception being an encounter in 'Trespassers'. The unifying feature of the stories is Dunton's exceptional ability to inhabit and lend convincing voice to his characters, whether they are male or female, rich or poor, naïve or sophisticated.

These strengths come most clearly to the fore in 'Evidence of Love. Signs of a Marriage'. This is written in the person of a young woman, married to a drunk, Saul, and in love or lust with his brother, Ibe. The story contains splendidly vivid, detailed descriptions both of Ibe's torso (presumably the inspiration for the cover photograph of this volume) and of the detail of the room in which the narrator lives with her husband and small children. It is the provision of this detail that lends to the reader an intimate understanding of the life and mindset of the central character. This is a truly distinguished piece of work.

Less successful is the title story, 'Boxing', which shows a farmer seething with rage and frustration at the difficulty of getting his produce sold except through the corrupt medium of one of the village businessmen. He then encounters a Ghanaian teacher in a bar, who recounts the difficulties caused by the corruption of his headmaster. The story centres, however, around a tale told to him by his school security guard – of a boxing match, to illustrate the proverb 'When it come to a fight, it's not the size of the dog that counts. It's the size of the fight in the dog.' The slightly too obvious moral about finding strength through cooperation with others strains Dunton's generally attractive ability to convey vivid detail.

Taking the other stories in the order in which they appear in the volume, this quality is manifested variously and attractively as follows: in 'Seeing Pedro, Being Pedro' a series of encounters occur between a teacher and a salesman, the Pedro of the title. Dunton conjures up some of the irritating difficulties of everyday life in West Africa with his depiction of futile efforts to procure a length of garden hose. The situation is perceived not only from the point of view of the (nameless) teacher, a reasonable man driven to incivility by the sheer awkwardness of the dealings, but also from that of the would-be salesman, Pedro, riven by self-hatred at his own futility.

In 'Kwame's Night', Kwame is desperately in love with his schoolmate Teresa, but too shy and awkward to do anything sensible about it. He makes a colossal mess of the school production of *Midsummer Night's Dream* because he is distracted by his inability to make contact with Teresa at the appropriate level. On the way home, he realizes that the reason for his inability to make progress is that Teresa, too, is crippled with shyness. Dunton conveys affectionately the awkwardness of teenage love and so manages to give us a happy ending without the indigestible saccharine quality that such endings often manifest.

'Remarkable People' shows two men holidaying together: Bernard, anglophone, probably white, and Obi, black, both apparently heterosexual. Paradoxically, the reader's uncertainty about whether Bernard is black or white adds strength to the story. It is a wonderful rendition of the sheer irritation factor of being with this Bernard. Not that he is a bad man, just generally annoying, always with a series of facts or thoughts to impart. Again, a great strength here lies in the descriptive detail, a particular example being the car windscreen breaking in the desert, so that there is nothing between the men and the desert air.

In 'Whenever I Open My Eyes' a fourteen-year-old boy working in a bar becomes gradually enmeshed in a corrupt transaction, and in due course loses his moral vision to the extent that he has no problem becoming part of a car-stealing ring. Here, Dunton succeeds in presenting a convincing account of moral decay without either losing sympathy with his central character or preaching to his readers.

'Trespassers' has businessman Olu, staying in a hotel and becoming infatuated with a prostitute, whom he has brought up to his room. Later, Olu observes his slightly boring colleague, Eustace, saying goodbye to a waiter who has been visiting him in his room. Eustace is the only gay character in the collection, and although he is depicted through another character's eyes, he comes across as a sympathetic, poignantly real person.

In 'A Meteorite' Usman, a bush petrol-seller, is exploited almost beyond belief by the corrupt owner of the petrol business. He has a great rebellious fantasy which occupies all of the central part of the story. But fantasy is all that it is. The story ends with Usman's poetic reflection: 'if I could be a meteorite. Then – then I would know where to fall.'

In general, the volume is nicely produced. 'A Meteorite' is the only one of the stories that contains a couple of obvious typographical errors. And, as indicated above, these are thoroughly readable and worthwhile stories. At £11.95, however, the volume does seem rather expensive, given that it comprises only 86 pages.

Chris Dunton's academic persona comes to the fore in his very useful short introduction to the Institute of Southern African Studies' 2005 edition of Tunde Fatunde's 1999 play *Shattered Calabash*, first published as *La Calabasse Cassée* in 2002 by Bookcraft Limited of Ibadan. This is a two-act play about corruption in an African state, which though nameless is probably Cameroon. Corrupt Eteki, Director of the national gas company, is living a life of drunkenness and fornication, paid for by funds presumably obtained illegally. He has on his side Kolingba, a pastor and hypocrite who gets money from running international prostitution rings, Pierre, a Swiss banker, and Yoro, Minister of State. Ranged against him are Sabine, his long-suffering and intelligent schoolteacher wife, his son Njoya, and daughter-in-law Salimatu, as well as Christopher, son of Pierre. These latter seek to expose corruption by using as a platform the Sovereign National Conference, which is being undermined by the government, trying to turn it into an exercise in window-dressing.

Act 1 ('Atmosphere') is set in the home of Eteki and his family. He has no hesitation in using the national guard to have his family arrested when they defy his wishes, especially in regard to his wife demanding that he make a will that leaves the house to her and the children. Act 2 is set in prison where the family are incarcerated and where they remain, having refused to do a deal with the government.

The overall moral of the play is that self-interest will always breed corruption and that therefore, in an apparently Trotskyist perspective provided by Eteki's son Njoya: 'What this implies is that the struggle must be permanent.' However, the play does not altogether come off. The satire at the expense of the establishment is all a bit too obvious and heavy-handed, where something more subtle might have worked better. There is too much of a need to play it for laughs, to underline the ridiculousness of the corrupt Establishment. The play is also let down (at least in translation) by some decidedly clunky dialogue. For example, we are told that: 'Mr Pierre and you have actively participated in the destruction and pillage of our economy and have contributed enormously to the moral decadence of our youth', and 'We're brothers in the struggle, Njoya. As for me, I realize that the best way to strengthen democracy in this country is to fight for a stronger democracy in my own.' Even more tortured: 'Ever since you befriended Pastor Kolingba, your moral values have tremendously declined.' These are all selected from dialogue given to the virtuous characters, so any sense of parody is presumably unintentional.

The play wears on its sleeve a heart that no doubt has many good anti-corruption, feminist and democratic principles, but it is just too much like hard work. In his introduction, Chris Dunton quotes from his own 1998 critique of Tunde Fatunde's earlier play *No More Oil Boom*, thus: 'Fatunde's expository/agitprop-style methods do not always seem adequate to his subject-matter.' Sadly, the accuracy of that assessment is demonstrated by this translation of *Shattered Calabash*. It is clear that the situation in Cameroon needs to be exposed and indeed held up to ridicule, if that is what is necessary in order to achieve reform. In 2006 it was reported in a British newspaper that: 'Cameroon has discovered 45,000 ghost workers on its civil service payroll' and that '[in 2005 Cameroon's] public service ministry found that more than half of its 2,700-strong workforce did not exist.' This in a country which 'was ranked the world's most corrupt country in Transparency International's 1999 Corruption Perception Index'. (*The Guardian*, 12 August 2006.) There is a crying need for the subject-matter of *Shattered Calabash* to be given as wide an airing as possible. But it needs a more flexible and convincing vehicle than this translation.

The final point to make here is that, again, this edition is really quite expensive at £11.95 for a relatively short text and introduction.

Andrew Wyllie
University of the West of England

Flora Veit-Wild, *Writing Madness: Borderlines of the Body in African Literature*
Oxford: James Currey, 2006, 174 pp., £14.95; ISBN 0-85255-583-0

In many respects, *Writing Madness* imitates its subject. Veit-Wild's book is a fragmented text, crossing boundaries between genders, sexualities, regions, languages, and orature and literature. Veit-Wild is most sure of her ground when discussing Southern African literature but her inclusion of work from elsewhere in the continent allows her to make some interesting comparisons. Writing in the *Journal of Southern African Studies* in 1997, Veit-Wild commented that white Africanists of her generation had lived 'in constant fear of applying European models of interpretation to African literature' (553). Comparing Rimbaud with Césaire and German folk-tales with African oral tales in *Writing Madness*, she now takes a cross-cultural and comparative approach to African literature

In her historical survey, Veit-Wild gives examples of colonial ways of seeing 'the' African body and 'the' African mind as abnormal and of how this led to the control of Africans through confinement and surveillance. She asks how illness can be defined in African societies, given that African healing systems traditionally concentrate on healing a community, not an individual. To illustrate this, she analyses the white South African doctor,

Wulf Sachs's *Black Hamlet* in which Sachs describes his psychoanalysis of the black Rhodesian traditional healer, John Chavafambira in the 1930s. For Veit-Wild, Sachs's practice and the effect it has on Chavafambira, rather than initiating an exchange between African and European healing, reveals the madness that can occur when a subject is submitted to two belief systems. It is strange, though, that there is little discussion of the work of Frantz Fanon, especially as, in her introduction, Veit-Wild acknowledges that his theories 'laid the foundation for analysing the psyche of the colonised' (1). There are fleeting references to Fanon throughout *Writing Madness* but no sustained engagement with his work.

In a chapter on surrealism, Veit-Wild discusses both European surrealism's appropriation of Africanness and Black surrealism's liberatory use of language. Surrealism is linked to madness through the unconscious's exploration of dreams, madness and the irrational – what Veit-Wild refers to as 'borderline experiences'. This introduces ideas that Veit-Wild develops in relation to the work of Dambudzo Marechera, Lesego Rampolokeng and Sony Labou Tansi. Veit-Wild applies her extensive knowledge of Marechera's life and work in her exhilarating discussion of *Black Sunlight* and Marechera's poetry. She argues not only that Marechera fits the role of 'mad genius', powerfully commenting on the society from which he is an outcast but also that his madness can be seen as a form of spirit possession. In her detailed commentary on the South African rap poet Lesego Rampolokeng, she skillfully analyses the ways in which Rampolokeng's direct, explicit, carnivalesque language challenges colonialism, neo-colonialism and religion. Her analysis of Sony Labou Tansi draws on the work of Achille Mbembe on the grotesque as oppositional practice in the postcolony. Veit-Wild's translations from Sony and her analysis of passages from his novels provide an introduction to his work for the Anglophone reader.

A chapter on African oral culture draws on theories of rites of passage and liminality. Veit-Wild is particularly interested in representations of sexual organs, extremities and uncleanness in folk-tales. She extends her discussion of female monstrosity, as symbolised in the vagina in the work of Marechera and Sony, to show the ways in which African orature depicts fears and anxieties about male/female social relations and the actual or potential fragmentation and disintegration of the body. The chapter includes a spirited reading of a West African tale about the spider trickster's punishment of an old woman who dares to express her sexual desire.

Following on from her analysis of female sexuality in orature, Veit-Wild turns her attention to three transgressive women writers, Bessie Head, Rebeka Njau and Tsitsi Dangarembga. According to Veit-Wild, they cross borderlines in their representation of women going astray in male-dominated societies. This chapter begins with historical examples of women, spirit possession and madness, drawn from Southern Africa during the colonial period. The study of key works by each of these writers is brief in comparison to the attention paid to the male writers. It is as if Veit-Wild thinks that too much has already been written on madness in *A*

Question of Power and anorexia in *Nervous Conditions.* A more focused
analysis of the literary texts would have brought out the linkages between
history, theory and the fiction more effectively. However, Veit-Wild does
undertake a detailed examination of Dangarembga's *Kare Kare Zvako*, a
short film based on a Shona tale in which a man dismembers his wife's
body.

The book ends without a formal conclusion. This is indicative of the
methodology Veit-Wild has employed: *Writing Madness* does not provide a
chronological overview of representations of madness in African literature
and history. Too many large ideas are brought in and left underdeveloped
and the definition of what constitutes madness shifts throughout the text.
One suspects, though, that this is deliberate and that Veit-Wild wanted to
challenge the reader's expectation of a guided study. Her range is impressive, as is her engagement with the literature and cultural practices she
analyses. There is much to admire and enjoy in this eclectic and synchronic
approach.

Pauline Dodgson-Katiyo
Anglia Ruskin University (Cambridge)

Gerd Meuer, *Journeys around and with Kongi – half a century on
the road with Wole Soyinka*
Neumarkt: Verlag Thomas Reche, 2008, 232 pp., 12 Euros. ISBN 978-3-929566-73-4
Available from the Africa Book Centre, http://www.africabookcentre.com

On 28 June 2006, Gerd Meuer emailed Wole Soyinka telling him he had
'assembled some 25 stories or so in English … (and asked) if you can, at all,
agree to that kind of book.' Soyinka replied 'Bankole had mentioned this,
and I'd given my okay.' (162-3) Some two years after this idiosyncratic and
somewhat elliptical exchange, *Journeys around and with Kongi* was
launched in Nigeria – actually in the presence of Soyinka. This whole
sequence was somewhat surprising because, although he has written very
revealingly about himself and some of his relationships, Soyinka has rarely
'okayed' biographical ventures. Indeed, he has kept anyone who would
play James Boswell to his Samuel Johnson at a distance, and it should be
emphasised that Meuer is strictly constrained. There is, for example, no
critical engagement with the positions Soyinka adopts.

Meuer's 'stories or so' include accounts of escapades, incidents,
episodes, endeavours and encounters; the book also contains a 1976
interview with Soyinka and a longish quotation from his writing about
Obatala (86-9). In this *macédonie,* Meuer sheds light on his friendship with
Soyinka that began in Ibadan in 1962, and has continued as Meuer has
moved around, and as Soyinka has been variously pursued, rewarded,
scape-goated and lionised. From a perspective affected by admitted hero

worship, Meuer describes Soyinka as a 'Black Prussian', but he is also joyously aware of Soyinka as oenophile and 'number one restaurant detective'. Soyinka's Teutonic concern with reliability, time-keeping and discipline is balanced, Meuer suggests, by a capacity for celebration and for savouring good food and wine. These last qualities come through, for example, in an affectionate sketch of the life-enhancing Soyinka who 'rescues' the situation after a concert. At this point in the narrative, Meuer is organising a seven-week West African tour by a German musical group, and it looks as is they have arrived at a 'Senior Service University Club' in a Nigerian city after closing time. Soyinka saves the night by announcing 'Nobody is to stay hungry here' and, leading by example, by stirring the kitchen staff into action. (46)

Because he has so often been a point of access for Germans and German organisations wanting to contact Soyinka, Meuer has been seen by some as the laureate's agent. He is at pains to make it clear that he has never filled this role; he has never been 'a ten percenter'. He has been a mediator of African culture in Germany. In that capacity, he has enjoyed numerous cross cultural events, many of them involving Soyinka. He has also, sometimes, been embarrassed by his countrymen and countrywomen (172). We see this, for example, in his accounts of the comportment of a director filming in Aké (203–13) and of Soyinka's visit to an art exhibition in Munich (214–17).

This reference requires some amplification. Meuer writes about Soyinka being invited to read at the Villa Stuck, Munich, when it was showing an exhibition entitled, I think, 'The Short Century of Africa: Independence and Liberation Movements in Africa 1945–1994'. A major project, the exhibition had been curated by Okwui Enwezor, and went on from Munich to Berlin, Chicago and New York. I think Meuer gets the date wrong, making it 2002 rather than 2001, but there is no reason to doubt the authenticity of the passage he reproduces from the catalogue and attributes to Chinweizu: it sounds a tediously familiar refrain.

Writing under the title 'Black Conradism: The Tigritude Image of Black Africa', Chinweizu takes forward his attack on Soyinka by associating him with those who 'lent their considerable talent to the colonialist program of vilification'. He describes Soyinka as the leader of 'the small crew of comprador intellectuals, the native agents of foreign interests', and claims that Soyinka had created 'a remarkable gallery of black African villains'. Chinweizu alludes to Jero, the Kadiye, Baroka and the members of the Court of Mata Kharibu and suggests that 'Soyinka's portraits conform to colonialist prescription.' In fabricating the argument that, 'judging by Soyinka's works, there is nothing good in Africa's past and nothing good in its present', Chinweizu turns to 'To My First White Hairs'. After quoting the opening lines, he exposes the weakness of his position by writing: 'Behind this Euromodernist jargon, Soyinka … is making an exhibition of his racial self-loathing…' Meuer is forthright in condemning this ridiculous line of attack, referring to Chinweizu as 'spreading his gall-bladder content against Kongi again'. This is spirited stuff that provides insights

into cross-cultural encounters as well as useful reminders of literary skir-
mishes.

Generally, and certainly in the case of Chinweizu, Meuer's targets
deserve the criticism directed at them. However, in recounting his differences with Manfred Loimeier, serious allegations are too hastily thrown
about: the extensive use of capitals and exclamation marks suggests the loss
of critical focus (218–20).

There are a number of points at which a tighter control of material is
desirable and one of them has taken on such significance over the years that
it deserves some attention. Meuer was in Ibadan in the early 1960s as a
post-graduate student when his 'planned empirical research was seriously
endangered by the violence accompanying the elections' in the Western
Region (28). Although Soyinka's activities would have been central to that
study, Meuer has not sorted out exactly what happened to the person he
constantly refers to in his book as 'the man'. Those trying to understand the
details of the 1965 radio-station hold-up and of the trial that followed must
set the version in *Journeys around* beside other sources. In a crucial passage
about the trial, Meuer writes 'Wole was found "not guilty" by the presiding
judge and was freed on a technicality.' Meuer summarises the conflicting
evidence thus: 'according to the radio technician on duty, the "invader of
the studio" had been sporting a beard. But when Wole appeared in court he
was … clean-shaven' (33). That version must be compared with the more
reliable account in *The Mystery Gunman* by Kayode Eso, who had been 'the
presiding judge'. Eso makes it clear that Soyinka's colleague, Geoffrey
Axworthy, testified to having seen Soyinka clean-shaven on the University
of Ibadan campus on *the afternoon of the hold up*, and it was in the context
established by this testimony that staff at the radio station reported that the
intruder who drew a gun on them *in the evening* was unmasked and, as
Meuer rightly has it, bearded. In *The Mystery Gunman*, Eso quotes himself
as having said in his judgement:

> While I can understand a bearded man at five o'clock in the evening becoming
> clean-shaven at 7 p.m., I cannot unravel the mystery of a clean-shaven man at 5
> p.m. becoming bearded at 7 p.m. except he is somehow masked. (239–40)

Eso acquitted Soyinka because of this 'sharp contradiction in the
evidence of the prosecution' (241). The judge was not, as Meuer's report
suggests, ignorant about the power of the razor and foolishly unable to
grasp that a man could shave off a beard between holding up a radio station
and appearing in court. I have no 'inside track' about how Soyinka
prepared for the radio-station hold-up, but I think an awareness of the
resources of any green room offers a solution to the mystery that faced the
judge. An actor with a box of stage make-up would not find it difficult to
appear clean-shaven in the afternoon and bearded in the evening.

Meuer places near the beginning of his book the invitation extended to
him by Soyinka to join the Order of the Ultimate Consumation. This is,
Meuer indicates, a brotherhood established some thirty years earlier by
Soyinka, Femi Johnson and Doig Simmonds (10). This order and this invi-

tation recalls the emphasis on friendship that runs through Soyinka's *You Must Set Forth,* and it establishes *Journeys around* as something of a 'companion volume' to that book. Both books prompt recollection of a quotation from another, a long, long dead 'Johnson', the one who was often accompanied by the original Boswell. Samuel Johnson said: 'A man, Sir, should keep his friendship in constant repair.' Both Soyinka and Meuer seem to say 'Amen', or rather 'Ashe', to that. This is a book by a close friend which sheds light on Soyinka's reception in Germany and in which opportunities for critical reflection are passed up.

James Gibbs

Index

Lightning Source UK Ltd.
Milton Keynes UK
UKHW02f0101221117
313105UK00007B/632/P